SURVIVING AWAY FROM HOME

ASPEN WEST

64th printing

PERMISSIONS: Page 45, soup label reprinted with permission from Campbell's Soup company. Page 22, Mayo Clinic Healthy Weight Pyramid reprinted with permission from the Mayo Clinic Permissions Department, Rochester, MN.

Aspen West Publishing Co., Inc.
P.O. Box 522151
Salt Lake City, Utah 84152
801-867-4502
www.aspenwest.com
email - aspenwestpub@gmail.com

Library of Congress TX 145F731983

Paperback
    ISBN-10: 1-885348-04-5
    ISBN-13: 978-1-885348-04-3

Book Cover: Kelly McGinnis
Graphic Designer: Michele James

For information on volume orders,

contact our office or email us at aspenwestpub@gmail.com

NOTICE OF LIABILITY: This publication is designed to be an informational guide in regards to the subject matter covered. It is sold with the understanding that the publisher is not engaged in rendering medical or other professional services. Where professional services are required, the services of a competent professional person should be sought.

Dedicated to all of our mothers who never stop worrying about us no matter how old we are.

———

*Mom, thank you for teaching me
how to survive on my own.*

Love, Kent

Introduction

Since we first published *Where's Mom Now That I Need Her? Surviving Away From Home,* over 30 years ago, some things have changed – such as information on nutrition and health, and some things have stayed the same – such as the traditional tasty recipes my mother originally included in this book.

Betty Rae "Mom" Frandsen was a fantastic cook and a talented homemaker. Like most mothers, she had learned to streamline the essentials of life into some basic steps. Like most children, I wasn't aware of her magic until after I left home.

My mother believed that the true test of a mother is not how well her children thrive under her care, but how well they survive on their own.

I know it was her wish that our book keep pace with changes in modern living so that *Where's Mom?* will always be a real-life, usable, day-to-day handbook for people living on their own for the first time. That is why we compiled this *new edition,* expanding the nutrition and health chapters, adding vegetarian main dishes and creating a section on microwave cooking.

When I first moved away from home in 1976, I was always asking Mom for basic survival tips. She shared with me her tricks-of-the-trade for cooking, staying healthy, doing laundry and household cleaning. Meanwhile, everyone else kept pestering her to put together a book of favorite family recipes.

Seven years later, we wrote and published *Where's Mom Now That I Need Her? Surviving Away From Home.* The book launched a successful family business.

Today *Where's Mom?* has sold more than a million copies. From the growth of this one book, Aspen West Inc. has expanded into publishing and distributing self-help books, graduation gifts and novelty items for graduates, newlyweds and even summer campers – anyone needing to survive away from home.

Since that time, we have also published *Where's Dad Now That I Need Him?,* providing tips on outdoor cooking, home and vehicle maintenance, finances – just about anything and everything Dads know and learn over the years.

Aspen West lost a vital element of the business when my mother passed away unexpectedly May 4, 1998. Unfortunately, like a lot of other people, I did not get my favorite recipes written down. The book provides that vehicle. Where's Mom? I think she's probably somewhere nearby still keeping an eye on me.

Please enjoy the fruits of our labor.

Kent P. Frandsen, author

P.S. And as my mother would always autograph the books:
May you and your families always enjoy good health and happiness!

Contents

Chapter 1 **What Are You Eating?** 1
Know Your Nutrients
Power Packed Proteins 2
Simple & Complex Carbohydrates 4
Good & Bad Fats 4
Water Will Keep You Well 7
Vital Vitamins & Minerals 8
Fiber Will Fix It 14
USDA Food Guide Pyramid 18
Watch Your Weight 18
Weight Loss Pyramid 22

Chapter 2 **Conquering the Grocery Store** 27
Find the Best Food Buys
Choosing & Storing Quality Foods 30
We'd Like to Propose a Roast! 36
Yogurt is Good Bacteria 38
Finding a Good Egg 39
Avoiding Food-Borne Illness 40
Reading Food Labels 44

Chapter 3 **First Things First** 47
Cooking & Housecleaning Basics
For Good Measure 48
Simple Substitutions 50
Common Cooking Terms 52
Tried & True Cooking Tips 55
Add a Little Spice 58
Making Life Easier 61
Recipes for Things You Can't Eat 70

Chapter 4 **Home Is Where the Food Is** 73
Recipes You Can Live By
Breakfast 74
Eggs 87

Sandwiches 95
Soups 105
Salads 115
Main Dishes 125
Vegetarian Main Dishes 155
Side Dishes 165
Breads 175
Beverages 189
Cakes, Pies & Puddings 197
Cookies & Bars 207
Candies & Sweet Treats 217
Easy Microwave Cooking 225

Chapter 5   Keeping Up Appearances 239
Laundry & Clothing Repair
The Shrinking Laundry Pile 240
Quick & Dirty Stain Removal 243
Keeping Clothes in Repair 253
Pressing Matters 256

Chapter 6   Easing the Pain 259
Basic First Aid

Chapter 7   Just a Cold or Pneumonia? 269
When to See A Doctor
Common Illnesses 270
Serious & Chronic Diseases 279
Sexually Transmitted Diseases 292
Drug Abuse & Addiction 296

Chapter 8   Getting From Here to There 299
Maintenance & Safe Traveling
Keeping up a Bicycle 300
Automobile Maintenance 301
Personal, Travel & Home Safety 303
Your Mom's Best Advice 306

Index 310

CHAPTER **1**

What Are You Eating?
Know Your Nutrients

The nutritional war has been waged for centuries. Children, eager to tumble on the warm lawn after a batted baseball, sit instead, lower lip stuck out, stubbornly refusing to eat those soggy canned vegetables. Mother's voice booms from the steamy kitchen: "If you don't eat them now, you'll eat them cold, for breakfast."

You may remember from your childhood that you had to eat meat, drink a lot of milk, snack on fruits, gobble up vegetables and even choke down liver. Mom knew best that a nutritious and balanced diet builds strong bodies. Once you are grown and on your own, nutritional eating is still important to keep you healthy, help you resist disease and infection, and make you mentally alert and physically strong.

The chemistry behind nutrition is complex – which chemical agents work and how – but the basics of nutrition are simple. Six essential nutrients make up a balanced diet: proteins, carbohydrates, fats, water, vitamins and minerals. Adequate daily fiber is also essential to good health.

1

Meat and dairy carry more calories and fat, while plant sources of protein provide more fiber, vitamins and minerals. For a healthy balance, eat some combined plant sources every day for your protein needs!

Power Packed Proteins

Called the *building blocks* of the body, proteins fight infections and grow, maintain and repair tissue. Protein is in our hair, muscles, skin, tendons and cartilage.

The body uses proteins to create antibodies and regenerate vital hormones such as insulin, adrenaline and thyroxin. Proteins create enzymes to aid digestion and support biochemical reactions.

The body cannot store protein. Space your intake of protein throughout the day to stay well fueled. Proteins should make up 10 to 15 percent of daily nutrients, about 50 grams in a 2,000-calorie diet. *(Metric tip: estimate 28 grams to an ounce.)*

Eat some meat, dairy and plant sources each day to satisfy protein needs. Most Americans eat too much meat and too much protein – four to five times more than we need every day! Extra protein means more calories and fat. High-protein diets stress the liver and kidneys. Too much protein also causes us to sacrifice carbohydrates, vitamins, minerals and fiber found in other foods.

The body needs eight essential amino acids. Proteins consist of chains of amino acids. Of the 22 amino acids found in animal and plant foods, eight are essential to human health and can only be obtained through diet. Complete proteins provide all essential amino acids.

Animal proteins found in eggs, milk, cheese, beef, pork, fish and poultry, are popular choices because each one alone provides a complete protein. So, if you eat a chunk of cheese, you meet the protein requirement for that meal. Ditto for a breast of chicken, a piece of fish, a pork chop or a tender steak.

Incomplete proteins contain small amounts of one or more essential amino acids. Most plant foods alone are incomplete, such as legumes, nuts, seeds, grains and vegetables. Some soybean products, such as tofu, however, do provide a complete protein.

Plant sources easily combine to make a complete protein. If you don't eat animal products or if you want to cut down on fatty meats, choose plant combinations, like rice and beans, for your daily protein needs instead. Certain combinations will provide a complete protein. Simply eat any whole grains with any dried beans; soy and whole grains; soy and seeds; whole grains and nuts; dried beans and dairy; or legumes, nuts and seeds. (Legumes include dried peas, lentils and dried beans, like kidney, pinto and lima beans.)

For example, whole grains and nuts make a complete protein, so spread some peanut butter on a slice of whole-wheat bread and there's your protein requirement for one meal. To combine nuts and dairy, just pour low-fat milk over nutty granola for breakfast. Dried beans and dairy? Wrap some refried beans and cheese in a warm tortilla for lunch.

Plant protein sources have advantages over animal sources. Meat and dairy products are higher in calories and fat, while combined plant sources of protein are richer in vitamins, minerals and fiber. For a healthy balance, choose foods from animal, dairy and combined plant sources every day.

DAILY NUTRITIONAL NEEDS		
(based on a 2,000 calorie diet)		
NUTRIENT	**DAILY NEED**	**DAILY PERCENTAGE**
Protein	50 grams	10 to 15 percent
Carbohydrate	300 grams	55 to 60 percent
Total Fat Saturated fat Cholesterol	65 grams less than 20 grams under 300 milligrams	25 to 30 percent (under 10 percent)
Fiber	25 to 30 grams	See the Vitamins and Minerals chart on page 11.
Water	64 ounces	

Source: United States Food and Drug Administration

Simple & Complex Carbohydrates

Carbohydrates provide the energy our bodies need to function and are contained in starchy and sugary foods. Carbohydrates also help protein perform. Without carbohydrates, protein can't do its job. And without sufficient protein, the body can't grow, maintain or heal itself.

Approximately 55 to 60 percent of your daily calories should come from carbohydrates. That adds up to about 300 grams in a 2,000-calorie diet. Choose fresh foods first. Take pride and pleasure in preparing your food. Processed and packaged foods contain high amounts of sugar, salt and preservatives that can harm the body.

You can get carbohydrates (and quick energy) by eating the simple sugars in candy, honey, syrup, jam, jelly, cake, pie and other sweet snacks, but your body will function better if you avoid the highs and lows that sugary foods give you.

Look for the best carbohydrates in fresh and dried fruits, potatoes, legumes, corn, wheat bread, brown rice, pasta and whole-grain cereals like oatmeal or creamy wheat. These foods, made up of complex carbohydrates, take longer to break down in the body, providing energy for an extended period of time.

Good & Bad Fats

At first glance, it would seem that we would want to eliminate fat altogether from our diet, but the right kinds of fat play an essential role in good health. Americans simply eat too much of the wrong kinds of fat, which makes us fat.

Fat stores energy, cushions organs from shock and insulates against temperature extremes. Fat makes skin supple and hair bright. Fats, in fact, are part of the structure of every cell.

We ingest three main types of fat: saturated, polyunsaturated and monounsaturated. Fats should make up 25 to 30 percent of daily calorie intake, but less than 10 percent should come from saturated fat.

Saturated fat, *the bad fat,* **is solid at room temperature.** Main sources are meats and whole-milk dairy products. Too much saturated fat clogs arteries, impedes blood flow and increases the risk of heart disease, heart attack and high blood pressure.

Monounsaturated and polyunsaturated fats, *the good fats,* **provide essential fatty acids.** The human body cannot create essential fatty acids on its own and must obtain them from food. Monounsaturated and polyunsaturated fats, which are mostly liquid at room temperature, come mainly from plant and fish oils.

Essential fatty acids keep cells healthy and transport fat-soluble vitamins to tissues. They also help control cholesterol levels in the blood. Cholesterol is an important cousin to fat. It builds brain and nerve tissues, constructs cell membranes and helps produce steroid hormones and bile acids for processing food.

We do not need to consume dietary cholesterol. The liver makes all the cholesterol our bodies need, but most diets contain substantial amounts of cholesterol in fatty meats, egg yolks, whole-milk dairy products and some shellfish. Too much cholesterol will form fatty deposits in arteries and cause heart disease.

Two essential fatty acids must come from food:

Linolenic acid, called **Omega-3**, comes from cold water fish such as tuna, cod, salmon, shellfish, trout, mackerel, bluefish, herring, sardines and anchovies. Non-meat sources of linolenic acid include canola oil and olive oil, or foods made with or prepared in them.

Linoleic acid, called **Omega-6**, is in corn oil, safflower oil, sunflower oil and liquid or soft margarines with liquid vegetable oil as the first ingredient. Omega-6 is also found in seafood and in breast milk.

*Did you know?
Despite traditionally
high-fat diets, native
Greeks and Eskimos
have lower rates
of heart disease
than Americans.
Their staple foods,
olive oil in Crete
and cold-water fish
in Alaska, provide
fatty acids that
lower cholesterol.*

Lipoproteins are made of large molecules of fat and protein that transport cholesterol in the bloodstream. LDL, or low-density lipoproteins, carry cholesterol to body tissues and can clog arteries.

HDL, also called high-density lipoproteins, take cholesterol away from body tissues and protect against heart disease.

Monounsaturated fat, found in canola and olive oils, lowers LDL levels and *increases* HDL levels.

Polyunsaturated fat, found in vegetable and fish oils, lowers LDL *and* HDL levels, but also provides essential fatty acids.

Don't overdo vegetable oils. To reap the benefits of Omega-6 fatty acids, you need to ingest only 2 tablespoons of any vegetable oil a day. That includes the oil you use to cook foods in and the soft margarine you spread on your bread.

Although there is no official recommended daily allowance (RDA) for essential fatty acids, research does show that the cardiovascular system will benefit greatly from as little as 200 milligrams (mg). *(Metric Tip: A milligram is one-thousandth of a gram.)* That adds up to as little as one or two servings of fish per week.

In addition to plant and fish oils, you can get essential fatty acids in smaller amounts from walnuts, soybeans, wheat germ, flaxseed oil, peanut oil, soybean oil and cottonseed oil.

The Skinny on Fat

Eat more fish.

Use olive oil and liquid or soft margarines.

Cook foods in canola oil or peanut oil.

Do not eat foods made with lard or shortening.

Eliminate foods fried in saturated fat.

Decrease consumption of meat, butter and whole-milk dairy products.

Water Will Keep You Well

You are half water. Water comprises just over 50 percent of your weight. Every cell, tissue and organ needs water to function. In fact, water is the nutrient your body needs in the greatest amount. The body will function best when 64 ounces – that's eight 8-ounce glasses – of water is consumed every day.

Often overlooked as a nutrient, water is part of the blood and lymph systems that transport all essential elements to cells and carry away wastes. You can survive as long as six weeks without food, but without water you could die in a week.

Water lubricates and cushions joints and organs, regulates body temperature, prevents constipation, protects against heat exhaustion and hydrates the skin, eyes, mouth and nose.

Drink a lot of water as part of your daily routine. Carry a full water bottle in the car, in your backpack, totebag or briefcase; to school, to work, to recreational events, to exercise class, to the library, to the park or on a walk. Especially take water with you on any activity that will require physical exertion.

Once you regularly drink the large amount of water your body needs every day, you will crave liquids. Don't try to meet your fluid needs with alcohol, coffee, tea or caffeinated soft drinks. These act as diuretics and actually pull water from the body.

Decaffeinated teas, hot or cold, are good choices for fluid needs. Studies show that antioxidants in decaffeinated green and black teas may reduce the risk of heart disease and cancer. Antioxidants are compounds that protect against disease by neutralizing unstable molecules in the body. Beta-carotene, vitamin C and vitamin E are antioxidants. You can also meet fluid needs with herbal teas, juices, milk and soups.

Mom says:
Drink eight 8-ounce glasses of water every day.
Carry a water bottle with you in your car, backpack or briefcase.
Even slight dehydration can cause headache and fatigue.
So, take several water breaks throughout the day.

Vital Vitamins & Minerals

Researchers have found about 20 vitamins that are essential for health. If you eat a balanced diet, you will likely get all of them but vitamin D, which is formed in skin exposed to the sun. Water-soluble vitamins dissolve in body fluids. Fat-soluble vitamins A, D, E and K dissolve in fat, and excess is stored in fat cells. No vitamin or mineral works alone. Nature made them dependent upon one another to nourish the body.

Fat-Soluble Vitamins

Vitamin A. Known to promote good vision, vitamin A also helps maintain mucous membranes and protect against infection. Vitamin A promotes healthy skin and strong tooth enamel. Sources include broccoli, carrots, corn, spinach, sweet potatoes, winter squash, apricots, cantaloupe, peaches, cheese, margarine, egg yolks and liver. The RDA (recommended daily allowance) for vitamin A is 5,000 International Units (I.U.) per day. Fat-soluble vitamins are measured in I.U.

Vitamin D. The skin produces vitamin D when exposed to the sun. Vitamin D enables the body to utilize calcium for strong bones and teeth. Food sources include oily fish, egg yolks, butter and fortified milk. The RDA for vitamin D is 400 I.U.

Vitamin E. Critical to the formation of red blood cells, vitamin E is essential for steady growth and disease resistance. Because it is necessary for reproduction and lactation, a vitamin E deficiency can cause miscarriage and sterility. As an antioxidant, vitamin E protects cells from environmental and chemical pollutants. The main sources to look for are plant-based margarines and cooking oils. Whole grains, almonds and sunflower seeds are also good sources. The RDA for vitamin E is 30 I.U.

Vitamin K. Essential for blood clotting, vitamin K supports bone formation and boosts metabolism. A shortage of this vitamin can lead to hemorrhage and loss of calcium from bones. Vitamin K is produced by beneficial intestinal bacteria. Some food sources include potatoes, green leafy vegetables, cabbage, cauliflower, peas, cereals and beef liver. The RDA for vitamin K is 80 µ g (micrograms).

Should I Pop a Pill?

Yes, if you eat poorly, you should take a supplement with 100% RDA of all essential vitamins and minerals.

Definitely take a supplement if you drink alcohol or smoke heavily, take medications regularly or have a chronic illness; or if you are a woman who is pregnant, nursing, menopausal or taking birth control pills.

Watch vitamin levels in any supplement as fat-soluble vitamins can become toxic. Do not take an extra multi-vitamin just to get higher doses of a single vitamin or mineral. If you need more than the RDA of a specific one, like vitamin C during cold season, buy it separately.

Store supplements in a dry, cool place, away from sunlight. A kitchen cupboard is a good place. Always keep supplements out of the reach of children.

Remember to take any multivitamin with a full meal. Without food in the stomach, you'll lose the supplement's benefit in the first three hours, and you will likely experience stomach upset and nausea.

Water-Soluble Vitamins

Vitamin B-1, Thiamin, enables the body to utilize carbohydrates, promotes normal appetite, supports digestion and helps the nervous system function. Sources include pork (three times richer than other meats), beef, poultry, oysters, eggs, whole-grain breads, soybeans, rolled oats, fortified cereals, broccoli, legumes and liver. The RDA for thiamin is 1.5 mg (milligrams).

Vitamin B-2, Riboflavin, helps the body utilize energy and maintains healthy skin, eyes and lips. Sources of riboflavin include milk, ice cream, cheese, cottage cheese, beef, fish, poultry, eggs, yogurt, enriched cereals, whole-grain breads, peanuts and beef liver. The RDA for Vitamin B-2 is 1.7 mg.

Vitamin B-3, Niacin, helps the body use oxygen and assimilate other vitamins, bolsters the nervous system, promotes mental and emotional health and enables the digestive system to function smoothly. Sources of niacin include beef liver, pork, tuna, turkey, milk, fortified cereals, whole-grain breads and peanut butter. The RDA for niacin is 20 mg.

Vitamin B-6, Pyridoxol, is needed to metabolize protein and fat, form red blood cells, support the nervous system and promote healthy skin. Sources are whole grains, meat, spinach, bananas, nuts, tomatoes and wheat germ. The RDA for B-6 is 2 mg.

Vitamin B-12, Cobalamin, is essential in forming red blood cells, building genetic material, promoting normal growth and supporting the nervous system. Good sources include clams, liver, oysters, mackerel, sardines, meat, eggs and milk. The RDA for B-12 is 6 µg.

Biotin is necessary in the formation of essential fatty acids and helps the body derive energy from carbohydrates. Sources include dark green vegetables, egg yolks and liver. Biotin is also produced by intestinal bacteria and can be destroyed by raw egg whites. The RDA for biotin is 300 µg.

Vitamin C, Ascorbic Acid, is necessary for the body to form the collagen that holds cells together. Vitamin C tones the blood vessels and helps the body resist infection, heal wounds and repair broken bones. Sources include oranges, tangerines, grapefruit, lemons, limes, tomatoes, green peppers, broccoli, cabbage, brussels sprouts, kale, spinach, potatoes, sweet potatoes, strawberries and cantaloupe. The RDA for vitamin C is 60 mg.

Folic Acid acts with vitamin B-12 to build genetic material (determinants of heredity) and is critical to the formation of hemoglobin in red blood cells. Women who use oral contraceptives require extra folic acid and should take a supplement or eat foods rich in folic acid. A deficiency of this nutrient during pregnancy can lead to abnormalities in the baby. Sources include orange juice, spinach, broccoli, asparagus, wheat germ, beef liver, dried beans and peas and brewer's yeast. The RDA for folic acid is 400 µg.

Pantothenic Acid helps form hormones and is essential to the nervous system. It helps the body use proteins, carbohydrates and fats. Made by intestinal bacteria, pantothenic acid is destroyed in heavily refined and processed foods. Good sources of pantothenic acid include dark green vegetables, milk, whole grains, eggs, nuts, soybeans and beef liver. The RDA for pantothenic acid is 10 mg.

Macro Minerals

Calcium is essential to life. It helps regulate heart rhythm, maintain cell membranes, strengthen nerve function, absorb vitamin B-12 and build strong bones and teeth. Calcium also helps blood clot and muscles contract. The best source of calcium is low-fat milk. Others include salmon, sardines, yogurt, oranges, sesame seeds and cheese. The RDA for calcium is 1,000 mg. Older women should take extra calcium to prevent osteoporosis, a thinning of the bones.

Chloride is found in regular table salt and natural salts. It helps regulate starch-splitting enzymes, body fluids and stomach acids. The RDA for chloride is 3,400 mg.

Sodium regulates internal water balance and helps transmit nerve impulses throughout the body. Most Americans get too much sodium by eating too much salt. Sodium is found in cottage cheese, cheese, milk, spinach and shellfish. The RDA for sodium is 2,400 mg.

Magnesium is essential in releasing energy from muscles. It also helps the body conduct nerve impulses,

Daily Vitamin and Mineral Needs
(based on a 2,000 calorie diet)

Sodium	2400 mg.
Potassium	3500 mg.
Vitamin A	5000 I.U.
Vitamin C	60 mg.
Calcium	1000 mg.
Iron	18 mg.
Vitamin D	400 I.U.
Vitamin E	30 I.U.
Vitamin K	80 µg
Thiamin B-1	1.5 mg.
Riboflavin B-2	1.7 mg.
Niacin B-3	20 mg.
Vitamin B-6	2 mg.
Folic Acid	400 µg
Vitamin B-12	6 µg
Biotin	300 µg
Pantothenic acid	10 mg.
Phosphorus	1000 mg.
Iodine	150 µg
Magnesium	400 mg.
Zinc	15 mg.
Selenium	70 µg
Copper	2 mg.
Manganese	2 mg.
Chromium	120 µg
Molybdenum	75 µg
Chloride	3400 mg.

Nutrients are listed in the order required to appear on labels for packaged foods.

I.U.	= International Units
mg	= milligrams
µg	= micrograms

Source: United States Food and Drug Administration

11

Shake the Salt Habit

We eat too much salt! On the average, each of us downs about 15 pounds a year.

Most Americans consume up to 6,000 milligrams (mg) of sodium a day. A healthy amount is at least 500 mg and no more than 2,400 mg.

The best daily intake of sodium is about 1,800 mg. That adds up to less than 1 teaspoon of salt a day.

Too much salt increases the risk of high blood pressure, causes water retention, taxes the kidneys and pulls calcium from the bones.

We can easily identify salt in foods like potato chips, pretzels and peanuts, but salt also hides in foods like gelatin desserts, puddings and soups. Soup and gravy mixes are especially high in salt.

Highly processed and packaged foods usually have too much salt. Anything under 140 mg per serving is low in sodium. Any item exceeding 480 mg is high in sodium.

• Cook without adding salt. People can add it at the table.

• Try tasting the food before you add salt. Really, this works!

• Check your medications. Antacids are typically high in sodium.

• Healthy packaged or processed food choices have no more than 360 mg of sodium per serving.

• Drain and rinse all canned produce, then cook it in fresh water.

• Eat low-sodium cheese, butter and margarine.

utilize proteins and build strong bones. Magnesium may protect against heart disease, help lower blood pressure and slow down bone loss. Sources include soybeans, wheat germ, sunflower seeds, seafood, dairy, meat, nuts, whole grains and vegetables. The RDA for magnesium is 400 mg.

Phosphorus is essential in the formation of genetic material. It helps maintain cell membranes, bones and teeth. Phosphorus also helps utilize energy from other nutrients and promotes proper blood acid balance. Sources include milk, cottage cheese, fish, poultry, meat, eggs and legumes. The RDA for phosphorus is 1,000 mg.

Potassium is critical for utilizing energy. It helps maintain fluid levels, transmit nerve impulses and contract muscles. Potassium also helps excrete extra sodium from the body, alleviating water retention and lowering blood pressure. Some sources are bananas, dried fruits, orange juice, peanut butter, potatoes, legumes, bran, milk, tea, coffee and cocoa. The RDA for potassium is 3,500 mg.

Trace Minerals

Chromium is necessary for insulin activity. It can relieve low blood sugar, lower risk for diabetes and protect the heart. Sources are fruit juices, broccoli, black pepper, barbecue sauce, meat, cheese, whole grains and peanuts. The RDA for chromium is 120 µg.

Copper is critical in forming red blood cells, and is essential to several respiratory enzymes. Sources include nuts, cocoa, cherries, shellfish, mushrooms, whole grains, gelatin, corn oil, liver and legumes. The RDA for copper is 2 mg.

Iodine is an element in thyroid hormones needed for reproduction and growth. Iodine helps prevent goiter, a swelling of the neck. Sources include spinach, lobster, shrimp, oysters, milk and iodized salt. The RDA for iodine is 150 µg.

Iron is critical in forming blood hemoglobin and comprises many proteins and enzymes. Sources are red meat, liver, tofu, pumpkin seeds, dried apricots, prune juice, spinach, blackstrap molasses, whole grains and legumes. The RDA for iron is 18 mg.

Manganese is needed for a healthy reproductive system. It also improves the nervous system, protects bones and creates enzymes for metabolism of nutrients. Sources include whole grains, nuts, vegetables, fruit, tea, coffee and cocoa. The RDA for manganese is 2 mg.

Molybdenum is an essential component of several enzymes. It may help prevent certain cancers and thwart tooth decay. Sources are legumes, whole-grain breads, cereals, milk and milk products. The RDA for molybdenum is 75 µg.

Selenium is an antioxidant that prevents the breakdown of body substances, battles heart disease, boosts immunity and benefits mood. Sources are fish, oysters, whole grains, bagels, mushrooms, Brazil nuts and dairy products. The RDA for selenium is 70 µg.

Zinc is part of more than 100 enzymes and helps the body grow and heal. Known to shorten cold symptoms, zinc maintains your sense of taste, improves memory and protects vision. Zinc also promotes healthy sexual development. Sources include oysters, crab, lean beef, poultry, eggs, liver, milk and whole grains. The RDA for zinc is 15 mg.

Fiber Will Fix It

Fiber, found in abundance in whole grains, fruits, vegetables and legumes, isn't a nutrient at all, but fiber is just as essential to health as proteins, carbohydrates, fats, water, vitamins and minerals. Classified as water-soluble and water-insoluble, fiber is the indigestible cell walls of plants sometimes referred to as *roughage*.

You should consume about 20 to 35 grams of fiber every day. The average American diet of processed and packaged food offers only eleven to twelve grams of fiber a day.

Soluble fiber lowers cholesterol and controls blood sugar. Sources include fresh vegetables, legumes, seeds, brown rice, fresh fruits and oat, barley and rice bran.

Insoluble fiber prevents constipation and moves wastes. This fiber can lower the risk of colorectal cancer, alleviate some digestive disorders and prevent hemorrhoids. Sources include wheat bran, corn bran, whole grains, vegetables, fruit skins and nuts.

Cooked legumes, lentils, kidney, pinto or lima beans are some of the best sources of fiber, but they can also cause gas and bloating. To reduce gas, soak dried beans until about double in size, rinse them and cook them in fresh water.

This represents 35 grams of fiber in real food for one day:

1/2 cup bran cereal	=	12 grams
2 slices wheat bread	=	4 grams
Lettuce w/tomatoes	=	2 grams
Medium apple	=	3 grams
1/2 banana	=	1 gram
Baked potato	=	4 grams
1/2 cup peas	=	2 grams
1 cup lettuce salad	=	1 gram
1 cup strawberries	=	3 grams
1-ounce peanuts	=	3 grams

If you increase fiber, also increase your fluid intake. Eating unprocessed bran or other bulk producers dry can obstruct the esophagus or lead to gas, bloating and constipation. So drink plenty of water – eight 8-oz glasses every day. Add fiber gradually to your diet so that intestinal bacteria can adjust, or you may experience gas and diarrhea. Only use fiber supplements if instructed by your physician or a dietitian. Only use laxatives or enemas as a last resort because your system can become dependent upon them.

To Increase Daily Fiber:

- Add fruit to your cereal.
- Buy whole-grain breads.
- Snack on fruits and nuts.
- Use brown rice instead of white rice.
- Try bran in baked goods.
- Eat a bran cereal daily.
- Eat whole fruits with peels.
- Eat popcorn instead of potato chips.
- Replace meat with plant protein sources twice a week.
- Eat generous helpings of fresh vegetables more often with meals.
- Prepare a cooked vegetable *and* a green salad with dinner.
- Drink plenty of water to keep fiber moving through the body.

Just Say No to Sugar

The average American eats about 100 pounds of processed white sugar a year. Sugar tastes good, but it has virtually no vitamins or minerals – only calories.

White sugar is blamed for many ills like obesity, tooth decay, diabetes, hyperactivity and heart disease. Statistics show that sugar added to food makes up about 25 percent of an adult's daily calorie intake. The figure is closer to 50 percent for teenagers.

If you are eating 300 grams of carbohydrates a day, only 30 grams should be from sugar. Sugar includes the sucrose, glucose, fructose, lactose and maltose found naturally in fruits, vegetables, whole-grain flour, cereal and milk. Processed foods usually contain additives including corn syrup and white, brown or powdered sugar. Most added sugar comes from sugar cane or sugar beets. Of all sweeteners, honey has some nutrients and blackstrap molasses has the most.

Sugar craving is a vicious cycle. A quick dose of it causes the blood sugar to rise rapidly. In order to handle the overdose, the body releases more insulin, which forces the sugar levels to plummet. This brings on another sugar craving. Eat more sugar for quick energy and the cycle continues.

To fight sugar cravings, nibble on nonprocessed foods. Choose from roasted nuts, sunflower or pumpkin seeds, raw vegetables, fresh or dried fruits, cheeses and hard-boiled eggs. Snack every two or three hours and take nutritious items to work or school. If you hit a sugar slump, get up and move. A few jumping jacks or a 10-minute walk will stabilize blood sugar levels.

Eat more complex carbohydrates. Increase your intake of whole grains, raw vegetables and fresh fruits. These will keep your blood sugar at an even level because they break down more slowly than the simple sugar in sweets. Complex carbohydrates also fill you up and keep you satisfied so that you won't be tempted to reach for a sugar snack.

The trick to not binging: Don't deprive yourself completely. Have a *small* forbidden treat once a week or eat low-sugar alternatives such as animal crackers,

---

To Reduce Sugar Intake:

Drop the soft drinks and candy altogether. A 12-ounce soft drink has nine teaspoons of sugar. A candy bar has about seven.

Avoid processed junk food. Snack instead on fresh fruits, vegetables, crackers, popcorn, nuts and cheese.

Substitute apple juice for the liquid in a recipe and eliminate the sugar, or cut the amount of sugar called for in half.

Get creative with dessert. Instead of ice-cream, eat a bowl of fresh raspberries topped with sugar-free whipped topping.

Get back to home cooking. Most packaged foods we buy have too much sugar. You may find you even enjoy cooking!

Buy a diabetic cookbook. Then you won't be deprived of your favorite desserts, cakes, candies and cookies.

Read food labels very closely. Ingredients are listed in order of amounts. If sugar is one of the first on the list, don't buy it.

Choose low-sugar snacks: Fruit topped with yogurt, ice milk or sherbet; hot milk with cinnamon and vanilla extract; gelatin with added fruit; angel food cake; or cinnamon toast.

fig bars, ginger snaps, vanilla wafers or graham crackers. Stay away from soft drinks. They equal 20 percent of all sugar consumed. Even drinks with artificial sweeteners only feed your desire for sugar.

Food Guide Pyramid

Do you remember as a student in elementary school, ripping out magazine pictures of all your favorite foods and pasting them onto construction paper to make up the Basic Four Food Groups: Milk, Meat, Fruit-Vegetable, and Grains? Times have changed. The United States Department of Agriculture has developed a new guide. Now, think pyramid. Five food groups make up *The Food Guide Pyramid:*

The Bread, Cereal, Rice and Pasta Group (6-11 servings daily) forms the base of the pyramid. The Vegetable Group (3-5 servings) and the Fruit Group (2-4 servings) make up the second level. The Milk, Yogurt and Cheese Group (2-3 servings) and the Meat, Poultry, Fish, Dry Beans, Eggs and Nuts Group (2-3 servings) comprise level three. The peak, Fats, Oils and Sweets, isn't even considered a food group, so use these items sparingly.

The Food Guide Pyramid replaces the old "Basic Four" that many of us grew up with. The old way offered variety, but didn't reflect what we now know about restricting fat and increasing fiber, vitamins and minerals.

In all five groups, try to eat nonfat and lean selections as often as possible. Choose nonfat or 1% milk instead of 2% or whole milk. Choose low-fat cheese, yogurt and salad dressing. Eat lean meat instead of fatty cuts. Eat natural whole-grain breads and cereals that are not processed with fat and sugar. Fill up on vegetables and fruits. The USDA's campaign of "5 A Day" reminds children to eat at least three servings of vegetables and two servings of fruit each day. It is wise advice for adults, too. The more vegetables and fruits, the better.

Did you know?
If you eat whole grains, fruits and vegetables without added fats, plus lean meat for protein, you can eat big meals and still lose weight. Quality foods high in fiber, vitamins and minerals boost your metabolism, helping you burn excess fat.

How Much is One Serving?

<u>Bread, Cereal & Grains</u>
(at least 6 servings daily)
1 slice whole-grain bread
1 medium muffin
1/2 hot dog/hamburger bun
1/2 bagel or English muffin
4 small crackers
1 corn or flour tortilla
1 cup cold cereal
1/2 cup cooked cereal
1/2 cup cooked rice
1/2 cup cooked pasta

<u>Vegetables</u>
(at least 3 servings daily)
1/2 cup cooked vegetables
1/2 cup raw vegetables
1 cup raw leafy vegetables
3/4 cup vegetable juice

<u>Fruit</u>
(at least 2 servings)
1 whole medium fruit
1/4 cup dried fruit
1/2 cup canned fruit
3/4 cup fruit juice

<u>Dairy</u>
(at least 2 servings)
1 cup milk or yogurt
2 slices cheese, 1/8" thick
1/2 cup cottage cheese
1 1/2 cups ice cream

<u>Protein</u>
(at least 2 servings)
3 oz. cooked lean meat
2 eggs
7 oz. tofu
1 cup cooked legumes
4 Tbsp. peanut butter
1/2 cup nuts or seeds

*Source: United States
Department of Agriculture*

USDA Food Guide Pyramid

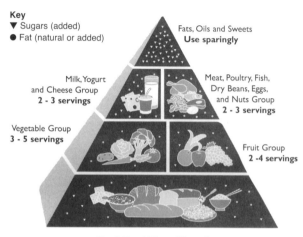

Key
▼ Sugars (added)
● Fat (natural or added)

Fats, Oils and Sweets
Use sparingly

Milk, Yogurt and Cheese Group
2 - 3 servings

Meat, Poultry, Fish, Dry Beans, Eggs, and Nuts Group
2 - 3 servings

Vegetable Group
3 - 5 servings

Fruit Group
2 - 4 servings

Bread, Cereal, Rice and Pasta Group
6 - 11 servings

Source: United States Department of Agriculture (USDA)

If you want to lose weight, eat the minimum number of servings recommended on the Food Guide Pyramid. If you want to gain weight, eat the maximum number of servings.

Watch Your Weight

(But Don't Obsess)

First and foremost, see your doctor if you plan to lose weight, change your diet or increase physical activity. With an OK from your physician, you may try some of these weight management strategies.

People wanting to maintain a healthy body weight should stay away from *empty calories*. Processed foods and snacks, fattening desserts, candy and carbonated drinks that contain no nutritional value will simply fill you up with empty calories.

For example, a slice of bleached white flour bread is all empty calories, while a slice of whole-grain wheat bread provides vitamins, minerals and fiber in addition to energy (calories). *Remember: High-nutrition food equals high-octane body fuel.*

There's no magic to weight loss or gain. There are 3,500 calories per pound of fat. If you want to lose one pound a week, cut your daily intake of calories by 500. If you eat 2,000 calories a day, which is average for an adult woman (2,500 for men), then eat a balanced diet of only 1,500 calories. After seven days, you've ingested 3,500 calories less – goodbye pound. Eat 500 more calories daily if you want to gain weight. Of course, sticking to a balanced eating plan takes discipline. Follow these tips to help:

Eat breakfast like a king and dinner like a pauper! You need the calories and nutrients in a balanced breakfast to kick start your metabolism. Likewise, if you eat a huge dinner then go to sleep, your body will store the unused calories as fat.

Eat the right kinds of foods more often during the day to help you stay on a lower-calorie diet. Then you will be more satisfied and less likely to binge on high-calorie snacks. The more water and fiber you ingest, the better. Both will fill you up and keep you on track.

Pack your daytime snacks. Choose from apples, oranges, grapes, strawberries, crackers, string cheese, peanuts, pretzels, oatmeal cookies, hard-boiled eggs, carrots, celery, yogurt, milk, fruit or vegetable juices and other portable items. Take them to work, school and play. Be prepared for a snack attack.

If you want to lose weight faster, *burn* calories by exercising. Studies show that the best weight-loss plan combines a reduced-calorie diet and moderate exercise at least three times a week. Plus, the more you exercise, the more muscle you build, and muscle burns more calories than fat. Better muscle tone will also speed up your resting metabolism so you burn more calories even when you're not exerting yourself.

Keep in mind that muscle weighs more than fat. If you are building muscle, don't watch the scale. Watch your inches and clothing size instead. When

Mom says: To keep your energy up and your weight down, eat every three hours or so during the day. Have breakfast around 7 a.m., a snack at 10 a.m., lunch at noon, a snack at 3 p.m., a small dinner at 6 p.m. and maybe some warm milk and wheat bread around 9 p.m., just before bedtime.

you exercise, you will lose more inches than weight at first, so don't get discouraged if the scale doesn't show progress immediately. It will catch up soon enough as you continue your eating and exercise routine.

Exercise even if you don't lose weight. When you move your body, get your heart pumping and use more oxygen, the activity not only burns calories but also tones muscles, relieves stress and releases endorphins in the brain. Endorphins make you happy, energetic, serene and just more fun to be around.

New studies show that people with a little extra weight on them are *not* dying earlier. The *Healthy Height and Weight Table* reflects weights of people who live the longest in each height category.

You are considered overweight if you are ten to 20 pounds over your healthy weight range. If you are overweight, a weight loss of just 10% of your total weight, or ten pounds, can greatly improve your health simply by causing a reduction in blood pressure and cholesterol levels.

What's Your Frame Size?

Extend arm in front of body, and bend elbow at 90-degree angle.

Keep fingers straight and turn inside of wrist away from body.

Put other thumb and index finger on the two prominent bones on either side of the bent elbow.

Measure distance between bones with a tape measure.

Compare this measurement to the medium-frame chart.

Determine your height while in your bare feet.

If you are below the listed inches, your frame is small. If you are above, your frame is large.

Elbow Measurement for a Medium Frame

Women	Elbow Breadth
4'10" – 4'11"	2 1/4" – 2 1/2"
5'0" – 5'3"	2 1/4" – 2 1/2"
5'4" – 5'7"	2 3/8" – 2 5/8"
5'8" – 5'11"	2 3/8" – 2 5/8"
6'0" – taller	2 1/2" – 2 3/4"

Men	Elbow Breadth
5'2" – 5'3"	2 1/2" – 2 7/8"
5'4" – 5'7"	2 5/8" – 2 7/8"
5'8" – 5'11"	2 3/4" – 3"
6'0" – 6'3"	2 3/4" – 3 1/8"
6'4" – taller	2 7/8" – 3 1/4"

Healthy Height and Weight Table

WOMEN	Small	Med	Large	MEN	Small	Med	Large
4'10"	102-111	109-121	118-131	5'2"	128-134	131-141	138-150
4'11"	103-113	111-123	120-134	5'3"	130-136	133-143	140-153
5'0"	104-115	113-126	122-137	5'4"	132-138	135-145	142-156
5'1"	106-118	115-129	125-140	5'5"	134-140	137-148	144-160
5'2"	108-121	118-132	128-143	5'6"	136-142	139-151	146-164
5'3"	111-124	121-135	131-147	5'7"	138-145	142-145	149-168
5'4"	114-127	124-138	134-151	5'8"	140-148	145-157	152-172
5'5"	117-130	127-141	137-155	5'9"	142-151	148-160	155-176
5'6"	120-133	130-144	140-159	5'10"	144-154	151-163	158-180
5'7"	123-136	133-147	143-163	5'11"	146-157	154-166	161-184
5'8"	126-139	136-150	146-167	6'0"	149-160	157-170	164-188
5'9"	129-142	139-153	149-170	6'1"	152-164	160-174	168-192
5'10"	132-145	142-156	152-173	6'2"	155-168	164-178	172-197
5'11"	135-148	145-159	155-174	6'3"	158-172	167-182	176-202

Source: Metropolitan Life Insurance Company

Weights are listed for ages 25 to 59 based on lowest mortality
and according to frame size, with clothing and shoes.

Weight Loss Pyramid

To help people lose weight and maintain healthy weight loss, the Mayo Clinic in Rochester, Minnesota, developed the *Mayo Clinic Healthy Weight Pyramid*. It differs from the *USDA Food Guide Pyramid* in that the Mayo Clinic plan stresses large amounts of fruits and vegetables daily and regular exercise for weight loss.

The pyramid is based on research and patient evaluations by Mayo Clinic doctors and dietitians. The studies were conducted by weight-loss experts at Pennsylvania State University and the University of Alabama at Birmingham.

Important Aspects of This Pyramid Include:

• A focus on *low-energy-dense* foods, like fresh fruits and vegetables, that make you feel full on fewer calories. Energy density refers to the calories (energy) in a given serving. Foods with *high-energy density* contain a high number of calories in a small amount of food.

• An unlimited allowance of whole vegetables and fruits in the daily diet – a practice first tried by University of Alabama researchers and found to be effective for proper weight management.

• In addition to fruits and vegetables, whole-grain carbohydrates such as wheat bread, whole cereals, pasta, baked potatoes and brown rice also occupy a large volume in the pyramid. These nutritious, fiber-rich foods take a longer time to eat, leading to lower overall calorie intake and higher satiation.

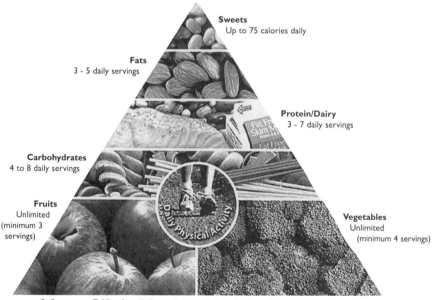

Sweets
Up to 75 calories daily

Fats
3 - 5 daily servings

Protein/Dairy
3 - 7 daily servings

Carbohydrates
4 to 8 daily servings

Fruits
Unlimited
(minimum 3 servings)

Vegetables
Unlimited
(minimum 4 servings)

Daily Physical Activity

Mayo Clinic Healthy Weight Pyramid ™

Mayo Foundation for Medical Education and Research. See your doctor before you begin any healthy weight plan.

Mayo Clinic Pyramid Daily Servings

Fruits...3 servings minimum
Vegetables..4 servings minimum
(Unlimited amounts of fruits and vegetables encouraged)
Whole-Grain Carbohydrates.............4 to 8 servings
Protein and Low-Fat Dairy.................3 to 7 servings
Fats..3 to 5 servings
Sweets ....75 calories

Level 1 is made up of unlimited amounts of vegetables and fruits. You should eat a minimum of four servings of vegetables a day and three servings of fruit a day. One serving of vegetables should equal 25 calories. One serving of fruit should equal 60 calories. That's two cups of a leafy vegetable, one cup of a solid vegetable or 1/2 cup of fruit. The plan encourages snacks and whole meals from these two categories.

Level 2 is made up of carbohydrates, including whole grains, pasta, bread, rice and cereals. The plan recommends four to eight servings each day. One serving of carbohydrates should equal 60 calories. That is 1/2 cup grain or cereal or one slice wheat bread.

Level 3 is made up of protein and dairy with both plant-based and animal-based recommendations, including beans, fish, lean meat and low-fat dairy products. You should have three to seven servings each day. One serving should equal 70 calories. That's 1/3 cup of beans, three ounces of meat or fish, or one cup of skim milk.

Level 4 is fats, which include heart-healthy olive oil, nuts, canola oil and avocados. The Mayo Clinic recommends three to five servings a day. One serving of fat should equal 45 calories. That's one teaspoon oil or one tablespoon nuts.

Level 5 is sweets, including candy and other processed-sugar snacks. You should have no more than 75 calories a day or 525 calories a week. That's about four carbonated sodas a week. Avoid this category – it's full of empty calories.

Mom says:
Sneak fruits and vegetables into your day. Snack on raw veggies instead of potato chips, add fruit to your breakfast cereal, choose the salad bar when you go out for lunch, drink juices instead of coffee, tea or soda.

*M*om says:
Aim for a healthy weight in a healthy way. Be a friend to your body. Get up and out and move every day. Eat nutritious snacks. Treat your body as if it were your child – feed and nurture it well!

A person with 50 pounds or more of extra weight is medically obese. Studies show that 59% of men in the United States are overweight and 20% are obese. Statistics for women show that 50% are overweight and 25% are obese.

An obese person is at higher risk for diabetes, heart disease, stroke, gall bladder disease and cancer of the breast, prostate and colon. Carrying too much weight weakens the immune system and over taxes bones and ligaments. In a society where thin is in, obesity can also bring discrimination and damage a person's self esteem.

If you are obese, see your family physician. *Willpower alone isn't enough.* Obesity is a chronic disease that is often hereditary. A physician, dietician or nutritionist can create a plan that includes healthy eating, exercise, behavior modification and, sometimes, safe medications for weight loss.

Strive for a healthy perspective of your weight. Some people obsess about their weight and appearance to the point of developing addictive and dangerous eating disorders. Such a person uses overeating, purging or starvation to cope with life. Teenagers and women in their 20s are most at risk for:

Binge Eating, episodic compulsive overeating that can lead to massive weight gain. Sufferers eat when not hungry and continue until painfully full. Binge eating disorder results in the same health risks as obesity and, if untreated, can cause premature death.

Bulimia, characterized by rapid consumption of food followed by self-induced vomiting, laxative use, diuretics, fad diets, fasts and vigorous exercise to lose weight. Bulimics are usually normal weight or overweight. Without treatment, bulimia can be fatal.

Anorexia Nervosa, self-starvation marked by extremely low body weight for a prolonged period of time. If left untreated, anorexia is often fatal. People with bulimia or anorexia are malnourished. Both disorders can lead to loss of hair, severe tooth decay and permanent damage to the digestive system, the heart and the brain.

If you or someone you know suffers from an eating disorder, seek professional help. Treatment usually consists of psychological counseling and nutritional education. With treatment, people with eating disorders can recover and live healthy lives.

Avoid fad diets, magic pills or amazing drinks that melt fat. If you are eating well daily and exercising at least three times a week, but you are not a size six or you don't have six-pack abs, relax, be good to yourself and embrace who you are!

Mom Says:
No matter your size,
shape or looks,
you can pursue
your interests
and talents,
succeed at what
you like most
or do best,
enjoy fulfilling
relationships,
get a good job,
keep a home,
have a family,
make a friend
and even change
the world!

Cut Back on Fast Food

It's a real temptation to dash into a fast-food restaurant, sink your teeth into a delicious double burger, gobble up some fries, savor a creamy shake and be on your way again.

But that's not a good idea if you're watching your weight or your budget. A fast-food meal can equal as many calories as you should have in an entire day and can cost you $5 a pop.

If you have a cheeseburger, fries and a shake for lunch that's about 1,000 calories. Have a 10-inch pizza for dinner and you've consumed 2,000 calories for the day and not much nutrition.

Two pieces of deep-fried fish, fries and cole slaw is about 1,000 calories. Add another piece of fish for 350 calories. A roast beef sandwich, fries and a shake adds up to 1,200 calories

Even chicken isn't immune. Expect to find over 1,000 calories with two pieces, potatoes, corn and a roll.

We should all pack our own lunch and take the time to make our own dinner. Here's a reality check: We humans enjoy immediate gratification – the "quick fix", especially when we are hungry and in a hurry.

If you must eat fast food, order a milk or juice instead of a soft drink. Pass on the French fries. Get a sandwich without mayonnaise or cheese, but with tomatoes and lettuce. Many fast food restaurants now offer salads. Use only half of your usual helping of salad dressing.

For pizza, order thin crust and light on the cheese. Don't eat the whole thing yourself! Treat yourself to fast food only once a week. Your body and your wallet will thank you.

Notes

....

....

....

....

....

....

....

....

....

....

....

....

....

....

....

....

....

....

....

....

....

....

....

....

....

....

....

....

2

Conquering the Grocery Store
Find the Best Food Buys

You have your shopping cart, and you're standing in the middle of a crowded grocery aisle. Along the shelves are rows of cans with brightly colored labels, clear plastic bags of curly macaroni and boxes that say, *"Just add water!"* The produce section overflows with fruits and vegetables, and the cooler stocks meats, eggs and cheese. What do you do now?

Shopping well – selecting the very best produce, determining the best buys, avoiding potential food poisoning and getting the most for your hard-earned money – requires some basic knowledge, routine and discipline. By following these guidelines, you can get good food at bargain prices.

Make your money work for you. Getting the most from your food dollar involves some time and effort, not only in the aisles of the grocery store, but at home, before and after you shop. You will want to plan nutritious meals, make a grocery list and decide on a food budget. It sounds tougher than it really is.

Mom says:
Always eat before
you shop.
Then, you won't
purchase unhealthy,
expensive snacks and
you will more likely
stick to your list.
Allow enough time
to compare items
and prices to get
the best bargains.

Check out grocery stores in your community. Prices vary from store to store. Food co-ops and food warehouses often feature lower prices on non-perishables (foods that do not require refrigeration), but many don't carry meat, eggs, cheese, milk and fresh produce. Save money by purchasing dry goods and staples at a food warehouse and shopping for perishables at another store.

Look for a farmers' market. Get a good price on fresh fruits and vegetables from growers who compete with one another. The produce is also fresher and better tasting. This is not true of produce stands where owners usually buy from farmers then mark up the price.

Plan a week's menu before you go shopping. Carefully plan three meals each day. Plan around leftovers; for example, if you eat baked chicken one night, you can put the leftovers in a salad the next day for lunch or in a casserole for dinner. Check your recipes and make a list of every item you'll need for that week.

Keep an ongoing shopping list. Tape a piece of paper to your cupboard for staples and when you're running out of an item, write it down. Also keep a list on the refrigerator for perishables. Then include those items on your final shopping list.

Accurately calculate how much food you'll need. It's no bargain if you buy a large quantity to save money then waste the leftovers. Find out the prices of the foods you regularly buy, then plan meals to stay within your budget.

Learn to read the labels. Food labels tell you serving size, ingredients, calories per serving and recommended daily allowance percentages for protein, carbohydrates, fats, fiber, sugar, sodium, vitamins and minerals for that particular food item.

Compare various forms of the same food type. Do consider personal likes, but remember you can save by buying a less expensive form of the same food. Fresh peas in the pod, for example, often cost more than canned or frozen peas.

Buy less expensive cuts of meat, especially if the meat will be slow cooked. Even inexpensive cuts will be tender when simmered in stew or soup. Also, whole chickens cost less per pound than chicken parts. Use the leftovers in soups and casseroles.

Compare the brands of the same kind of packaged foods. Many large grocery chains have house brands that cost less than national brands. Many generic products are as good as brand names, and nutritional quality is the same by law.

Resist the temptation to grab extras. Stores purposely tempt you to buy on impulse. To get the milk, you must walk down an aisle of delicious snacks. The checkout line has candy bars, magazines and trinkets. Don't give in to the temptation.

Be flexible when it comes to bargains. Stick to your list but if you spot a bargain, be willing to substitute if it means you will save some cash. For example, if you plan to eat corn for dinner and green beans are on sale, make the switch.

Buy milk in one-gallon containers. Skim milk or milk with 1% fat content costs less and is better for you. Milk in plastic jugs freezes well, too, so take advantage of a good milk sale.

In general, avoid prepared or prepackaged foods. You can buy a box of mix then just add meat and water to make dinner, but you will save money if you buy fresh produce and pasta and make it yourself. Meals from scratch also taste a lot better.

As you buy fresh produce, pay attention to amounts. It's a temptation to grab the largest bunch of grapes, but don't buy more than you will eat. Food that goes to waste is a waste of money.

Buy whole-grain products. Whole-grain cereals, breads, crackers and snacks give you more nutritional bang for the buck. Also buy foods labeled enriched, fortified or vitamin C added.

Choose whole-grain cereals you prepare yourself, like oatmeal and creamy wheat, instead of pre-packaged cereals. Steer away from sweetened cereals, drink mixes and heavily processed foods.

Keep an eagle eye at the checkout counter. Mistakes can be made *especially on sale items.* Monitor the price of each item as it is rung up on the cash register, and point out any errors to the clerk. Likewise, be honest if a mistake is in your favor.

Choosing & Storing Quality Foods

How can you tell whether that musky-smelling cantaloupe is really ripe? Do you thump it? Do you shake it? Do you scratch it? Do you smell the end? Which apples are the best for eating, which ones for baking? Which mushrooms should you pick from a crowded bin? There are no great secrets involved, just read through the following information to determine how to choose the best quality fruit, vegetables, meat and dairy products, and how to store those items to keep them fresh.

Fresh Fruit:

Apples: Rich, deep, uniform color. Avoid bruised, soft or blemished fruit. Store at room temperature. If cut, sprinkle with lemon juice and store covered in refrigerator.

Apricots: Deep in color, and firm, with rosy plush. Avoid bruised, soft or shriveled fruit. Store covered or uncovered in the refrigerator.

Avocado: Dark, with either smooth or pebbled skin. When held in the palm, yields to gentle pressure. Avoid fruit that is too dark and soft or green and hard. Store avocados covered or uncovered in refrigerator. Store at room temperature if they need ripening.

Bananas: Firm, uniform in color, from green to yellow. Will ripen during storage. Avoid fruit that is soft, bruised, spotted or brown. Store at room temperature. Bananas that are green will need time to ripen and should be stored at room temperature in a paper bag.

Berries: Medium in size, uniform color, firm, solid and plump. Avoid berries that have started to juice or mold. Store unwashed, spread out in the refrigerator, covered. Check frequently for mold.

Cantaloupe: Webbed skin with yellowish coloring on the underside. Smoothly rounded depression at ends. The stem end yields to slight pressure. Fragrant aroma. Avoid fruit that is sunken or that has a calloused scar on the end. Store at room temperature to ripen, then refrigerate. Once the cantaloupe is cut, store it covered in refrigerator.

Casaba Melon: Large, round, heavy for size, slightly softened tips, deep yellow ridged skin. Avoid fruit that is misshapen, sunken or rigid at the tips. Store at room temperature or in the refrigerator.

Coconut: Should be well-rounded, and heavy for size, sloshing sound when shaken. Avoid softened or those with greenish color. Store at room temperature. When cut, cover and store in refrigerator. Store milk covered in refrigerator.

Crenshaw Melon: Bright yellowish green or yellow in color. Has a firm pear shape and yields to pressure on ends. Pleasant aroma. Avoid fruit that is misshapen, mostly green, or sunken. Store either at room temperature or in the refrigerator.

Grapefruit: Heavy for size with smooth, thin skin. Avoid fruit that is light, has puffy skin, or has sunken, withered or soft areas. Store at room temperature or in refrigerator. When grapefruit is cut, store covered in the refrigerator.

Grapes: Plump, deep, uniform color, tight clusters on dark green stems. Avoid those with brown stems or grapes that

are soft and discolored. Store grapes covered or uncovered in the refrigerator.

Honeydew Melon: Large (5-7 pounds), firm, pale yellow or creamy white. Avoid soft, small or greenish fruit. Store at room temperature. When cut, store melon tightly covered in the refrigerator.

Lemons: Heavy for size, deep yellow with uniform color and smooth, thin skin. Avoid fruit with greenish tinge or thick skins. Store lemons at room temperature. Will yield more juice if warmed in hot water before juicing. When cut, store covered in refrigerator.

Limes: Heavy for size, dark green uniform color. Avoid those with pale color or those that are soft and wrinkled. Store whole limes at room temperature. When cut, store tightly covered in refrigerator.

Nectarines: Smooth, shiny skin, deep color with rosy blush, firm but not hard. Avoid nectarines with brown spots or bruises. Store covered or uncovered in refrigerator.

Oranges: Should be heavy for size, with smooth, thin skins. May be deep orange or tinged with green, firm but yielding to pressure. Avoid sunken, light for size, withered oranges with thick skin. Store at room temperature or in refrigerator when cut.

Peaches: Firm, deep uniform color with rosy blush. Avoid those with a green tint or

*D*id you know? *"An apple a day keeps the doctor away" is no myth. Recent studies show that apples have a complex chemical makeup like no other fruit that provides phytochemicals, pectins and d-glucaric acid to lower cholesterol levels, antioxidants to protect cells from pollutants and flavanoids to reduce the incidence of heart disease and cancer. Apples also contain vitamin C and agents that allow the vitamin to be better absorbed.*

Did you know? Sweet blueberries are nature's number one source of antioxidants among all whole fruits and vegetables. Antioxidants are vitamins and minerals that fight free radicals (pollutants) that are in the body. Much of that power comes from the pigments that give blueberries their color. And like cranberries, blueberries will also fight urinary tract infections. Just 1/2 cup of blueberries on your cereal each day will improve your health.

those with soft, brown or bruised areas. Store covered or uncovered in refrigerator.

Pears: Best if firm with some softness at stem. Choose slightly under-ripe and turning yellow. Will ripen during storage. Avoid brown spots or bruises. Store at room temperature until yellow.

Pineapple: Tight crown with sweet smell and bulging eyes. The center leaves come out easily when gently tugged. Makes dull, solid sound when thumped. Avoid the ones that are greenish, have a slight fermented odor or whose center leaves do not come out easily when tugged. Store at room temperature. When cut, store in the refrigerator.

Plums: Uniform color either purple, blue, red, yellow or pale green, firm and slightly soft. Avoid fruit that is spotted, too soft or wrinkled. Store uncovered in refrigerator or at room temperature if they need to ripen.

Pomegranates: Round, full, firm, and uniform in color. Avoid those with spots, dents or bruises. Store at room temperature. When cut, cover and store in refrigerator.

Tomatoes: Firm, but yields to pressure. Heavy for size, deep red color, can ripen during storage. Avoid those that are mushy, light for size or extremely hard. Store at room temperature to ripen. When ripe or cut, store covered in the refrigerator.

Watermelon: Rounded with smooth surface, creamy color on underside. When scraped with fingernail, skin should yield thin green shaving. Avoid those with shiny surface or creamy color on more than half of melon. Can be stored at room temperature or in the refrigerator. When cut, store tightly covered in refrigerator.

Fresh Vegetables

Artichokes: Small in size with tightly closed leaves. Avoid if leaves are spreading or discolored. Keep in the refrigerator, either covered or uncovered. Should be used within just a few days to avoid toughening.

Asparagus: Tender, firm stalks with compact tips, six to eight inches long. Avoid stalks that are whitish, too large or too long. Store covered in the refrigerator and use within just one to three days.

Beets: Small (about three inches in diameter), uniform, deep red color. Remove tops, store at room temperature.

Broccoli: Tight, closed bud, uniform green. Avoid broccoli with yellow flowers, yellow buds or smudgy spots. Store covered in the refrigerator. Use before the ends begin turning yellow.

Brussels Sprouts: Should be deep green with tight heads. Avoid those that have started to wilt. Store covered in the refrigerator.

Cabbage: Pick small heads that are heavy for their size, light to bright green. Avoid cabbage with holes which indicates worm infestation. Store covered in refrigerator.

Carrots: Uniform, bright orange color, no longer than six inches and one inch in diameter at its widest point. Avoid big, woody carrots. Cut off the tops and store uncovered in the refrigerator. Unpeeled carrots may be stored at room temperature.

Cauliflower: Flower clusters tight, head firm, flowers well-formed and white. Avoid those with smudgy or dirty spots which are indicative of insect infestation. Store covered in the refrigerator.

Celery: Light, pale green. Avoid celery that is too dark or visibly wilted. Store in a paper bag in refrigerator or in water after cut. Do not store in plastic bag.

Corn: Tip of ear should be blunt, not tapered, and the silk should be dark and dry. When pierced with fingernail, kernel should spurt. Avoid corn with tapered end and moist silk or dry kernels. Watch for worms. Corn will stay fresher longer if not husked. Store in refrigerator either covered when husked or uncovered in husks.

Cucumbers: Medium to dark green, long and slender, firm. Avoid those that are yellow, soft or wrinkled. Store them in a paper bag in the refrigerator.

Eggplant: Glossy shine, deep purple, firm. Avoid those with green spots. Store covered in the refrigerator.

Green Pepper: Firm, thick-walled, deep green color. Avoid peppers that are wrinkled, soft, or have uneven color. Store covered in refrigerator.

Lettuce: Heavy for size, firm head, deep green leaves, scratch the core and sniff for freshness. Avoid those with bitter smell or wilted heads. Store lettuce in a paper bag in refrigerator, not in plastic.

Mushrooms: Light in color, tightly closed around the stem and well-rounded in shape. Avoid those that are spotted, discolored or decaying. Do not forage for wild mushrooms. Store in the refrigerator in a paper bag.

Okra: Pods two to three inches long, uniform and green. Avoid soft, shriveled okra. Store covered in refrigerator.

Onions: Full, firm and slightly flat with brown shriveled tops. Avoid those with wet necks, soft spots or mold. Store at room temperature.

Parsnips: Small, uniform and tannish yellow in color. Avoid those that are large, woody or split. Store in the refrigerator or at room temperature.

Peas: Look for small pods that are well filled and deep green in color. Avoid pods that are bulging, withered, yellow, dry or discolored. Store peas in the refrigerator, with a cover if hulled.

33

Mom says:
After shopping,
take time to cut
veggies for snacks.
Clean refrigerator of
old leftovers and
store food properly,
especially produce,
dairy and meat.

Potatoes: Firm, with a netlike texture on skin, shallow eyes and even color. Avoid those with rot, unpleasant odor or green color. Store in a dark, cool, well-ventilated place. Do not store in the refrigerator. Cover cut potatoes with water and a few drops of vinegar then store for up to three days in the refrigerator.

Rhubarb: Deep red color, tender young shoots. Avoid those stalks that are large, thick and stringy. Store in a paper sack in the refrigerator up to three days.

Snap Beans: Young, tender and small. Avoid any large or dry-looking beans. Store in the refrigerator.

Squash: Summer squash should be small and tender, with skin that pierces easily with fingernail. Winter squash has hard rinds. Avoid squash with blackened or dried stems, watery or soft spots. Store covered in refrigerator when cut. Store at room temperature when uncut.

Sweet Potatoes: Small and firm, uniform rose to bronze in color. Avoid those that are soft, shriveled or turning black. Store unpeeled at room temperature.

Dairy Products

Butter or Margarine: Store covered in the refrigerator. If butter is hard, leave it out briefly until softened. Do not leave butter unrefrigerated for a long period of time.

Cheese: In the U.S., choose U.S. Grade A or AA. Leave cheese in original wrapper in refrigerator. After opening, wrap cheese in foil or plastic wrap. To freeze, wrap tightly in moisture-proof wrapper.

Eggs: Choose eggs with dull shells. Always check to see if any eggs in the container are cracked. Avoid eggs with shiny shells, eggs that have been cracked or eggs with an odor. Use large eggs for eating, medium for baking. Buy only those that have been refrigerated. Store in carton in the refrigerator for up to four weeks. Never wash eggs before storing, as film protects against bacteria. Store whites covered in the refrigerator and yolks in water in refrigerator no longer than four days.

Instant Nonfat Milk: If in the United States, choose U.S. Extra Grade. Store powdered milk covered in cool, dry place. Refrigerate after mixing. Never freeze.

Shortening: Choose a can that is properly sealed. Store covered at room temperature.

Various Food Items

Bread: Store in an airtight plastic bag. Can be frozen for up to three months in airtight wrapping.

Brown Sugar: Store at room temperature in tightly closed plastic bag or an airtight jar. If sugar hardens, add a cracker or bread crust to soften.

Canned Produce: Store at room temperature in dry, cool place. When opened, store covered in airtight container in refrigerator.

Cottage Cheese: Turn the carton upside down, place it on a saucer and store it in the refrigerator.

Crackers: Keep wrapped at room temperature. In high humidity, store in a jar with screw-on lid.

Cream: Store covered in refrigerator for up to one week. Can be frozen in a glass jar with a screw-on lid for up to six months.

Flour: Keep in an airtight container. Metal containers are best, since they prevent insect and rodent infestation.

Frozen Produce: Keeps for up to twelve months in the freezer. Once any thawing begins, do not refreeze.

Honey: Store in a small, airtight container at room temperature. If the honey becomes crystallized, put container in a pan of hot water until it liquifies again.

Ice Cream: Put the original carton in a plastic bag and seal it closed to avoid freezer burn.

Jam and Jelly: Store with screw-on lid in refrigerator.

Marshmallows: Store in a moisture-proof, airtight bag in the freezer.

Peanut Butter: Store in jar with screw-on lid for up to six months in cupboard. Do not refrigerate.

Popcorn: Store in a jar with a screw-on lid in the freezer.

Soup: Store in refrigerator in airtight container. Will keep for up to three months in the freezer in a jar with screw-on lid.

Sugar and Spices: Best if stored at room temperature in airtight containers.

Meat Products

Beef: Look for flecks of fat throughout lean part of meat, dark purplish-red to bright red color, firm fine textured muscle, little fat. Avoid meat that is discolored in any way, dark brown or greenish, has extra fat or an offensive odor. Wipe with paper towel, wrap and store in the refrigerator. To freeze, wrap in an airtight, moisture-proof container. Beef will keep in the freezer for up to twelve months. Ground beef keeps frozen for three months.

Hot Dogs and Sandwich Meats: Check the labels. Meat should be listed as the first ingredient. Avoid those that list variety meats. Store in the refrigerator loosely covered. It is best to use fresh deli meats promptly.

Fish: Bright, clear, bulging eyes, tight shiny scales, firm, elastic flesh, fresh odor, reddish-pink gills without slime. Avoid fish with slimy gills, sunken eyes, loose

Garlic Breath Is O.K.

Just a clove of fresh garlic a day – one segment, not a whole bulb – added in cooking may reduce your risk of stroke and heart attack.

Compounds in garlic make the blood less sticky, preventing clots. Studies show that eating garlic daily may also reduce cholesterol levels by as much as ten percent.

Store bulbs at room temperature, uncovered. Keep peeled cloves in jar of cooking oil with screw-on lid or tightly covered in the freezer.

Mom says:
Stir-fry meat. Add
a small amount
of steak, pork or
chicken to a veggie
stir-fry to savor the
flavor of meat for a
fraction of the
calories and cost.

scales, sagging flesh or foul odor. Store in refrigerator covered and use within a few days. Freeze up to six months. Thaw in milk or cook frozen.

Pork: Lean, bright pink to grayish pink with little fat. Avoid pork that is at all discolored, fatty or has a foul odor. Wipe with paper towel and store covered in the refrigerator. Pork can be frozen for up to six months in airtight moisture-proof wrapping. Sausage will freeze for up to three months.

Poultry: Young poultry with meaty flesh, smooth skin, flexible breast bone, well-distributed fat. Avoid poultry that is blemished or in a damaged package. Keep frozen until ready for use. Thaw in refrigerator, not at room temperature, for 24 hours. After cooking, store covered in refrigerator. Use within a few days. Remove stuffing and store separately.

What About Soy?

Products made from the soybean are known to contain plant protein that can substitute for meat protein, reducing intake of saturated fats. Soy protein also has *isoflavones* that help lower cholesterol levels.

Certain compounds in soy protein can help keep blood vessels flexible and help prevent blood clots.

Try soy milk beverages, flavored soy nuts, tofu and soy protein powder. The taste of soy may take some getting used to, but, as with skim milk, your palate will eventually adjust.

We'd Like to Propose a Roast!

On a tight grocery budget, roast, beef, lamb, veal or pork, may be overlooked entirely. But look again.

A good roast may mean a larger initial expense, but it's economical because it will provide many meals. Serve it first accompanied by potatoes and carrots, then use the leftovers in soup, stew, tacos, casseroles, sandwiches and salads.

When deciding exactly what size roast to buy, plan to serve six ounces of cooked meat per person. To figure out cooking time, set your oven to 325 degrees and use the following chart:

Meat	Weight	Minutes Per Pound
Beef	3 to 6 lbs.	30 to 35 min.
Pork loin	3 to 6 lbs.	30 to 35 min.
Pork shoulder	5 to 8 lbs.	35 min.
Pork butt	3 to 6 lbs.	40 to 50 min.
Ham	10 lbs. or less	20 min.
Half hams	all weights	25 min.
Picnic ham	5 to 8 lbs.	30 to 35 min.
Veal loin	4 to 6 lbs.	30 to 35 min.
Lamb shoulder	4 to 6 lbs.	35 min.
Leg of lamb	5 to 8 lbs.	35 min.

To Make a Tender Roast: Preheat oven. Place roast, straight from refrigerator, fat side up, in shallow roasting pan. Season before cooking. Insert meat thermometer into thickest part, not touching bone or fat. *Do not add water or cover roast.* Roast according to timetable above. Remove roast when thermometer registers 135-140 degrees (medium rare) or 150-155 degrees (medium).

Tent the roast loosely with aluminum foil. Let stand 15 minutes. Roast temperature will continue to rise about five to ten degrees to final desired doneness and will be easier to carve. Carve across the grain when possible. You may add vegetables to the pan within the last 30 minutes of roasting. Do not put vegetables in at the beginning as they will be overdone. For a quick and almost flawless roast, use a seasoned roasting bag found in most supermarkets.

A Fish by Any Other Name...

Well-prepared fish can be a real treat. To make certain that a meal of fresh fish is enjoyable, pay close attention to what's available in the market and ask questions.

Also ask for store recipes on how best to prepare a particular type of fish.

Fish fillets are boneless and some are also skinless. Some tiny bones may remain in fillets because they are virtually impossible to remove, but the fish shouldn't contain any bones large enough to cause trouble during eating.

While most bones in *fish steaks* have been removed, the backbone typically remains. Some are skinless and some are not.

A *whole fish* has the head and tail attached. Some have had internal organs removed, but some are sold with organs. If you can't tell by reading the packaging, check with the butcher.

TIP: To prevent fish from smelling while you cook it, squeeze lemon juice on all surfaces and let stand in the refrigerator for an hour before cooking. To get rid of smell on hands, rub with stalk of celery.

Yogurt Is Good Bacteria

We usually look to get rid of bacteria in foods, but with yogurt, the more the merrier!

Yogurt is "contaminated" with beneficial bacteria, called acidophilus, that also naturally occur in the human intestine. Sugars in milk transform into lactic acid, which causes the milk to have a tart yogurt taste.

Yogurt is relatively low in calories and provides phosphorus, vitamin B-12, calcium, protein and riboflavin. It's easy to digest and soothing to the stomach.

Yogurt can be used in cooking a variety of dishes. For fewer calories and fat and more nutrition, substitute yogurt for sour cream in recipes.

If you take antibiotics, friendly bacteria in your intestinal tract can be destroyed. Eating yogurt will replenish that good bacteria. If you suffer recurrent yeast infections and bloating, yogurt can clear that up.

You can buy yogurt in different varieties and flavors: smooth and fruity, custard style, drinkable, frozen – even in a squeezable tube.

Finding a Good Egg

Eggs, one of the best sources of protein, are a real bargain compared to the cost of meat, but bigger is not always better. The size and quality of eggs have nothing to do with each other.

In the United States, eggs are sized as jumbo, extra large, large, medium and small, and graded from AA to C. If you buy an egg to poach, scramble, fry or hard-boil, get Grade A or AA. If needed for a recipe, you can use small Grade B eggs.

Only buy eggs that have been refrigerated in the store, and check them for cracked shells. A crack can let in bacteria and lead to food poisoning. Shells should be dull. *Don't* wash the shells before you store the eggs or you'll remove the film that protects against bacteria. To get the best bargain, buy only the size and grade you need. If less than eight cents difference, buy the larger.

Did you know? The egg has as many as 17,000 tiny pores over its surface. Through them, the egg can absorb flavors and odors. Storing them in their carton helps keep them fresh.

Let's Do Breakfast

For starters, never ever skip a good breakfast!

Your brain and your nervous system need glucose – protein, carbohydrates, and fat broken down into accessible energy.

Let's say the last time you ate was at 9:00 p.m. The next day, you skip breakfast and wait until noon for lunch – you've gone 15 hours with nothing to eat! Your brain is starved, so your body has to work extra hard to help you think, walk and talk.

The day's first meal is called breakfast because you literally *break* the eight or nine-hour *fast* you started at bedtime.

Eating breakfast will improve your concentration, mental performance, memory, mood and physical strength.

Without breakfast you are at a disadvantage compared with co-workers or classmates who ate this morning.

A quick bowl of oatmeal with milk and fruit is all you need to get the day started.

Breakfast establishes the foundation for healthy eating habits. Meal skippers have a hard time fitting important nutrients into their daily diet.

Say you don't have time for breakfast? Take along a small bag of whole-grain cereal, a yogurt, a small box of skim milk, some juice, or an apple and orange.

Or pack along whole-grain crackers, hard-boiled eggs, low-fat granola bars, low-fat string cheese or even a peanut butter sandwich. Come on, get some breakfast in your belly!

Avoiding Food-Borne Illness

Some 250 types of bacteria, viruses and parasites exist that cause food-borne illness. Some can lead to disease or death, but most cause discomfort such as diarrhea, fever, vomiting, cramps and dehydration.

Food-borne illness, also called food poisoning, occurs when micro-organisms contaminate bottled or canned foods, dairy, meats, seafood and produce. Food poisoning can occur when food is not properly handled. One way to prevent food-borne illness is simply to wash your hands. Food poisoning doesn't always affect food appearance, taste or odor. But you can suspect contamination from certain signs.

Wash hands and kitchen surfaces often. Don't use a sponge to clean your kitchen counters, cupboards, sinks or stove. Sponges are breeding grounds for bacteria. Use mild disinfectant soap, warm water and disposable paper towels or a clean dishcloth.

Avoid cross-contamination. Store meat, fish and poultry sealed. When thawing, place meat on a plate on the bottom refrigerator shelf to catch juices. Use one plate to carry raw meat to grill and another for serving. Boil marinade for three minutes before serving. Use separate spoons for stirring and sampling.

Treat cutting boards with care. If you use a cutting board and knife to cut uncooked or raw meat, wash the utensils with hot, soapy water and dry completely before using them to cut vegetables.

Refrigerate foods within two hours of cooking. Be cautious at buffets with food that should be kept cold or hot. If questionable, pass it up.

Thaw frozen foods in the refrigerator, not on the counter. Keep freezer at eight degrees and refrigerator at 40 degrees. If food begins to thaw, cook it or discard it. Never refreeze food, especially meats.

Avoid processed or fast foods. Foods you prepare yourself are less likely to be tainted if you cook and store them properly.

Suspect Contamination If:

• Fruits or vegetables have started to decay. Look for brown spots, soft spots or discoloration.

• There is visible mold on fruits or vegetables.

• Eggs are cracked in the carton.

• Cans are dented or bulging at either end.

• The contents of can forcefully spray out when opened.

• The food inside can is bubbly or frothy.

• Meat feels slimy or has an iridescent sheen to it.

• Food is discolored, smells strong or tastes unusual.

Sources & Types of Food Poisoning

The following circumstances can lead to food poisoning. Seek medical help immediately if serious symptoms develop.

Contaminated Canned Goods: Called *Botulism,* this highly fatal form of poisoning strikes within four to thirty-six hours after the consumption of contaminated food. Symptoms are dizziness, weakness, difficulty breathing, abdominal pain, bloating, nausea, vomiting and blurred vision. Paralysis of facial muscles follows and progresses downward. Sources include canned foods, home-prepared bottled fruits and vegetables, and herbal oils. See a doctor immediately. **Botulism is often fatal.**

Contaminated Water: In one to three days, symptoms include sudden onset of explosive watery stools, abdominal cramps, loss of appetite, nausea and vomiting. *Giardiasis* is mainly associated with contaminated water. The illness can be transmitted by uncooked foods that were contaminated while growing or after cooking by an infected food handler. At risk are hikers, children and travelers. **Giardiasis is serious but rarely fatal.**

Internal Temperatures for Cooked Foods	
Use an instant-read thermometer to see that meats reach these USDA recommended temperatures:	
180°	Whole Poultry
170°	Poultry breast or well-done meats.
165°	Stuffing, ground poultry, reheated leftovers.
160°	Medium meats, pork, egg dishes, ground meat.
145°	Medium-rare beef, veal and lamb.
140°	Buffet foods kept hot at warming tables.

Food Left in Warming Trays for Extended Periods: Symptoms of *Perfringens* food poisoning generally appear eight to twelve hours after eating in a restaurant and include abdominal pain and severe diarrhea. This food-borne illness is caused by a failure to keep meats and meat products hot. The organisms thrive at between 120-130 degrees. Gravies and stuffing must be kept above 140 degrees. An instant-read thermometer is a must for foods in warming trays. **Perfringens is rarely fatal.**

*Did You Know?
Disease causing
germs like E. Coli
and Hepatitis A can
survive on cloth
even after you've
laundered it.
Wash underwear,
towels and kitchen
linens separately
from other clothes.
Use hot water,
chlorine bleach or
an antibacterial
detergent. Cloth
kitchen and
bathroom towels
provide refuge for
bacteria. Use paper
towels to wipe off
countertops and to
dry your hands after
you wash them.*

Improper Hand Washing and Food Handling: Food becomes contaminated with the *Shigellosis* toxin when a human carrier doesn't wash hands thoroughly in hot soapy water then handles liquid or food that is not thoroughly cooked. Symptoms appear within one to seven days and include abdominal cramps, diarrhea, fever, vomiting and blood or mucus in stool. The *Shigellosis* toxin is often found in milk and dairy products, poultry and potato salad. **Shigellosis is rarely fatal.**

Improper Cooking or Refrigeration: The *Staphylococcal* toxin is produced when food that is contaminated with the bacteria is left too long at room temperature. Symptoms may include abdominal cramps, diarrhea, fever, nausea and vomiting. Sources include meats, poultry, eggs, tuna, potato and macaroni salads, and cream-filled pastries. Foods containing mayonnaise should be kept in the refrigerator. **Staphylococcal poisoning is rarely fatal.**

Raw or Undercooked Meats: The *E. Coli* bacteria is found in meat – especially undercooked or raw hamburger – tainted produce, and unpasteurized milk or juice. Symptoms appear within 24 to 72 hours after eating and may include some abdominal pain, nausea, vomiting and diarrhea. Symptoms may also include a flu-like illness with fever, chills, muscle pain, and stiffness in the muscles and joints. Seek medical attention immediately. **E. Coli can be fatal, especially to infants.**

Campylobacteriosis may develop within five days of eating raw or undercooked meat. Symptoms include diarrhea, abdominal cramps, fever and bloody stools. Campylobacteriosis is contracted from undercooked poultry or meat and unpasteurized milk. Bacteria on poultry, cattle and sheep can often contaminate meat and milk. Symptoms last seven to ten days. **The illness is not fatal.**

Salmonella can manifest itself within eight to twelve hours after eating. Symptoms include stomach pain, diarrhea, nausea and vomiting. Salmonella bacteria can be found in raw and undercooked food, especially chicken or eggs. Chicken from warming trays or buffets is always suspect. **Salmonella is rarely fatal.**

Seafood: A food-borne illness, called *Vibrio infection,* is contracted from bacteria that live in coastal waters, and can infect humans either through open wounds or consumption of contaminated seafood. Lips and fingertips start to tingle within five to thirty minutes, followed by chills and fever, loss of strength in muscles and difficulty breathing. At high risk are people with liver conditions, low stomach acid and weakened immune systems. **Vibrio infection can be fatal.**

With *Hepatitis A,* symptoms begin with malaise, appetite loss, nausea, vomiting and fever. After three to ten days, jaundice and darkened urine may appear. Oysters, clams, mussels and scallops can carry the virus when their beds are polluted by untreated raw sewage. Raw shellfish are potent carriers, but even cooking does not always kill the virus. The best way to prevent the illness is to eat at reputable restaurants and to wash hands thoroughly after using the toilet. **Hepatitis A can cause liver damage and death.**

Listeriosis is a serious disease for pregnant women, newborns and adults with weakened immune systems. Listeria bacteria may be found in frozen cooked crab meat, cooked shrimp and cooked imitation shellfish. The bacteria can also contaminate soft cheeses, unpasteurized milk and fruits or vegetables grown in contaminated soil or water. Listeria bacteria resist heat, salt and acidity better than other pathogens. Symptoms appear within 72 hours or sometimes as late as seven to 30 days after eating contaminated food and include fever, headache, nausea and vomiting. **Listeriosis can cause fetal or infant death.**

Reading Food Labels

You can select good quality food if you learn to read labels. The name of the product is just the beginning.

1) Labels give directions for use of the product.

2) They also include storage information such as, *promptly refrigerate*.

3) The product brand name – in this case, *Campbell's*.

4) The name of the item – in this case, *Chicken Noodle Soup*. In some cases, such as the one illustrated here, there may also be a description of the item, such as *condensed*. Other product descriptions may include *cream-style, evaporated* or *crinkled*.

5) Some labels provide extra information on product use. This one has a serving suggestion, while others may have a recipe using their product. Some cereal boxes, give instructions to send the cereal box top with a small amount of money for various products. Others list ideas for a variety of different ways to use the product.

6) Some labels contain guarantee information if the manufacturer has decided to guarantee satisfaction. This information is valuable if you are dissatisfied and need to file a claim.

7) Nutrition information is required on all labels and is listed per serving, not for the entire amount of food in the container. The nutrition information on the sample is one-half cup of condensed soup – this can would contain two and a half servings. Typical nutrition information includes the number of calories in a serving and amount of nutrients in percentages of the U.S. Recommended Daily Allowance (RDA).

8) By law, labels must contain information about the weight of the product in pounds and ounces. This is critical when using a recipe that calls for a certain size can or package of an ingredient. For example, your food

would be ruined if you used a five-ounce can of tomato paste when the recipe called for a 16-ounce can.

9) Ingredients are listed in descending order. The ingredient with the most volume is listed first. *Campbell's Chicken Noodle Soup* contains more chicken stock than anything else. On some labels, additives such as flavoring or coloring are listed by their chemical names. On other labels, they are listed simply as added color and added flavor.

10) Labels contain the place of origin of the product. This can of Campbell's soup originated in Camden, New Jersey.

Pay special attention to labels of products that contain meat. By law, a product that contains meat can also contain natural amounts of fat. Check to see what percentage of calories comes from fat. Products labeled *All Meat* cannot contain any type of extender, such as cereal. A product labeled *All Beef* can contain only beef, no other type of meat.

Also note that chicken-flavored soup has been flavored to taste like chicken, while chicken soup contains chicken pieces or broth. This also applies to juice. Look for 100% juice, not juice cocktail.

Notes

First Things First
Cooking & Housecleaning Basics

Y ou retrieve the frying pan from the kitchen cupboard, you have all the necessary ingredients spread out on the counter and you're ready to start whipping up something delicious and nutritious. Hold on! Between now and mealtime, there are plenty of things you will need to know and do. Measuring and mixing are just the beginning.

Maybe you've seen a practiced cook pinch a bit of salt here, toss in a handful of raisins there, spoon in a little cream and dump in a bunch of flour. That system really doesn't work for the rest of us.

One of the time-honored secrets to good cooking is to follow the recipe thoroughly. Accurate measuring is a top priority and shouldn't be taken lightly. While it seems simple enough, measuring requires a bit of skill. You'll need three basic tools:

1) A set of measuring spoons,
2) A set of nested measuring cups, and
3) A liquid measuring cup with a spout for pouring.

Kitchen Essentials
Cooking Utensils

❑ 9 x 13 baking pan
❑ Aluminum foil
❑ Bread pan
❑ Casserole dish
❑ Can opener
❑ Colander, strainer
❑ Cookie sheet
❑ Flour sifter
❑ Frying pan with lid
❑ Grater
❑ Large pot with lid
❑ Measuring cups
❑ Measuring spoons
❑ Meat thermometer
❑ Mixing bowls
❑ Mixing spoons
❑ Muffin tin
❑ Pancake turner
❑ Paring knife
❑ Pitcher with lid
❑ Place setting for four including forks, spoons, knives, glasses, mugs, bowls, small plates and large plates
❑ Plastic wrap
❑ Saucepan with lid
❑ Spatula
❑ Tongs
❑ Two 8" round cake pans
❑ Wax paper
❑ Wire whip

For convenience:

❑ Crockpot or slow cooker
❑ Electric mixer
❑ Electric rice maker
❑ Oriental wok

For Good Measure

Salt, spices, baking powder and baking soda. Fill the measuring spoon to overflowing, then level the spoon off using the blunt straight edge of a dull knife.

Flour or powdered sugar. Spoon the flour lightly into the measuring cup until overflowing. Use a knife to push excess flour off and level the cup. Don't pack the flour or shake cup as you level. If the recipe calls for sifted flour, sift the flour onto a plate or a square of waxed paper before spooning it into the measuring cup.

Brown sugar. Spoon the brown sugar into the measuring cup, and pack it down tightly with the back of the spoon. Keep packing it until the sugar is level with the top of the cup.

Granulated sugar. Spoon the sugar into the measuring cup to overflowing and level with the edge of a knife. If sugar is lumpy, sift before measuring.

Milk, water or other liquids. Set the liquid measuring cup on a level surface (such as a counter top), lower your head so you're at eye level with the cup and slowly pour the liquid into the measuring cup until it reaches desired level.

Shortening. You will have mess if you don't do this properly. Try one of these methods for easy measuring and quick cleanup.

1) Pack the shortening into the measuring cup and scrape off the excess. Briefly set the bottom of the measuring cup into hot water – the shortening will slide right out.

2) If the recipe calls for less than a cup of shortening, use the liquid measuring cup, subtract the amount of shortening needed and fill

Cooking Codes

Common Recipe Abbreviations	
cup	c.
gallon	gal.
hour	hr.
minute	min.
ounce	oz.
pint	pt.
pound	lb.
quart	qt.
tablespoon(s)	Tbsp.
teaspoon(s)	tsp.

the rest of the cup with cold water. For example, if you need 1/4 cup shortening, fill the 1-cup measuring cup with 3/4 cup cold water. Then drop in spoonfuls of shortening until the water level reaches the 1-cup mark. The shortening will float and is easily spooned out to add to your recipe.

Of course, measuring isn't always that simple, especially when you run across a recipe that calls for a pound of flour. Do you break out the bathroom scale? How do you figure out how much cheese you need if a recipe calls for three cups grated? Or how many eggs make one cup? How much do you buy?

If the Recipe Calls for . . . You Will Need

1/2 cup butter	1 stick or 1/4 pound
2 Tbsp. butter	1 ounce
1 pound butter	4 sticks
1 square baking chocolate	1 ounce
2 1/4 cups brown sugar	1 pound
3 1/2 cups powdered sugar	1 pound
2 cups granulated sugar	1 pound
4 cups white flour	1 pound
3 cups cooked rice	1 cup uncooked
2 cups cooked noodles	1 cup or 4 oz. uncooked
1 cup bread crumbs	2 slices of bread
1 cup cracker crumbs	12 graham crackers OR 20 saltine crackers OR 23 vanilla wafers
2 cups grated cheese	1/2 pound
1 cup chopped nuts	1/4 pound
1 cup chopped celery	2 medium stalks
1 cup chopped onion	2 medium onions
1 cup chopped tomato	2 large tomatoes
1 cup diced green pepper	1 large pepper
1 cup chopped apples	1 medium apple
2 cups sliced strawberries	1 pint strawberries
3 Tbsp. lemon juice	1 lemon
8 Tbsp. orange juice	1 orange
1 tsp. grated lemon peel	1 lemon
2 tsp. grated orange peel	1 orange
1 cup egg yolks	14 eggs
1 cup egg whites	10 eggs
2 cups cooked hamburger	1 pound hamburger

Cooking Essentials
Food Staples

- ❏ Baking powder
- ❏ Baking soda
- ❏ Biscuit mix
- ❏ Bouillon cubes, granules
- ❏ Bread crumbs, crackers
- ❏ Brown sugar
- ❏ Condensed milk
- ❏ Cooking oil
- ❏ Cornmeal
- ❏ Cornstarch
- ❏ Corn syrup
- ❏ Cream soups
- ❏ Dry soups, gravy mixes
- ❏ Dry yeast
- ❏ Evaporated milk
- ❏ Gelatin
- ❏ Granulated sugar
- ❏ Honey
- ❏ Iodized salt
- ❏ Macaroni or pasta
- ❏ Olive oil
- ❏ Powdered milk
- ❏ Powdered sugar
- ❏ Rice
- ❏ Shortening
- ❏ Vanilla extract
- ❏ Wheat and white flours

Perishables:

- ❏ Butter or margarine
- ❏ Eggs
- ❏ Ketchup
- ❏ Mayonnaise
- ❏ Milk
- ❏ Prepared mustard
- ❏ Salsa or hot sauce

Simple Substitutions

After rifling frantically through your kitchen cupboards, you're ready to wave the white flag of surrender. You just don't have all the ingredients you need to make that favorite recipe.

Don't give up. Countless simple ingredients can work double-time, giving you great versatility and saving you a trip to the grocery store. Next time you can't find buttermilk, cornstarch or baking chocolate, scan this chart for a substitute.

If the Recipe Calls for . . . Use This Instead

Dairy Products

If the Recipe Calls for	Use This Instead
1/2 cup butter	1/2 cup shortening plus 1/4 teaspoon of salt
1 cup whipping cream	1/3 cup butter plus 3/4 cup of milk
1/2 cup buttermilk	1/2 cup milk plus 1 1/2 tsp. vinegar
1/2 cup sour milk	1/2 cup milk plus 1 1/2 tsp. lemon juice
1 cup whipped cream	1 egg white whipped with 1 sliced banana
1 cup whole milk	1 cup water, 4 Tbsp. plus 2 tsp. melted butter OR 1/2 cup water plus 1/2 cup evaporated milk
1 cup skim milk	1 cup water plus 4 Tbsp. nonfat instant milk
1/2 cup honey butter	2 Tbsp. butter or margarine plus 1/4 cup honey
1/2 cup sour cream	1/2 cup plain yogurt
1 egg	2 egg yolks plus 1 Tbsp. water OR 1 tsp. unflavored gelatin mixed with 3 Tbsp. cold water and 2 Tbsp. boiling water
2 egg whites	1 egg white plus 1 Tbsp. ice water

If the Recipe Calls for . . . Use This Instead

Baking Ingredients

1 tsp. baking powder	1/2 tsp. cream of tartar plus 1/4 tsp. baking soda
1 Tbsp. flour to thicken	2 egg yolks OR 1/2 Tbsp. cornstarch OR 2 tsp. quick-cooking tapioca
1 tsp. double-acting baking powder	1 1/2 tsp. regular baking powder plus 1 1/2 tsp. vinegar
1 cup cake flour	1 cup regular flour sifted twice, minus 2 Tbsp.
1 cup bread flour	1/2 cup flour plus 1/2 cup cornmeal, bran or whole-wheat flour
1 package dry yeast	2 tsp. dry yeast OR 1 cake compressed yeast
1 square unsweetened chocolate	3 Tbsp. cocoa plus 1 Tbsp. butter or margarine
1/2 cup molasses	1/2 cup honey
1 cup tomato juice	1/2 cup tomato sauce plus 1/2 cup water
1 cup wine	1 cup apple juice
1 cup beer	1 cup water
1 cup orange liqueur	1 cup orange juice
1 large marshmallow	10 miniature marshmallows
1 cup honey	1 1/4 cups sugar plus 1/4 cup water
1/2 cup graham cracker crumbs	1/2 cup saltine cracker crumbs
1 can cream of celery soup	1 can cream of mushroom OR 1 can cream of chicken soup

Seasonings

1/2 cup ketchup for cooking	1/2 cup tomato sauce, 1 Tbsp. vinegar and 1 cup sugar
1 tsp. dry mustard	1 tsp. prepared mustard
1 cup chopped onion	1/3 cup dehydrated onions

If the Recipe Calls for . . . Use This Instead

Seasonings cont'd.

I tsp. instant onion	4 Tbsp. chopped fresh onion
I Tbsp. fresh parsley	I tsp. parsley flakes

Fruits and Vegetables

Mandarin oranges	pineapple tidbits
8-oz. can grapefruit	I medium fresh grapefruit
1/2 lb. fresh mushrooms	4-oz. can mushrooms
10-oz. frozen peas	8-oz. can peas
8-oz. whole tomatoes	8-oz. can stewed tomatoes

Miscellaneous

I can chow mein	I can potato shoestrings OR 3 cups cooked rice
I cup hominy	I cup cooked rice
I cup cooked rice	I cup cooked noodles
I cup seasoned bread crumbs	I cup regular bread crumbs with I tsp. black pepper OR 3 slices of bread (cubed) with I tsp. black pepper
1/2 cup pecans	1/2 cup walnuts OR almonds
I lb. ground pork	I lb. ground beef
1/2 cup cubed ham	1/2 cup chopped luncheon meat
8-oz. can chili beans	8-oz. can kidney beans with 2 tsp. chili powder

Common Cooking Terms

Every recipe has one thing in common after the list of ingredients – the instructions, orders on how to put the ingredients together and emerge with a steamy pot of soup, a crusty loaf of bread or a chewy batch of cookies. The science of cooking has a jargon all its own. The following definitions should help you understand almost any recipe.

Bake. To cook, either covered or uncovered, in an oven.

Baste. To keep foods moist during cooking by pouring or brushing liquid, such as meat drippings, melted fat or another liquid, over them.

Beat. To make mixture creamy, smooth or filled with air by whipping in a brisk motion.

Blanch. To precook food briefly in boiling liquid, usually to loosen the skin. For example, drop tomatoes in boiling water for less than a minute and the skin comes off easily.

Blend. To stir two or more ingredients together until they are smooth and uniform.

Boil. To cook at a liquid boiling temperature (212 degrees at sea level). When boiling a liquid, bubbles will form rapidly, rise continually and break as they reach the surface of the liquid.

Braise. To brown meat quickly in fat, then cook it in a covered pan on stove top or in the oven.

Bread. To coat a raw food with bread crumbs. Such crumbs are often mixed with a beaten egg, or the food is first dipped in the beaten egg and then coated with bread crumbs.

Broil. To cook food by placing it on a rack that is directly under the source of heat.

Pan Broil. To cook food in a heavy, ungreased pan on top of the stove. Grease from the food is poured off while cooking so that the food doesn't fry.

Chill. To place food in the refrigerator for several hours, until cold throughout.

Chop. To cut food in pieces about the size of small peas.

Cool. To remove food from the source of heat and let stand at room temperature. Do not put food in the refrigerator in an attempt to bring the temperature down more quickly.

Cream. To mix one or more ingredients until creamy and soft.

Cut in. To use a knife or pastry blender to add shortening to dry ingredients. The shortening is actually cut into tiny pieces during the blending process.

Dice. To cut food into small, uniform cubes.

Dredge. To coat raw meat with a dry mixture, usually flour or cornmeal, prior to frying.

Fold in. To add a new ingredient gently to an already-beaten mixture. The new ingredient is poured on top of the mixture. With a large spoon, the new ingredient is gently brought down through the middle of the mixture, and the mixture is scraped off the bottom and brought to the top. The procedure is often used to add egg whites, berries or other fruit to batter.

Fricassee. To braise small, individual serving pieces of meat or poultry in broth or sauce.

Fry. To cook food in hot fat or oil. No water is added and no cover is used. To pan-fry, food is cooked in a small amount of oil in a frying pan. To deep-fry, food is cooked in a large kettle that contains enough hot fat

*M*om says:
When you are trying a new recipe for the first time, take things step-by-step, slow and methodical. The final creation will be the reward for your patience.

53

to cover the food or allow it to float.

Glaze. To cover a food with a mixture that hardens, adds flavor and makes the food glossy.

Grate. To cut food into fine particles using a grater.

Grill. To cook food on a rack directly under or over the source of heat.

Knead. To make a dough or dough-like substance smooth and elastic by folding, stretching and pressing continuously until it reaches desired texture. (When fondant for candies is kneaded, it gets satiny rather than elastic.)

Marinate. To make foods more flavorful or tender by letting them stand in liquid for several hours or overnight. The food is completely covered. Most marinades consist of cooking oil and vinegar or lemon juice with spices added for flavor.

Mince. To chop food into very fine, small pieces.

Mix. To stir ingredients until they are well blended.

Parboil. To partially cook a food in boiling liquid.

Poach. To simmer in hot liquid slowly. Poaching should be a gentle process and food should hold its shape.

Pot-roast. To brown a roast or other large piece of meat in fat quickly, then cook it in a covered pan in the oven or on top of the stove. A small amount of liquid is usually added to make the roast more tender.

Purée. To blend a cooked fruit or vegetable until it is smooth and uniform.

Roast. To cook a food, usually meat, in the oven, uncovered, without added liquid.

Sauté. To cook food quickly in melted butter until it's tender. Chopped onions are cooked until transparent.

Scald. To heat liquid to just below the boiling point.

Scallop. To cook a food in a sauce. Many scalloped foods are cooked in a cheese or cream sauce and topped with browned bread crumbs.

Sear. To brown meat rapidly by using extremely high heat.

Shred. To cut food into narrow, long pieces with a grater.

Simmer. To cook food in hot liquid just below the boiling point (usually between 185 and 210 degrees). Bubbles will form slowly, but break just before reaching the liquid's surface.

Soft peaks. To beat egg whites or cream until the peaks hold their shape but droop slightly when beaters are lifted out of the bowl.

Steam. To cook with steam, food is put on a rack or in a perforated pan and placed in a covered container with a small amount of boiling water in the bottom. The steam from the boiling water cooks the food.

Steep. To simmer food in liquid below the boiling point over an extended period of time.

Stew. To simmer food slowly in liquid for several hours.

Stiff peaks. To beat egg whites or cream until the peaks stand up straight without drooping when beaters are lifted out of the bowl.

Stir. To combine two or more

ingredients thoroughly, using a circular motion – generally with a spoon.

Toss. To combine two or more ingredients lightly and gently, with a slight lifting motion.

Whip. To beat a food rapidly so that air is added to it. Whipping will increase the volume but lighten the consistency of the ingredients.

*D*id You Know? Any cooking that minimizes the time, temperature and amount of water needed will help preserve nutrients.

Tried & True Cooking Tips

Baking Hints

When using raisins or berries, put them in a paper bag with flour and shake to coat, then they won't sink to the bottom of the batter during baking.

To keep cake from sticking, take out of the oven and put the pan on a wet towel to cool.

When baking bread, put a dish of water in the oven during baking to keep the crust soft.

To reheat biscuits, put them in a brown paper sack, twist it closed, then sprinkle the sack generously with water. Place the sack in the oven and bake at 350-degrees for five minutes.

When melting chocolate, grease the pan it's melting in and the chocolate won't stick.

To cut marshmallows, rub butter on scissors.

To form popcorn balls, rub butter on hands.

Grating and Slicing

Chill cheese before grating.

Nut breads and raw meats slice easily when partially frozen.

Meatloaf is easier to slice if you wait ten minutes after taking it out of the oven before cutting it.

Freshly baked bread is easier to slice when placed on its side.

Eggs and Dairy

To keep hard-boiled eggs from cracking during cooking, gently submerge them in cold water, add a teaspoon of salt to the water, and let them heat slowly to boiling. If shell does happen to crack, add some vinegar to the water as the eggs cook to seal the crack.

After cooking, put hard-boiled eggs (still in the pan) under cold, running water before removing the shells.

To store egg yolks, cover them with a mixture of cold water and a teaspoon of salad oil, then keep them in the refrigerator.

To double the volume of whipped cream, add one egg white to one cup of whipping cream then whip as usual.

Soups, Stews and Sauces

When using flour to thicken a liquid, sprinkle the flour with salt first and the liquid won't turn lumpy.

55

*M*om says:
Cooking is an art.
Make the time to
cook and enjoy the
process. Take pride in
preparing your own
meals using fresh
food, herbs and spices.
The food you make
yourself tastes better
and is better for you.

Metric Conversions

If your recipe uses metrics, refer to this chart to make accurate measurements.

For cooking weights and measures, all you need are milliliters (ml) and liters.

5 ml	= 1 tsp.
15 ml	= 1 Tbsp.
60 ml	= 1/4 cup
70 ml	= 1/3 cup
120 ml	= 1/2 cup
160 ml	= 2/3 cup
180 ml	= 3/4 cup
240 ml	= 1 cup
30 ml	= 1 ounce
60 ml	= 2 ounces
120 ml	= 4 ounces
240 ml	= 8 ounces
480 ml	= 1 pint
.95 liters	= 1 quart
3.8 liters	= 1 gallon

To thicken soup or stew, use instant mashed potato flakes. Stir in 1/4 cup to 1/2 cup until soup reaches desired consistency.

To absorb the grease in soup or stew, drop in a clean leaf of lettuce. Remove the lettuce when the cooking is finished.

If the soup or stew is too salty, add equal amounts of sugar and vinegar, or add chunks of raw potato. Remove potato before serving – it will have absorbed the salt.

Meat and Poultry

To make juicy hamburgers, Place a chip of ice on top of the patty just as it begins to cook.

To cut down baking time for meatloaf, bake in single-serving size muffin tins or mini loaf pans.

For juicier chicken, bake with the skin on to seal in juices, then remove the skin before serving.

For crispy chicken, rub the skin with mayonnaise before broiling.

To keep roast beef from drying out when reheating, simmer in broth in a saucepan. If the roast isn't heated all the way through, slice it, arrange the pieces on an ovenproof plate, and return to the oven for ten to 15 minutes.

Tasty Vegetables

When submerging spinach, beet greens, lettuce or other greens in water to wash, put a handful of salt in the water to remove the grit. Rinse thoroughly with clear water afterward.

When boiling cauliflower, add a small amount of milk to the water to keep the vegetable white.

When boiling vegetables, add a teaspoon of sugar to the water to enhance natural flavors.

Instead of boiling beets, bake them in the oven like potatoes.

To rebake leftover baked potatoes, dip them in water and bake at 350 degrees for 15 to 20 minutes.

To speed up baking time for potatoes, soak them in

salt water for 30 minutes before baking or cut the potatoes in half lengthwise and place them cut side down on a greased or buttered baking sheet. Bake for 35 minutes at 425 degrees.

To salvage soggy potato chips, crackers or cereal, spread them on a cookie sheet and bake at 250 degrees for three to five minutes.

Miscellaneous Tips

Sweeten leftover pancake batter with some baking soda and ginger-ale.

If food starts to burn while cooking, don't stir it! Remove or pour the unburnt food into a clean pot and continue cooking.

Whip it Good

Making whipped cream from real cream is a treat. For best results, before beating, place the beaters, bowl and cream in the refrigerator to chill well. Beat the cream on medium speed with an electric mixer. An egg beater or wire whip will also work. Watch carefully and whip only to the soft peak stage. If beaten too long, the cream will gather and turn into butter.

To sweeten the cream, add one to two teaspoons of powdered or granulated sugar. This helps make the cream smooth, thicken and hold its shape. You may also add 1/2 teaspoon of vanilla extract to taste.

Whipping cream can be substituted with.

• One can of evaporated milk that is thoroughly chilled or partially frozen before whipping.

• Or 1/2 cup of powdered nonfat dry milk with 1/3 cup water. Mix and chill, then whip until mixture stands in soft peaks. Then add one tablespoon lemon juice. Whip again and carefully beat in two to four tablespoons of sugar.

Add a Little Spice

That aromatic cinnamon in the corner of your cupboard has an impressive past. Spices were once considered as valuable as gold. Wars were fought over the likes of nutmeg and paprika.

Herbs and spices make the difference between bland boredom and exciting eating. There's virtually no limit to the way you can use them. Have you ever tried cinnamon on ham or paprika in a hamburger? Live a little and give it a try.

While the word "spice" generally means any aromatic vegetable product that adds zest to food, there are actually five distinct types of savory aromatics: *Spices,* obtained from the bark, root, fruit or berry of perennial plants, are used whole or ground. *Herbs,* leaves of annual and perennial shrubs, are used in fresh or dry form. *Aromatic seeds* of annual plants may be used whole or ground and include anise, caraway, celery, coriander and mustard. *Seasonings* are a blend of spices, herbs, seeds and/or salt. *Vegetable spices* include garlic, celery and onion powder, chives, crushed chili peppers, paprika and horseradish.

Handy Herbs

Basil: Tomatoes, chowders, shrimp, broiled fish, eggs, lamb, sausage, asparagus, eggplant, squash, onion, spaghetti sauce, all Italian dishes and bakes.

Bay Leaves: Stocks, soups, stews, beans, poached halibut and salmon, pot roast, chicken, tomatoes, sauces and marinades. *Remove whole bay leaves before serving.*

Dill: Cheese dips, seafood spreads, soups, shrimp, halibut, sole, omelettes, cottage cheese, beef, veal, lamb, chicken pot pie, cabbage, beets.

Marjoram: Mushrooms, crab, tuna, clams, halibut, salmon, omelettes, scrambled eggs, roast, pork, beef, veal, creamed chicken, stuffings, carrots, peas, zucchini, and chicken salad.

Oregano: Sausage, lamb, meat loaf, shrimp, clams, lobster, poultry stuffings, pizza sauce, spaghetti sauce, tomatoes, beans, lentils, minestrone, cabbage, broccoli, enchilada sauce.

Peppermint: Fruit, melon balls, pea soup, shrimp and prawn garnish, cream cheese, lamb, veal, carrots, potatoes, spinach, zucchini, coleslaw, fruit salads, mint sauce.

Rosemary: Fruit dishes, soups, salmon, halibut, omelettes, lamb, veal, beef, ham, poultry, peas, spinach and potatoes,

Saffron: Halibut, sole, all fish sauces, eggs, omelettes, cream cheese, veal, chicken, rice, desserts, cakes and frostings.

Sage: All chowders, halibut, salmon, cottage cheese, stews, pork, sausage, turkey, stuffings, eggplant, onions, tomatoes.

Savory: Vegetable soups, crab, salmon, deviled eggs, pork, veal, chicken, poultry stuffings, beans, rice, lentils, fish sauces.

Tarragon: Soups, veal, chicken, fish, eggs, mushrooms, chicken and seafood salads, tartar and mustard sauces.

Thyme: Fish spreads, seafood cocktails, gumbo, pea soup, clam chowder, tuna, scallops, crab, sole, cottage cheese, mutton, meat loaf, veal, liver, poultry and wild game stuffings, onions, carrots, beets.

Savory Spices

Allspice: Pot roast, fish and poultry marinades, stew, veal, pork, lamb, chili, barbecue and spaghetti sauces, fruit and spice cakes, apple and pumpkin pies.

Cardamom: Spareribs, ham, pork, barbecue sauce, cakes, breads, fruitcake and cookies.

Chili Powder: Beef, sauces, baked potatoes, Mexican dishes.

Cinnamon: Fruits, broiled grapefruit, bouillon for fish, ham, lamb and pork chops, beef stews, stuffing, milk drinks, pudding, pumpkin and apple pies.

Cloves: Baked fish, stocks, eggs, marinades for beef, pork, lamb and veal, meatloaf, ham, beets, sweet potatoes, sauces like spaghetti, chili and barbecue, all spice cakes, cookies and puddings. *Remove whole cloves before serving.*

Crushed Red Pepper: Pizza, pasta sauce, Mexican dishes, fish, chicken, hamburger, steak.

Cumin and Coriander: Meat sauces, pork roast, hamburgers, Mexican dishes and sauces.

Spice It Right

• Go easy on using spices. The flavor should be subtle.

• Save money by purchasing spices in plain containers. You pay more for fancy packaging. You can find many spices in Mexican and Oriental food aisles in plastic bags at half what bottled spices cost.

• Purchase spices in small containers and replace often. Aromatic oils evaporate and they can lose their flavor.

• Store herbs and spices in airtight jars in a cool, dark and dry place. If you usually buy them in cardboard containers, make the switch.

• Add whole spices as you *begin* making hot soups and stews.

• Add spices early to uncooked foods such as salad dressings, salads and beverages.

• Add ground spices just before you finish cooking. Prolonged heat can destroy their flavor and aroma.

Checklist

Herbs and Spices
These are must-haves:

- ❑ Allspice
- ❑ Basil
- ❑ Bay leaves
- ❑ Black pepper
- ❑ Celery salt
- ❑ Chili powder
- ❑ Cinnamon
- ❑ Cloves
- ❑ Curry powder
- ❑ Dry mustard
- ❑ Garlic powder
- ❑ Ginger
- ❑ Ground cumin
- ❑ Iodized salt
- ❑ Nutmeg
- ❑ Onion salt
- ❑ Oregano
- ❑ Paprika
- ❑ Parsley flakes

Eventually get these:

- ❑ Cardamom
- ❑ Cayenne pepper
- ❑ Chives
- ❑ Cilantro flakes or ground coriander
- ❑ Dill weed
- ❑ Mace
- ❑ Marjoram
- ❑ Peppermint
- ❑ Rosemary
- ❑ Saffron
- ❑ Sage
- ❑ Savory
- ❑ Tarragon
- ❑ Thyme
- ❑ Turmeric

Curry Powder: Dips, fish, deviled eggs, egg salad, lamb, pork, beef, chicken, vegetables, marinades, rice, Indian dishes.

Garlic, Celery, Onion Salt: Soups and stews, stocks, sauces, marinades, fish, beef, chicken, and vegetables.

Ginger: Fruits, puddings, fish, pot roast, steak, lamb, poultry stuffing and marinades, sweet potatoes, glazed carrots.

Lemon Pepper: Marinades for fish, chicken and steak, spinach.

Mace: Fruit, trout, scallops, fish, lamb, sausage, buttered carrots, cauliflower, squash, spinach, mashed potatoes, sauces for fish, veal and chicken, cooked apples, cherries and apricots, pancakes, puddings.

Mustard: Butter for fish and vegetables, crab, fried and broiled fish, beef, stew, Swiss steak, pot roast, ham, pork, potatoes, cabbage, brussels sprouts, asparagus, broccoli, green beans, vegetable and seafood salads, salad dressings, sandwiches and cream sauces.

Nutmeg: Milk and spiced drinks, eggnog, fish, Swedish meat balls, meat loaf, meat pie, chicken, glazed carrots, squash, cauliflower, spinach, cream sauce for chicken, seafood and veal, ice cream, cakes, cookies, pies, rice pudding and bread pudding.

Paprika: Cheese mixtures, deviled eggs, ground beef, dipping mixture for pork chops, veal cutlets and fried chicken, baked potatoes, sour cream.

Parsley: Garnish any dish, especially fish, poultry and rice.

Turmeric: Marinades for shrimp, salmon, lobster and chicken; eggs, curried beef and lamb, cream and mustard sauces, rice, seafood salad and Indian dishes.

Making Life Easier

Once you do it the right way, meal planning and cooking for yourself everyday can be fast, simple and even enjoyable. The same goes for other necessary tasks of life such as house cleaning, laundry, personal hygiene, finances and home maintenance.

Kitchen Tips

To clean a glass oven door, sprinkle baking soda onto a damp cloth. Use circular motions to wipe over the entire door. The soda will dissolve baked-on stains. Rinse with clean water and wipe dry.

To clean a food spill in the oven, sprinkle with salt while is still hot. Once the oven cools, scrape up with a spatula.

To extinguish small stovetop fires, keep a box of baking soda or a container of salt nearby and pour over flames.

To keep garbage cans clean, line with plastic trash bags.

To keep stains off of the oven floor and the covers under stove burners, line with foil. When the foil gets dirty, discard and replace with new.

If you don't have hot water to rinse dishes, dip the dishes in a solution of one gallon of cold water and 1/4 cup of liquid bleach. Wipe dishes thoroughly with a clean towel.

To make defrosting the freezer a breeze, wipe the inside thoroughly with a clean towel, put a small amount of shortening on a paper napkin and wipe the metal with it. Next time the ice builds up, it will fall off with ease.

To get a raw egg off of the floor, cover it with salt, wait five minutes and it will easily sweep up.

To remove coffee and tea stains from counter tops, cups and fabric, rub with a paste made of baking soda and water.

Mom says:
Once you get the basics of life down to a routine, you will have more time, energy and money to pursue other activities and interests that you enjoy.

To clean burnt pans, Coat area with paste of baking soda and water. Let stand for three hours then scrape with a plastic spatula.

For a shiny floor, add a cup of vinegar to mop water.

Removing Odors

To eliminate bathroom odors, simply strike a match.

To get rid of onion or fish smell on your hands, rub your hands with fresh lemon juice.

To absorb odors when cooking cabbage or sauerkraut, put half a cup of vinegar on the stove near the pot or add a chunk of red pepper to the pot.

To get musty odors out of a suitcase, wipe the inside with a mixture of baking soda and water and let it dry in the sun. Then put a few drops of cinnamon oil on a cotton ball and tuck it inside.

To get rid of onion odor on utensils and knives, rub them with either a raw potato or a piece of celery.

To freshen the air, sprinkle a few tablespoons of cinnamon or nutmeg in an aluminum tray or pie plate. Heat it on the stove until the spice is completely burned up. *OR* try putting a few whole cloves on a piece of orange peel in a tin and burn them until ashy. *OR* dab your vacuum cleaner bag with scented oil. As you vacuum, the scent will fill the house.

To get rid of body odor that didn't disappear during laundering, soak the clothing in a mixture of one cup salt to one gallon of water for at least an hour, then repeat laundering.

Cutting Costs

Utility bills can add up in a hurry, especially during extremely hot and cold weather. Cut costs and conserve energy by following a few simple guidelines:

Laundry: Wait to do laundry until you have a full load.

Buy permanent press or wrinkle free clothing. Remove clothes promptly from the dryer and hang them up immediately. If clean clothes are wrinkled, hang them in the bathroom during a warm shower or hang them on a door, spritz with clean water, tug firmly and smooth wrinkles, then leave to dry.

Avoid over-drying clothes. Hang dry whenever possible.

Cooking: Use the right-size burner for your pan, and use a lid when cooking.

Don't keep opening the oven door during baking and, if you can, bake more than one item in the oven at the same time.

Thaw foods completely before cooking them.

Air Conditioning: Keep curtains or window shades closed during the part of the day when sun shines directly in.

Dress in light-colored cotton clothing.

Keep thermostat set as high as you possibly can – 72 degrees or higher.

Heating: Open curtains and shades during the part of the day when the sun shines directly in.

Wear warm clothing. Several layers of light clothing are warmer than one layer of heavy clothing, and you can take one layer off at a time when you get too hot.

Check to make sure nothing is blocking your heat registers. Move furniture and other objects away so that registers are free and clear.

Lower thermostat to 60 degrees while you are out during the day.

Mom says:
Small actions over a long period of time add up to big savings. Be the master of your own space. Run the household instead of letting the household run you.

···

Protect Your Stuff

Life holds surprises, not all of them pleasant. No one thinks they'll be the victim of theft, robbery or burglary. Just to be safe, protect your valuables by taking the following steps:

• Write your name, address, telephone number and bicycle serial number on a card or paper and roll into a tight roll. Remove the seat and drop the roll into the frame of your bike. If the bicycle is stolen, you can easily identify it.

• If you have any expensive items, such as stereo or computer equipment, a home entertainment center, or a music or video collection, get renter's insurance. For small priceless heirlooms, rent a safety deposit box.

Keep the thermostat low at night – 60 degrees or lower – to save significantly on your heating bill. Use several blankets on beds during the winter months.

If you have a fireplace, make sure damper is closed when not in use.

Close off any rooms you may not be using.

Water Heater: Repair any leaking faucets.

When shaving or washing face, fill basin with hot water instead of letting the hot water run.

Take short showers. Turn the water off while you lather and turn it on again to rinse. You can save more than half the hot water that way.

When taking a bath, don't fill the tub all the way. If you do laundry at home, rinse all loads in cold water.

Refrigerator and Freezer: Don't overload refrigerator. Keep freezer defrosted.

Let hot foods cool down before placing in refrigerator.

Don't hold refrigerator door open unnecessarily. Decide what you want to get beforehand.

Keep refrigerator and freezer clean and tidy so food will be easy to find and leftovers won't go to waste.

When Even Your Water Is Dirty

If you're in an underdeveloped country, or have been the victim of a natural disaster, you may have reason to doubt the purity of your water. Use one of three easy methods listed below to make sure your water is safe for drinking and cooking.

Boiling. Boil the water vigorously for a full three minutes. Boiling will destroy bacteria but will not remove radioactivity.

Iodine. Add three drops of household iodine (2% tincture) to each quart of water, or twelve drops to each gallon. Double the amount of iodine if the water is cloudy.

Bleach. Use chlorine bleach containing 5.25% sodium hypochlorite. Use two drops per quart, eight drops per gallon and 1/2 teaspoon per five gallons of water. Double the amount of bleach you use if the water is cloudy. Thoroughly mix in the bleach and let the water stand for five minutes. Check to see if you can taste or smell the chlorine – a sign of safety. If you can't, mix in another dose and let the water stand for 15 minutes. Don't use the water until you can taste or smell the chlorine.

Can't I Just Be a Slob?

If you like to live in chaos, be a slob. All the rest of us are going to do our housework. Housecleaning is not rocket science. A few good daily habits will make the chore simple and even fun.

It takes less time and effort to keep a house clean than it does to clean the house once it becomes a disaster. A house doesn't get dirty all at once but a little at a time. Take a few minutes everyday to clean up a small mess. For example, do the dishes right after each meal. Then you won't have to spend Saturday morning doing a week's worth of encrusted dishes.

Checklist

Cleaning Supplies

❐ Broom
❐ Bucket
❐ Carpet sweeper
❐ Cleaning cloths/rags
❐ Cleanser
❐ Damp/scrubber mop
❐ Disinfectant cleaner
❐ Dust cloth or duster
❐ Dust pan
❐ Furniture polish
❐ Garbage bags
❐ Glass cleaner
❐ Nylon scrub sponge
❐ Old towels for drying
❐ Paper towels
❐ Toilet bowl brush
❐ Toilet bowl cleaner
❐ Upright vacuum with
   attachments

A well-stocked cleaning tote will help you do the job. But you don't have to have a bunch of supplies. A broom, a few rags – one for cleaning, one for rinsing and one for drying – any kind of soap and some good old elbow grease are enough to get a home clean.

Five Reasons to Clean House

1) So that your home functions well and you can find everything.

2) So that you will have clean clothes to wear and clean dishes for meals.

3) To scare germs, mice and bugs away. To keep things sanitary and healthy.

4) So that you can invite visitors in without the worry of embarrassment.

5) To care for yourself and show the world how good you feel about who you are.

Housecleaning 1-2-3

Step 1: Set aside a half hour the same time each day to do surface cleaning. Learn to top clean. Put dishes in the sink with hot water and detergent to soak. Make the beds, pick up papers, garbage and empty trash cans into a large bag that you carry with you. Spray window cleaner on sinks and mirrors, wipe with paper towels. Use a carpet sweeper or broom. Dust briefly with an old cloth. Do the dishes, dry and put them away. Go put your feet up and read the paper.

Step 2: Set aside an hour or two to do deep cleaning the same time each week. Get your roommates or family members involved. Turbo house cleaning is an art form. Be well armed. Have all your basic supplies in one carrying case. Pick up clutter and put it in its place. Then scrub top to bottom. Use disinfectant cleaner in kitchen and bathroom. Use cleanser in the bath tub and toilet. Wash down walls, sinks, appliances. Clean the floors. Dust shelves and furniture. Vacuum.

Step 3: Dejunk house every three months.
"A place for everything and everything in its place." If you are running out of places, it's easier and cheaper to get rid of some of your possessions than it is to find a bigger apartment or home to keep them in. If you don't use it or it's broken, throw it away. If you've grown tired of it or grown out of it, give it to someone who needs it.

<u>**Cleaning Hints**</u>

Living Room and Bedrooms: Sprinkle newspaper with water before you empty the vacuum cleaner bag onto it – dust won't scatter.

To clean a ceiling fan, cover your hands in a pair of old socks. Dip them in warm sudsy water and run your hand over the top and bottom of each blade. After cleaning and drying the blades of a ceiling fan, apply a thin coat of floor wax to both sides to keep dust from clinging.

Wipe miniblinds with a damp fabric softener sheet. This will help eliminate the static that collects dust.

Water rings on most surfaces can be removed by rubbing petroleum jelly thoroughly into the spot.

Clean cobwebs with an upward motion to lift them off. A downward sweep usually plasters them against the wall.

Use a clean sponge mop for walls and ceilings.

Bathroom and Kitchen: Out of glass cleaner? Dampen a soft rag with rubbing alcohol and wipe over the entire surface of mirrors and windows.

To remove rust stains from sinks and tubs, pour a few drops of hydrogen peroxide on the stain and sprinkle with cream of tartar. Let sit for half hour, then wipe off and rinse well.

Drop a denture cleaning tablet into the toilet for a fast cleanup.

Wipe bathroom fixtures with rubbing alcohol for a quick shine.

To remove water stains from your dish drainer, pour one cup of vinegar over it and let it stand overnight, then wipe it off with a wet sponge.

Hair spray buildup can be removed from a mirror by wiping the mirror with crumpled up newspaper.

Keep tile and fiberglass shower walls clean by washing them well, applying a thin coat of car wax and then buffing. This will prevent most soap build up and wipes off easily.

Wash and dry your stainless steel sink, then polish it with a few drops of baby oil and buff until shiny. This will help prevent water spots in the future.

Pour some baking soda down the drains weekly to keep the pipes clean.

Deodorize your garbage disposal by throwing in and grinding up leftover orange and lemon peels.

For a shiny finish on no wax floors, add one quarter cup of presoak laundry powder to soapy mop water.

To unclog drains that are plugged with hair, mix equal parts of vinegar, salt and baking soda. Pour down drain, let foam for 15 minutes, then flush with boiling water.

Miscellaneous:

To remove mildew from paper, sprinkle cornstarch over the mildew, let stand for at least 48 hours, then remove it with a soft brush.

To keep newspaper clippings from turning yellow,

spray them lightly with hairspray. Use two or three coats, waiting for each coat to dry.

To clean the telephone, use cotton balls dipped in rubbing alcohol.

To clean silk flowers, put them in a bag with some salt and shake. The dust will stick to the salt.

Baking Soda – Don't Be Home Without It

That humble box of baking soda in your kitchen cupboard can become your best friend. It cooks, cleans and refreshes!

Baking soda is the key to many baked goods, including cakes, breads, cookies, biscuits and pancakes. But did you know it can do some other amazing things, too?

Try using baking soda in some of these ways:

Personal Care

• **To kill odor,** sprinkle soda in shoes.

• **To treat an upset stomach,** mix a teaspoon of soda in a glass of warm water.

• **To soothe bee stings and insect bites,** mix soda into a paste with water.

• **To cool a sunburn or calm hives from allergies,** put half a box in tepid bath water.

• **To use as toothpaste,** combine it with salt and water.

• **To get combs and brushes sparkling clean,** soak them in a mixture of warm water, a little shampoo and a handful of baking soda.

• **To take care of soiled toenails and fingernails,** scrub with a paste made from soda and water.

• **To soak tired feet** at the end of long day, swirl it in warm water.

Household Uses

• **To freshen rooms,** sprinkle soda on the carpet and let stand for half an hour before vacuuming.

• **To eliminate food odors,** tuck a small bowl of baking soda in the corner of the refrigerator or freezer.

• **To extinguish small kitchen fires, especially those that involve grease or oil,** dump soda on the flames.

• **To clean car battery cables or polish the headlights and chrome,** dissolve half a cup of soda in a quart of water.

• **To keep whites bright,** dump a handful of soda in the washing machine.

• **To clean and deodorize tile, dish drains, silverware, nonstick pans, thermos jugs, lunch boxes, enamel surfaces, plastic dishes, tablecloths and place mats,** mix soda with water.

Recipes for Things You Can't Eat

Think of recipes and you might think of creamy cheesecakes, nutty brownies or cheesy casserole, but there's an exciting way to use some unusual recipes that can save money, too. Give them a try and see how they stand up to any commercial product you have tried. You just might be surprised!

> **WARNING:**
>
> Do NOT mix ammonia and chlorine bleach together. The combination of the two produces deadly fumes! Always mix and use chemicals carefully and in well-ventilated areas.

Window Cleaner

Mix in a quart bottle:
1/2 cup rubbing alcohol
1 1/2 tsp. ammonia
1 1/2 tsp. liquid dish soap

Combine ingredients in a quart bottle with a spray nozzle. Top with water, and shake vigorously. This solution is useful for cleaning windows, mirrors and porcelain.

Ant Killer

1 cup molasses
2 packages dry yeast
1/2 cup sugar

Mix into a paste. Coat one side of small squares of cardboard and place near ants. When the paste dries, replace squares and continue until the ants are gone.

Furniture Polish

2 cups mineral oil
6 drops lemon extract

Put mineral oil in a spray bottle. If you want a scent, add lemon extract. Shake well. Spray on furniture and polish with a clean cloth.

Outdoor Window Cleaner

1/2 gallon warm water
2 Tbsp. dishwasher detergent
1 Tbsp. liquid dishwasher
   drying agent

Mix ingredients. Brush or sponge on window. Immediately hose off. Water will sheet with no drying necessary. Be sure windows are tightly closed.

General Household Cleaner

1 Tbsp. ammonia
1 Tbsp. liquid detergent
2 cups water

Mix together and use for general cleaning. Put in a spray bottle for touch-ups if desired.

Wall Cleaner

1 gallon hot water
1 cup ammonia
1/2 cup vinegar
1/4 cup baking soda

Mix ingredients. Wash only a small area at a time. Wipe the area being worked on thoroughly with a second cloth of clean, warm water. This mixture will clean badly soiled, painted surfaces. Because the mixture can be drying to the skin, wear rubber gloves.

Carpet Cleaner

1 tsp. mild detergent
1 tsp. white vinegar
1 quart warm water

Mix ingredients. Apply with clean cloth, using only amount of cleaning solution needed. Be careful not to soak the carpet through and always absorb excess liquid with a clean rag.

Dusting Cloths

1 Tbsp. mild soap powder
1 quart warm water
1 Tbsp. ammonia
2 Tbsp. boiled linseed oil
   or furniture polish

Mix ingredients well. Dip soft cotton cloth into solution. After a few minutes, squeeze out, dry and store in covered glass, plastic or tin container. Treat cloths again after each washing.

Furniture Beauty Oil

3 Tbsp. boiled linseed oil
   (buy it as such)
1 Tbsp. turpentine
1 quart hot water

Mix ingredients in two-quart pan and heat to as warm as gloved hand can stand. Dip soft cloth into solution. Lift out and squeeze until it does not drip. Go over a small area. Follow immediately with a clean, absorbent cloth.

Septic Tank Recharger

2 cups brown sugar, packed
1 package dry yeast
1 quart of water

If you're in a rural area, chances are you have a septic tank, and septic tanks depend on the action of bacteria to break down solids and purify the resulting liquids. You can prevent sludge buildup and keep the bacteria working well by using this formula once a month. Mix thoroughly, pour into the toilet bowl and flush.

Notes

....

....

....

....

....

....

....

....

....

....

....

....

....

....

....

....

....

....

....

....

....

....

....

....

....

....

....

CHAPTER 4

Home Is Where the Food Is
Recipes You Can Live By

*M*ost of the recipes make enough to satisfy three or four people.

Cooking well will fill your stomach and keep you healthy, it will also help you win friends and influence people. Everyone likes to be fed. If you develop a reputation for whipping up great meals, you will never worry about eating alone. Of course, let other people contribute – no one is rich enough to feed a bunch of friends all the time. Make it a habit to prepare delicious meals and snacks for yourself and you'll always have something to offer a visitor. It's nice to hear: "Sit down and make yourself at home. Would you like a bite to eat?"

In this chapter, you will find easy, tasty recipes made with simple, inexpensive ingredients. Try the traditional favorites or some new treats for breakfast, eggs, sandwiches, soups, salads, main dishes, vegetarian main dishes, side dishes, beverages, breads, cakes, cookies and candies. If you're in a hurry to eat, there are microwave recipes, too! And feel free to write down your favorites. ***Mom's Old Standbys pages are set aside for you to write in your favorite family recipes.***

Breakfast

Since breakfast is the most important meal of the day, do it big. The *German Pancake* recipe is Mom's favorite, and the recipe in this book even inspired a university student to write his music thesis in honor of the yummy delight.

Wash hands with soap and water, rinse and dry them with a paper towel before beginning any recipe.

To cut down on fat: For any recipe calling for butter or margarine to be melted in a pan before you cook an item, simply substitute non-stick cooking spray. *"Grease"* baking pans with cooking spray as well. Use skim milk and fat-free cheeses in recipes.

Easy Pancakes

2 eggs, well beaten
1/2 cup milk
2 Tbsp. cooking oil
3/4 cup flour

2 tsp. baking powder
1/2 tsp. salt
1/2 tsp. sugar

Sift together flour, baking powder, salt and sugar in medium bowl. Beat together eggs, milk and oil. Stir egg mixture into flour mixture until all ingredients are well blended. Heat a greased griddle or frying pan. Pour small amount of batter into pan. Cook until bubbles form on top. Turn. Cook until bottom side is light brown.

Applesauce Roll Pancakes

2 eggs, well beaten
1/2 cup milk
1/2 cup flour
1/2 tsp. salt

1 Tbsp. sugar
1 cup applesauce
powdered sugar (optional)

Heat applesauce in small saucepan until warm. Mix eggs and milk in medium bowl. Add flour, salt and sugar. Beat until smooth. Grease small frying pan and heat until very hot. Pour 1/4 of batter into pan. Tip pan quickly until batter covers bottom. Turn and brown on other side. Remove from pan, spread with 1/4 cup warm applesauce and roll. Sprinkle with powdered sugar, if desired.

German Pancakes

These are Mom's favorite!

6 eggs
1 cup milk
1 cup flour

1/4 tsp. salt
4 Tbsp. butter or margarine

Preheat oven to 450 degrees. Combine eggs, milk, flour and salt in a bowl. Beat until fluffy and smooth. Put two tablespoons of butter in each of two pie pans. Put tins in the oven as it preheats to melt the butter. Pour half of the batter in each pan. Bake at 450 degrees for 20 minutes. Pancakes will puff up as they bake. Serve with syrup, warm jam or warm fruit.

Moist Oatmeal Pancakes

2 cups quick-cooking oatmeal
1 1/2 cups milk
1/2 cup granulated sugar
1 tsp. baking powder

2 eggs, beaten
dash of salt
1/4 tsp. cinnamon

Mix all ingredients in a large bowl. Beat into a thin batter. Heat a greased griddle. Pour a small amount of batter onto the griddle. If batter is not thin enough to pour, add a little more milk. Cook until bubbles come to the surface and the edges look dry. Flip over with a spatula and cook until light brown.

Potato Pancakes

Try these for a delicious dinner, too!

2 eggs
1 Tbsp. flour
1/2 tsp. salt
2 tsp. onion, minced

Dash of nutmeg
2 potatoes, grated
4 slices bacon, cooked and crumbled
1 cup warm applesauce

Combine eggs, flour, salt, onion, nutmeg and potatoes. Pour 1/4 cup of the mixture into a hot greased frying pan, one pancake at a time. Flatten and cook on both sides until lightly browned. Sprinkle with crumbled bacon. Spoon warm applesauce over the top of the potato pancakes, or serve the applesauce on the side.

Swedish Pancakes

3 eggs
1 1/4 cups milk
3/4 cup sifted flour

1 Tbsp. sugar
1/2 tsp. salt

Combine ingredients in bowl. Beat with wire whip or mixer on medium speed. Cook as thin pancakes on medium heat. Brown both sides, roll or fold in quarters. Serve with favorite topping.

Whole-Wheat Pancakes

2/3 cup whole-wheat flour
1 1/2 tsp. baking powder
4 tsp. granulated sugar
1/4 tsp. salt

1 egg, beaten
2/3 cup milk
4 tsp. cooking oil

Stir flour, baking powder, sugar and salt together in bowl. Combine egg, milk and oil. Stir into flour mixture. Pour batter onto hot, ungreased frying pan. Cook until brown.

Easy Waffles

1 cup flour
1 tsp. baking powder
1/4 tsp. salt
1/4 tsp. baking soda

1 cup milk
2 tsp. lemon juice or vinegar
2 Tbsp. butter or margarine
1 egg, beaten

Combine flour, baking powder, salt and baking soda. Stir in milk, lemon juice, butter and egg. Cook in greased waffle iron.

Best-Ever Waffles

1/2 cup butter or margarine, melted
1 Tbsp. sugar
4 egg yolks
2 cups flour, sifted

2 cups milk
4 egg whites, stiffly beaten
4 tsp. baking powder

Mix butter, sugar and egg yolks. Beat in milk and flour. Fold in egg whites and baking powder. Cook in greased waffle iron.

Bacon and Cheese Waffles

1 egg, beaten
1 cup milk
2 tsp. lemon juice
1/2 tsp. baking soda
1 cup sifted flour

1 tsp. baking powder
1/4 tsp. salt
3 Tbsp. butter or margarine, softened
1/2 cup cheese, grated
6 strips of bacon, cooked and crumbled

Beat egg, milk and lemon juice. Sift together baking soda, flour, baking powder and salt. Stir into the egg mixture. Fold in butter, cheese and bacon. Cook in greased waffle iron.

Gingerbread Waffles

1/4 cup butter or margarine,
    softened
1/2 cup brown sugar, packed
1/2 cup light molasses
2 eggs, beaten
1 cup milk
2 cups flour, sifted

1 1/2 tsp. baking powder
1 1/2 tsp. cinnamon
1 tsp. ginger
1/4 tsp. allspice
1/2 tsp. salt
2 bananas, sliced
1/2 cup whipped cream

Cream butter, brown sugar, molasses, eggs and milk. Mix flour, baking powder, cinnamon, ginger, allspice and salt. Add to molasses mixture. Cook in waffle iron. Top with bananas and whipped cream.

Nutty Whole-Wheat Waffles

1 cup whole-wheat flour
1 1/2 tsp. baking powder
1/2 tsp. salt
3 egg yolks

1 cup milk
3 Tbsp. butter or margarine, melted
3 egg whites, stiffly beaten
1/2 cup nuts, chopped

In small bowl, sift together flour, baking powder and salt. In separate bowl, beat together egg yolks, milk and melted butter. Pour into dry ingredients. Fold in egg whites and nuts, stirring just enough to combine. Cook in greased waffle iron.

Easy Maple Syrup

2 cups granulated sugar
1 cup water

1/2 tsp. maple extract

Bring sugar and water to boil. Remove from heat. Stir in extract.

Banana-Orange Sauce

1/2 cup orange juice
1/4 cup sugar
1 1/2 tsp. cornstarch

1 large banana, sliced
1 large orange, sectioned and chopped

Combine orange juice, sugar and cornstarch. Bring mixture to a boil. Simmer until thickened. Stir in bananas and oranges. Serve warm.

Brown Sugar Syrup

1 cup brown sugar, packed
1/2 cup water

1 Tbsp. butter or margarine
1/2 tsp. vanilla extract

Combine sugar and water. Bring to a boil and boil for two minutes. Remove from heat and stir in butter and vanilla. Serve warm.

Bubbly Apple Topping

1/4 cup butter or margarine
2 apples, cored and sliced
1/4 cup brown sugar, packed

1/4 cup nuts, chopped
1/8 cup water

Melt butter. Add apples and cook, stirring occasionally, until tender. Stir in brown sugar, nuts and water. heat through. Serve warm.

Creamy Cinnamon Syrup

1/2 cup light corn syrup
1 cup granulated sugar
1/4 cup water

1 tsp. cinnamon
1/2 cup evaporated milk

Bring corn syrup, sugar, water and cinnamon to a boil. Cook two to three minutes. Allow to cool for five minutes. Stir in milk. Serve warm.

Honey Maple Syrup

3/4 cup granulated sugar
1/2 cup light corn syrup

1/2 cup water
1/4 tsp. maple extract

Combine all ingredients in saucepan. Cook, stirring occasionally, until butter is melted and sugar dissolves. Serve warm or cold.

Breakfast Apple Pie

1 egg, beaten
4 Tbsp. cooking oil
1 cup milk
1 1/2 cups biscuit mix
1/2 cup sugar
1/2 cup chopped nuts

2 large apples, cut into wedges
2 Tbsp. sugar
1/2 tsp. cinnamon
1/4 tsp. nutmeg
2 Tbsp. butter or margarine

Preheat oven to 375 degrees. Beat together egg, oil and milk. Add biscuit mix, sugar and nuts. Beat well. Pour into greased 9-inch pie plate. Arrange apple wedges on top of pie. Sprinkle with sugar, cinnamon and nutmeg. Dot with butter. Bake at 375 degrees for 30 minutes.

Breakfast Sandwiches

A delicious way to use leftover waffles!

8 cooked waffles, heated
1/4 cup peanut butter

1/4 cup strawberry jam
2 bananas, sliced

Spread 4 waffles with peanut butter and top with banana slices. Spread 4 waffles with strawberry jam. Put peanut butter and strawberry jam waffles together. These sandwiches can be frozen. Wrap in foil to freeze. Heat in oven before eating.

Nutty Granola

4 cups quick-cooking oatmeal
1 1/2 cups shredded coconut
1 cup sunflower seeds
2 cups walnuts, chopped

1 cup cooking oil
1/2 cup water
2 tsp. vanilla extract

Preheat oven to 275 degrees. Combine all ingredients and spread on a cookie sheet. Bake at 275 degrees for two hours, stirring often. Serve with milk. Store in tightly covered container.

Easy Granola

3 1/2 cups quick-cooking oats
1/4 cup cooking oil
1/4 cup honey

1 Tbsp. vanilla extract
1/2 cup raisins
1/2 cup nuts, chopped

Preheat oven to 300 degrees. Combine all ingredients. Spread on cookie sheet. Bake at 300 degrees for 10 minutes. Serve with milk and shredded coconut, if desired.

Apple Granola Crunch

1 1/2 cups quick-cooking oatmeal
1 cup coarsely chopped walnuts
1 cup bran granule cereal

1 cup dried apples, chopped
1/2 cup brown sugar, packed

Preheat oven to 350 degrees. Combine all ingredients. Mix well. Spread on a greased cookie sheet. Bake at 350 degrees for 10 minutes, stirring several times. Store in tightly covered container. Serve with milk as cereal or alone as a snack.

Cinnamon Breakfast Cake

1 1/4 cups flour
1/4 granulated sugar
1 Tbsp. baking powder
1/4 cup shortening
2/3 cup milk
1 egg

2/3 cup nuts, chopped
4 Tbsp. flour
6 Tbsp. granulated sugar
3 Tbsp. butter or margarine, softened
1 tsp. cinnamon

Preheat oven to 400 degrees. Sift together flour, sugar and baking powder. Cut in shortening. Add milk and egg. Fold in nuts. Pour into greased 8x8 baking pan. Mix together flour, sugar, butter and cinnamon. Sprinkle over batter. Bake at 400 degrees for 25 minutes.

Fruited Grits

1 1/2 oz. instant-cooking grits
1/2 cup raisins
1 Tbsp. granulated sugar
1/2 tsp. cinnamon

1/4 tsp. nutmeg
1/4 cup nuts, chopped
1 1/4 cups boiling water

Stir together grits, raisins, sugar, cinnamon, nutmeg and nuts. Pour boiling water over mixture. Serve warm with milk.

Golden Apple Rings

1 cup biscuit mix
1 egg

1/2 cup milk
2 apples, cored

Mix baking mix, egg and milk together until smooth. Grease frying pan. Cut apples crosswise into 1/8-inch round slices. Dip slices into batter. Cook in hot pan until golden brown. Turn once. Serve hot with syrup, jelly or powdered sugar.

Four-Fruit Cocktail

2 cups orange juice
2 bananas, sliced
1 small can pineapple tidbits

1 orange, sectioned and diced
Shredded coconut (optional)

Pour orange juice over bananas, pineapple tidbits and orange pieces. Stir to combine well. Top with shredded coconut, if desired.

Cinnamon Spice Toast

1/4 cup butter or margarine
1/4 cup brown sugar, packed
1/4 tsp. nutmeg

1 tsp. cinnamon
Toast or muffins

Beat all ingredients until fluffy. Spread on hot toast or muffins.

Caramelized French Toast

2 Tbsp. butter or margarine
3 eggs
1/4 cup milk
Dash of salt

4 slices bread
1/2 cup brown sugar
1/4 cup water

Melt butter in frying pan. Beat eggs, milk and salt together. Dip bread into egg mixture and fry until light brown and egg is cooked through. Remove from pan. Add brown sugar. Stir until melted and sticky. Add water and stir. Place toast in caramel sauce. Turn to coat, then remove from pan.

Easy Cheesy Breakfast Bars

1/3 cup butter or margarine
1/2 cup granulated sugar
1 egg, beaten
1 tsp. vanilla extract
1/2 cup flour

1/4 tsp. baking soda
1/4 tsp. salt
1 1/2 cups quick-cooking oatmeal
1/2 cup cheese, grated
5 slices bacon, cooked and crumbled

Preheat oven to 350 degrees. Cream butter, sugar, egg and vanilla. Sift together flour, baking soda and salt. Add to creamed mixture. Beat in oatmeal, cheese and crumbled bacon. Smooth batter on greased cookie sheet. Bake at 350 degrees for seven to ten minutes. Cut into bars.

Quick Breakfast Cookies

1/3 cup butter or margarine
1/2 cup granulated sugar
1 egg, beaten
1/2 tsp. vanilla
1/2 cup flour

1/4 tsp. baking soda
1/4 tsp. salt
1 1/2 cup quick-cooking oatmeal
1/2 cup cheese, grated
5 slices bacon, cooked and crumbled

Preheat oven to 350 degrees. Cream together butter, sugar, egg and vanilla. Sift together flour, baking soda and salt. Stir into creamed mixture. Beat in oatmeal, cheese and bacon. Drop in large spoonful onto greased cookie sheet. Bake at 350 degrees for seven to ten minutes or until lightly browned.

MOM'S
OLD
Standbys

Mom's Old Standbys

MOM'S OLD Standbys

Mom's Old Standbys

Eggs

Easy Fried Eggs

To keep a fried egg tender, you must cook it quickly at medium heat. In a frying pan, melt one to three tablespoons butter or margarine. Break the eggs, one at a time, onto a saucer, then slip each egg into the pan. Reduce the heat to low. Spoon the melted butter or margarine over eggs periodically as they cook. Season with salt and pepper. A firmly cooked fried egg takes about 10 minutes to cook on the stove. For less fat, coat pan with non-stick cooking spray. Cook eggs until whites are firm on bottom. Add one tablespoon water to pan and cover to steam. Cook until yolks are soft, medium or hard, whichever you prefer.

Scrambled Eggs

Scrambled eggs should be cooked at a low heat with a minimum of stirring. For each serving, break two eggs into a bowl. Beat the eggs slightly adding three tablespoons milk and a dash of salt and pepper. Melt two tablespoons butter or margarine over medium heat. Pour into egg mixture. As egg begins to set in pan, lift cooked portion with a spatula so that uncooked portion flows to bottom. Continue this process for three to five minutes or until eggs are completely cooked. Stir slightly to break up eggs.

Soft-Boiled Eggs

Place desired number of eggs in a saucepan. Cover with cold water. Water should be at least two inches above eggs. Bring the water rapidly to boiling. Cover pan and remove from heat. Let stand for two minutes. Fill pan with cold water. Cool eggs for several seconds. To serve, break shelled egg in half with a knife, and scoop out soft egg with a spoon.

Hard-Boiled Eggs

Place desired number of eggs in a saucepan. Cover with water. Water should be at least two inches above eggs. Bring water rapidly to boiling. Cover pan and remove from heat. Let stand for 20 minutes. Cool eggs quickly by filling pan with cold water. For a quick way to remove shells, drain water off eggs, shake eggs briskly back and forth in saucepan until shells shatter. Rinse shells away under cold running water.

Poached Eggs

Fill a shallow pan or frying pan with about two inches of water. Heat water to boiling and reduce heat to low. One at a time, break eggs onto a saucer and slip each one gently into the simmering water. Cook eggs until firm, about 4-5 minutes. Add salt and pepper to taste during cooking time. Remove with a spatula or slotted spoon. Drain each egg on paper towels before serving. Serve on toast or a biscuit.

Baked Eggs

Lightly grease a small baking pan with butter or margarine, or spray with non-stick cooking spray. Heat oven to 325 degrees. Gently break eggs into the pan. Sprinkle with salt and pepper. Bake for 15 to 20 minutes, or until desired firmness.

Easy Cheesy Omelet

1 Tbsp. butter or margarine	Dash of pepper
3 eggs	1 Tbsp. milk
1/4 tsp. salt	1 1/2 cups cheddar cheese, grated

Melt butter in frying pan. Beat together eggs, salt, pepper and milk until fluffy. Pour into pan. Cook over medium heat. When eggs are still glossy, sprinkle cheese on top. Fold in half. Serve immediately. Try other stuffings, including cooked bacon or ham, onions, mushrooms, green peppers or fresh avocado.

The Camel's Eye

2 slices bread	2 eggs
1 Tbsp. butter or margarine	Salt and pepper

Cut circle from center of each bread slice. (A biscuit cutter or round cookie cutter is good for this.) Set aside. In small frying pan, melt butter. Place bread slices in pan. Crack one egg each gently into center of bread. Sprinkle with salt and pepper to taste. Cook over medium heat, turning after five minutes. Cook to desired firmness.

Classic Quiche Lorraine

9-inch pie shell, baked
6 slices bacon, cooked and crumbled
1 cup Swiss cheese, shredded
6 eggs, beaten

1 cup milk
1/2 tsp. salt
Dash of pepper
Dash of nutmeg

Preheat oven to 350 degrees. Sprinkle bacon and cheese in bottom of pie shell. Combine remaining ingredients in small bowl. Mix well. Pour over bacon and cheese. Bake at 350 degrees for 35-40 minutes or until knife inserted in center comes out clean. Let stand for five to ten minutes before cutting and serving. As a variation, try a totally veggie quiche with broccoli, onions, green peppers, tomatoes, mushrooms or any of your favorite vegetables.

Corned Beef and Eggs

6-oz can corned beef
4 eggs
3 Tbsp. chili sauce

4 slices toast
1 Tbsp. butter or margarine
Parmesan cheese

Crumble corned beef into pan and heat slowly. Beat eggs with chili sauce. Stir slowly into corned beef. Cook until soft but done. Spoon onto hot, lightly buttered toast. Sprinkle with cheese.

Creamed Ham and Eggs

2 Tbsp. butter or margarine
2 tsp. onion, minced
3 Tbsp. flour
1 tsp. salt
Dash of pepper

1/8 tsp. dry mustard
1 cup milk
3 hard-boiled eggs, sliced
1 cup cooked ham, cubed

Melt butter in frying pan. Cook onion until golden. Stir in flour, salt, pepper and mustard until it becomes a thick paste. Whip in milk. Cook, stirring constantly, until thickened. Stir in eggs and ham.

Easy Oven Omelet

4 eggs
1/2 cup milk
1/4 tsp. seasoned salt

1/2 pkg. sliced corned beef, (about 3 oz.)
1/2 cup cheese, grated
1 1/2 tsp. onion, grated

Preheat oven to 325 degrees. Beat eggs, milk and seasoned salt together. Tear corned beef into small pieces. Add to egg mixture. Stir in cheese and onion. Pour into greased baking pan. Bake at 325 degrees for 20 to 30 minutes, or until eggs are set.

Quick Quiche

3 slices bacon, cooked and crumbled
1 cup cheese, grated
1/2 cup onions, chopped
4 eggs

2 cups milk
1/2 cup biscuit mix
1/2 tsp. salt
Dash of pepper

Preheat oven to 350 degrees. Grease pie plate. Sprinkle bacon, cheese and onions over bottom. Beat eggs and milk together. Add remaining ingredients. Beat until well mixed. Pour into pie plate. Bake at 350 degrees for 50-55 minutes or until knife inserted in center comes out clean. Let stand five to ten minutes before cutting.

South-of-the-Border Scramble

2 Tbsp. butter or margarine
1 Tbsp. onion, minced
1/4 tsp. garlic salt
1/2 cup green pepper, chopped
1 small tomato, chopped

4 eggs, beaten
2 Tbsp. water
1/2 tsp. salt
Dash of pepper

Melt butter in frying pan. Cook onion, garlic salt, green pepper and tomato until tender. Beat together eggs, water, salt and pepper. Pour into frying pan with vegetables. Cook over low heat, stirring occasionally. Serve with hot sauce, if desired.

MOM'S OLD Standbys

Mom's Old Standbys

MOM'S OLD Standbys

Mom's Old Standbys

Sandwiches

Easy Tuna Salad

Small can tuna, drained
1/4 cup celery, diced
1 Tbsp. onion, minced
1/4 cup mayonnaise

2 tsp. lemon juice
Dash of paprika
Dash of pepper

Combine all ingredients and mix well. Smooth 1/4 of mixture between
2 slices of bread. Makes 4 sandwiches.

Baked Cheese Puffs

2 slices bread
2 slices cheese
2 slices tomato
1 egg white, beaten stiff

1/4 cup mayonnaise
1/2 tsp. salt
Dash of pepper

Preheat oven to 350 degrees. Trim and discard crusts from bread. Toast the bread
on one side under the broiler. On untoasted side, layer a slice of cheese and a slice
of tomato. Place on baking pan. Fold mayonnaise, salt and pepper into egg white.
Mix well. Put a spoonful of mayonnaise mixture onto the tomato. Bake at 350
degrees until puffy and brown.

Best-Ever Hamburgers

1/2 lb. ground beef
1 Tbsp. onion, minced
2 Tbsp. mustard
1 1/2 tsp. soy sauce
1 Tbsp. green pepper, minced
2 hamburger buns

2 Tbsp. sour cream
2 slices of tomato
1/2 red onion, thinly sliced and
   separated into rings
1 Kosher dill pickle, sliced lengthwise
2 Romaine lettuce leaves

Combine beef, onion, mustard, soy sauce and green pepper into patties. Fry until
cooked thoroughly on both sides. Place on buns. Garnish with sour cream, tomato,
red onion, pickle and lettuce.

Cheesy Tuna Burgers

Small can tuna, drained
3 Tbsp. mayonnaise
2 Tbsp. pickle, chopped

1 tsp. onion, minced
8 slices of cheese
4 hot dog buns

Combine tuna, mayonnaise, pickle and onion. Spread on hotdog buns. Top each bun with 2 slices cheese. Place on cookie sheet. Broil until bubbly.

Corned Beef and Slaw

4 Tbsp. mayonnaise
1 Tbsp. horseradish
2 tsp. mustard
1/2 tsp. salt

2 cups cabbage, shredded
8 slices rye bread
2 Tbsp. mayonnaise
8-oz. can corned beef, sliced

Combine mayonnaise, horseradish, mustard, salt and cabbage. Spread on 4 slices of bread. Spread other 4 slices with mayonnaise and top with sliced corned beef. Pair to make sandwiches.

Creamed Tuna on Toast

1 can cream of chicken soup
Small can tuna, drained
2 Tbsp. onion, minced

1 Tbsp. green pepper, minced
4 slices of toast

Heat soup, tuna, onion and green pepper. Simmer for seven to ten minutes or until onion and pepper are tender. Spoon over toast.

Deviled Ham and Cheese

2 slices French bread
4 1/2-oz. can deviled ham

1 small tomato, sliced thin
4 slices of cheese

Spread each slice of French bread with deviled ham. Top with sliced tomatoes and cheese. Broil until cheese is bubbly. Serve hot.

Exactly Egg Salad

4 hard-boiled eggs, chopped
1/2 cup sweet pickles, chopped

1/4 cup mayonnaise
4 slices of bread

Combine eggs, pickles and mayonnaise. Spread on bread. Ingredients that can be added include: crumbled bacon, cooked and diced chicken, beef, ham or fish, chopped pickle, minced onion or celery, diced green pepper or sliced tomato.

French Hamwiches

2 Tbsp. butter or margarine, softened
2 tsp. mustard
4 slices bread
4 slices Swiss cheese

2 slices cooked ham
1 egg, beaten
2 Tbsp. milk
1/2 cup applesauce

Spread two slices of bread with butter and mustard. Place a slice of Swiss cheese on each. Place a slice of ham on each. Top with remaining slices of bread. Beat egg and milk together. Dip sandwiches in egg mixture. Brown sandwiches on both sides in lightly buttered frying pan. Top each with a spoonful of warm applesauce.

Heated Creamy Salmon

1/2 cup mayonnaise
1/4 tsp. salt
Dash of pepper
1/2 cup evaporated milk
1 1/2 cups salmon, drained
4 sandwich buns

3 Tbsp. pickle, chopped
1/2 cup celery, diced
1 cup cream of celery soup
1/4 cup evaporated milk
3 Tbsp. water

In a bowl, combine mayonnaise, salt, pepper, 1/2 cup canned milk, salmon, pickle and celery. Spread on buns. Combine soup, 1/4 cup canned milk and water in small saucepan. Heat until bubbly. Pour over sandwiches.

Raisins and Peanut Butter

1/4 cup raisins, finely chopped
1/2 cup peanut butter

4 slices of wheat bread

Mix raisins and peanut butter well. Spread on bread and enjoy. For a tasty variation, substitute 1/2 mashed banana for raisins.

··

Hot Tuna Boats

1/2 cup cheese, grated
2 hard-boiled eggs, chopped
2 Tbsp. celery, chopped
2 Tbsp. green pepper, chopped

2 Tbsp. pickle, chopped
1/3 cup mayonnaise
1 small can tuna, drained
4 hot dog buns

Preheat oven to 300 degrees. Combine all ingredients. Fill hotdog buns. Wrap each bun in foil. Bake at 300 degrees for 20 minutes.

Cheese Make-Aheads

8 slices bread
2 Tbsp. butter or margarine
4 slices cheese

3 eggs
1 1/4 cup milk
1/4 tsp. salt

Butter bread. Place a slice of cheese each on four slices of bread, and top with remaining bread slices. Place sandwiches in lightly greased baking pan. Beat together eggs, milk and salt. Pour over sandwiches. Cover and refrigerate for two to four hours. Preheat oven to 350 degrees. Bake uncovered for ten to twelve minutes or until golden.

Philly Beef and Swiss

1 Tbsp. butter or margarine
1/4 cup green pepper, diced
1/4 cup onion, chopped
1/2 cup mushrooms, sliced
Garlic powder to taste

6 slices roast beef
2 Tbsp. water
Salt and pepper
4 slices of Swiss cheese
2 hoagie rolls

Melt butter in frying pan. Cook green pepper, onion and mushrooms with garlic powder until tender. Add roast beef, water, salt and pepper. Top with cheese. Simmer covered until cheese melts. Scoop half onto each hoagie roll. For toasted sandwiches, place opened under broiler for a few minutes.

Picnic Sandwiches

2 cups bologna, diced
1 hard-boiled egg, chopped
2 tsp. pimento, diced
1/4 cup pickle relish

1 Tbsp. evaporated milk
2 Tbsp. mayonnaise
Salt and pepper

Combine ingredients, mix well and chill. Spread on crusty buns, garnish with lettuce.

Pizza on a Roll

1 lb. loaf frozen bread dough
1/2 cup tomato paste or pizza sauce
1 cup pepperoni, chopped
OR 1/4 lb. ground beef, browned

1 tsp. oregano
1/4 tsp. garlic powder
1/4 cup onion, chopped
1 cup cheese, grated

Thaw bread for two hours. Roll out to 12x9 rectangle. Spread with sauce. Top with remaining ingredients. Roll up jelly-roll fashion from long side. Seal edges well. Place on greased baking sheet, seam side down. Brush with water, sprinkle with salt. Let rise until almost double in size, about one hour. Preheat oven to 375 degrees. Make three slashes across top of pizza roll. Bake 30 minutes or until light brown. Slice to serve.

Pizza Quick

1/2 lb. ground beef
1/2 cup cheese, grated
3 Tbsp. onion, minced
3 Tbsp. black olives, chopped
1/2 tsp. salt

Dash of pepper
1/3 cup tomato paste
4 slices of French bread
4 slices of cheese
1 tomato, thinly diced

Preheat oven to 425 degrees. Brown ground beef. Add cheese, onion, olives, salt and pepper. Cook until onion is tender and cheese is melted. Stir in tomato paste and heat through. Put _–1/4 of meat mixture on each slice of bread. Top with slice of cheese and tomato. Bake on a cookie sheet until cheese melts.

Barbecued Cheese Buns

2 hot dog or hamburger buns
1 cup cheese, grated
2 hard-boiled eggs, chopped
1/4 cup green pepper, diced
1/4 cup tomato, diced

1 Tbsp. onion, grated
1/4 cup evaporated milk
2 Tbsp. ketchup
1/2 tsp. salt
Dash of pepper

Split buns and place face up on cookie sheet. Set aside. Preheat oven to 400 degrees. Combine remaining ingredients in small bowl. Mix well. Spread evenly on buns. Place on cookie sheet and bake for seven minutes or until hot and bubbly.

....

Toasted Chicken Salad

1/2 cup chicken, cooked and cubed
1/2 cup celery, diced
2 tsp. onion, minced
2 tsp. lemon juice

1/3 cup mayonnaise
1/4 tsp. paprika
Butter or margarine
2 slices of bread

Preheat oven to 400 degrees. Combine chicken, celery, onion, lemon juice, mayonnaise and paprika. Spread butter on bread. Top bread with scoop of chicken salad and spread to cover. Bake on cookie sheet for twelve to 15 minutes or until bubbly.

Barbecue Beans and Franks

4 hamburger buns
4 hotdogs
2 Tbsp. butter or margarine
1 cup baked beans

1/2 cup cheese, cubed
2 Tbsp. barbeque sauce
4 slices of tomato
4 slices of onion

Preheat oven to 350 degrees. Slice hot dogs lengthwise and fry in butter until curled. Layer on buns. Combine beans, cheese and sauce. Spoon over hot dogs. Bake for ten to twelve minutes or until cheese melts. Top each with slice of tomato and fresh onion. Serve hot.

Western Eggs and Beef

1/4 cup green pepper, diced
1/4 cup onion, diced
2 Tbsp. butter or margarine
4 eggs, well beaten
2 Tbsp. milk

1/4 tsp. salt
Dash of pepper
1/4 cup ground beef, cooked
4 large rolls, split and toasted
4 slices of tomato

Sauté green pepper and onion in butter until tender. Beat eggs with milk, salt and pepper. Add to pepper and onions. Scramble until done. Cook ground beef. Stir beef into egg mixture. Spread on rolls. Top each with a slice of tomato.

Hoagie Sandwich

2 hoagie buns
1/4 cup Thousand Island dressing
2 Tbsp. mustard
4 slices cheese
4 slices luncheon meat

1 small tomato, thinly sliced
1/4 head lettuce, torn into leaves
1 small onion, thinly sliced and
   separated into rings
1 dill pickle, sliced thin

Split hoagie buns. Spread evenly with thin layers of dressing and mustard. On each, layer cheese, meat, tomato, lettuce, onion and pickle.

French-American Connection

1 loaf French bread, small narrow size
Equal parts of mayonnaise and sour cream
Prepared filling of your choice

American cheese
Seasoned salt to taste

Slice loaf of bread in half lengthwise. With spoon, scoop out some of the soft bread in each piece. Cover bread so that it will not dry out. Prepare favorite filling. (Possible fillings include: tuna, chicken or egg salad, corned beef, ham, tomatoes, bacon, cucumber, lettuce, avocado, or sprouts.) Spoon into bottom crust. Add cheese. Place top crust over fillings. Slice with sharp knife.

Carry Your Lunch

With a little creativity, lunchbox meals can be as delicious as meals at home.

Your lunch should be well-balanced. Be sure to include protein, vegetable, fruit, dairy product and whole-grain bread.

To keep your lunch cool, include a small can of frozen juice. When you're ready to eat, the juice will be thawed.

Choose meatless protein like peanut butter, egg, or cheese. Leave the shells on hard-boiled eggs to preserve their freshness.

In addition to carrot and celery sticks, try some raw cauliflower, broccoli, zucchini or other crunchy vegetables.

Include fresh fruits, like apples, oranges, grapes, plums, pears, peaches, grapefruit, watermelon, cantaloupe or honey dew.

You can take along fresh fixings for a chef's salad with lowfat dressing.

Use foods with cream or mayonnaise only if the lunch can be refrigerated until eaten.

Pack cottage cheese, yogurt or pudding for a dairy snack. Take along some wheat crackers, a bran muffin or make sandwich on whole-grain bread.

Sandwiches will be easy to pack if you cut them in quarters, and they won't get soggy if you wrap tomatoes and lettuce separately in foil or plastic bag. Put them on the sandwich just before you're ready to eat.

You can keep many foods fresh by packing them in a small jar with a screw-on lid. This prevents spilling, too.

When you get tired of sandwiches for lunch, buy a thermos and fill it with hot stews, soups or even pasta.

Mom's Old Standbys

MOM'S OLD Standbys

Soups

Easy Soup-in-a-Hurry

1 pkg. dry onion soup mix
4 cups water
3 cups frozen vegetables

1/2 tsp. salt
1/2 tsp. pepper
Grated cheese

Cook soup and water according to package directions. Heat to boiling. Add vegetables. Bring to boil, then reduce heat. Simmer until all vegetables are tender. Stir in salt and pepper. Sprinkle with cheese.

10-Minute Carrot Soup

6 medium carrots, grated
1 medium onion, minced
2 1/2 cups water

1 cup milk
2 chicken bouillon cubes
1/2 tsp. sugar

Simmer carrots and onions in water and milk for eight to ten minutes. Add bouillon cubes and sugar. Simmer two more minutes, stirring to dissolve bouillon. Garnish with croutons, if desired.

10-Minute Corn Chowder

2 Tbsp. butter or margarine
1/4 cup flour
1 cup water

1 chicken bouillon cube
2 1/2 cups milk
10-oz. pkg. frozen corn, thawed

Melt butter over low heat in medium saucepan. Add flour and water, stirring constantly. Add bouillon cube and milk. Cook until thickened. Add corn and heat through. Salt and pepper to taste.

Hamburger Soup

2 lbs. ground beef, browned and drained
6 cups water
2 cans tomatoes
1 cup dry noodles

2 pkgs. vegetable soup mix
1 can pork and beans
1 tsp. seasoned salt

Combine all ingredients and bring to a boil. Simmer 30 to 45 minutes.

Easy Meaty Chili

1 lb. ground beef
1 cup onion, chopped
Large can stewed tomatoes
2 cans kidney or pinto beans
2 Tbsp. chili powder

1 tsp. salt
2 Tbsp. sugar
2 Tbsp. vinegar
2 tsp. garlic powder

In a large saucepan, brown ground beef and onions until done. Drain. Add remaining ingredients and simmer for 20 minutes.

Quickest-Ever Beef Stew

2 1/2 cups stewing beef
1 Tbsp. cooking oil
3 cups water
1 pkg. dry onion soup mix

2 potatoes, peeled and cubed
10-oz. pkg. frozen vegetables
2 Tbsp. flour
1/4 cup water

Brown meat in oil. Cover and simmer until tender. In large saucepan, boil water. Stir in soup mix, potatoes and vegetables. Cook for ten to twelve minutes. In small bowl, stir flour into 1/4 cup water until well blended. Pour into soup, stirring until thickened. Add beef. Heat through.

No Lumps, Please

Some of Mom's favorite recipes give instructions to make a base of oil, flour and milk as a thickener for casseroles, soups, stews or gravies. The tough part is keeping the flour from turning lumpy.

Try these tips for smooth sauces. Instead of adding flour directly to oil in the pan, place flour and milk in a bowl and use a wire whip, egg beater or fork to mix until well blended. Or you can place flour and liquid in a small container with a screw-on lid and shake. Then add the flour/liquid mixture slowly to the pan of hot liquid, stirring constantly until thickened.

Cornstarch is also a good thickener. Substitute one tablespoon of cornstarch for two tablespoons of flour. Mix cornstarch with cold liquid until smooth, then add gradually to hot oil, meat drippings or soups. Stir constantly with a wire whip or fork until thickened.

To protect non-stick pans, use a large wooden fork or heavy-duty plastic utensil to stir in mixture, especially when stirring directly in the pan.

Chicken and Dumplings

4-lb chicken, cut up
8 cups water
1 onion, chopped

1/2 bay leaf
Salt and pepper

In large pan, place chicken, water, onion and seasonings. Cover and boil. Cook two hours. Remove chicken. Remove meat from bones. Discard bones and skin. Set meat aside. Strain broth.

Add to broth:
1 cup celery, chopped
1 cup carrots, chopped
Chicken meat

Salt and pepper
1 small onion, chopped
1/2 tsp. seasoning salt
1/2 tsp. poultry seasoning

Add vegetables to chicken broth adding more water, if needed. Bring to boil. Cook about 15 minutes. Top with dumpling dough.

To make dumplings:
1 cup flour
1 1/2 tsp. baking powder
1/2 tsp. salt

Salt and pepper
2 Tbsp. shortening
2/3 cups milk
1 egg, beaten

Sift together dry ingredients. Cut in shortening until mixture is crumbly. Mix egg and milk. Add to flour mixture. Stir only until flour is dampened. Dough will be lumpy. Drop spoonfuls on top of broth. Cover and steam 15 minutes without lifting lid.

Creamy Cheese Soup

2 Tbsp. butter or margarine
2 Tbsp. celery, finely chopped
2 Tbsp. carrot, grated
1 Tbsp. onion, finely chopped
1/2 tsp. salt

Dash of pepper
3 Tbsp. cornstarch
2 cups cold milk
2 cups cheddar cheese, grated

Sauté celery, carrot and onion in butter until tender. Add salt and pepper. Stir cornstarch into cold milk until well blended. Add to vegetables, stirring constantly. Heat until thickened and bubbly. Add cheese and stir until melted. Top with croutons.

Cream of Turkey Soup

A great idea for leftover turkey!

1 Tbsp. butter or margarine
1/2 cup onion, chopped
2 cups hot water
2 chicken bouillon cubes
2 cups potatoes, diced
1 cup cooked turkey, cubed

10-oz. pkg. frozen carrots, thawed
10-oz. pkg. frozen peas, thawed
1 tsp. salt
1/2 tsp. pepper
1 cup evaporated milk

Sauté onion in butter. Dissolve bouillon cubes in hot water. Add remaining ingredients except milk. Simmer for ten minutes. Stir in milk and heat through. Do not boil.

Easy Clam Chowder

2 large potatoes, peeled and diced
2 stalks celery, diced
1/4 cup butter or margarine

2 Tbsp. flour
1 cup milk
1 small can of diced clams, drained

Cook potatoes and celery in salted boiling water until tender, about ten minutes. Drain and mash. In separate saucepan, melt butter or margarine. Stir in flour. Add milk gradually, stirring constantly until thickened. Stir in potatoes, onions and clams. Heat through.

Corn and Bacon Chowder

3 slices bacon, cooked and crumbled
1/2 cup onion, chopped

2 medium potatoes, peeled and diced
1 can of corn, drained

Fry bacon. Bring onion, potatoes, corn, salt, pepper and water to a boil. Cover and cook over low heat until potatoes are tender, about ten minutes. Add milk and bacon. Heat until warm. Do not boil.

Potato and Ham Chowder

1 Tbsp. butter
1/4 cup onions, diced
1/4 cup green peppers,
    chopped
2 large potatoes, diced
1 cup water

1/2 tsp. salt
1/8 tsp. pepper
1/4 tsp. paprika
2 Tbsp. flour
1 cup milk
1 cup ham, cooked and diced

Melt butter in a large saucepan. Add onion and green pepper. Sauté until tender. Add potatoes, water, salt, pepper and paprika. Cover and simmer about ten minutes or until potatoes are tender. Combine flour and small amount of water into a paste. Add to soup. Add milk and cook until thickened, stirring constantly. Stir in ham and heat through.

Speedy Potato Soup

4 potatoes, cubed
4 carrots, sliced
4 stalks celery, sliced
1 onion, chopped

1 Tbsp. butter or margarine
1/2 cup flour
1 1/2 cups water
1 cup cheese, grated (optional)

Cover vegetables with water and cook until tender, about 20 minutes. Drain and mash. In separate pan, melt butter or margarine. Add flour and water, stirring constantly until thickened. Fold into potato mixture. Season to taste with salt and pepper. For variety, you can also add cheese until melted.

Hearty Tomato-Rice Soup

1 Tbsp. butter or margarine
1 cup onion, chopped
1/2 cup celery, chopped
1 large can tomatoes
2 beef bouillon cubes

1/2 cup uncooked rice
1 tsp. salt
1/2 tsp. chili powder
3 cups water

Sauté onion and celery in butter until tender. Add remaining ingredients and bring to a boil. Reduce heat and simmer for 20 minutes or until rice is tender. Serve immediately.

Spicy Tomato Soup

2 cups water
2 tsp. granulated sugar
3 bay leaves
5 whole cloves
1 1/2 tsp. salt

1/4 tsp. pepper
4 cups tomatoes, cooked
2 Tbsp. butter or margarine
3 Tbsp. flour

Mix water, sugar, bay leaves, cloves, salt and pepper in pan. Simmer for 15 minutes and strain. Add tomatoes. In separate saucepan, melt butter and stir in flour. Gradually add to tomato mixture, stirring constantly until thickened. Cook over low heat for ten minutes.

Simple Minestrone

3 beef bouillon cubes
2 cups boiling water
12-oz. can corn
16-oz. can tomatoes, undrained
18-oz. can lima beans, undrained

2 Tbsp. onion, chopped
1/2 tsp. salt
1/4 tsp. pepper
1/4 tsp. basil
1/2 cup macaroni, uncooked

Dissolve bouillon cubes in water in large saucepan. Add remaining ingredients. Cover and simmer about 30 minutes.

Classic French Onion Soup

2 large onions, thinly sliced and
    separated into rings
1/4 cup butter or margarine
2 tsp. flour

4 beef bouillon cubes
4 slices of French bread
1 cup Swiss cheese, grated
3 cups hot water

Brown onions in butter or margarine. Sprinkle with flour. Add hot water and bouillon cubes, stirring constantly. Simmer for 20 minutes or until onions are tender. Season with salt and pepper. Sprinkle French bread with cheese and melt under broiler. Place a piece of bread in the bottom of each soup bowl.

MOM'S OLD Standbys

Mom's Old Standbys

Salads

Easy Fruit Salad

1 can fruit cocktail, drained
2 bananas, sliced
1 can mandarin oranges, drained

1 cup crushed pineapple, drained
1/2 cup whipped cream

Mix fruit and fold in whipped cream.

Classic Waldorf Salad

1 cup apples, diced
1 tsp lemon juice
1 cup celery, diced
1/2 cup raisins

1/2 cup nuts, chopped
1/2 cup mayonnaise
2 Tbsp. milk
1 tsp. granulated sugar

Toss apple pieces with lemon juice until well coated. Add celery, raisins and nuts. Toss until mixed well. In small bowl, stir enough milk into mayonnaise to thin it. Stir in sugar until well blended. Toss salad with dressing until well coated. Chill and serve.

Cool Summer Salad

2 cups watermelon, cubed
1 cup cantaloupe, cubed
1 cup seedless green grapes

1 cup strawberries, halved
grated coconut

Combine all ingredients and chill.

Fruit Whip Delight

10-oz. carton frozen whipped topping, thawed
6-oz. pkg. cherry gelatin

1 can fruit cocktail, drained
1 pint small-curd cottage cheese, drained

Combine all ingredients and chill.

Spinach Parmesan Salad

1 bunch spinach leaves, torn
1 small red onion, minced
3 slices bacon, cooked and crumbled
1/4 cup fresh parmesan cheese, grated

2 Tbsp. cooking or olive oil
2 Tbsp. powdered parmesan cheese
1 Tbsp. fresh parsley, minced

Combine spinach, onion, bacon and fresh parmesan. Mix oil, powdered parmesan and parsley. Drizzle over salad and toss.

Stuffed Tomatoes

2 medium tomatoes
1 cup cottage cheese
1/4 cup carrot, grated

1/4 cup cucumber, sliced
1/4 cup green pepper, chopped
2 radishes, grated

Cut tomatoes in half. Scoop out pulp and seeds. Set aside. In small bowl, mix remaining ingredients. Add tomato pulp. Mix well. Salt to taste. Spoon mixture into tomato halves.

Three-Bean Salad

1 can cut green beans, drained
1 can yellow beans, drained
1 can kidney beans, drained
1 small green pepper, diced
1 small onion, diced

1/2 cup granulated sugar
1/3 cup vinegar
1 tsp. salt
1/4 tsp. pepper
1/3 cup cooking or olive oil

Combine all ingredients until well mixed. Chill before serving.

Best-Yet Macaroni Salad

3/4 cup macaroni, cooked
1 cup black olives, sliced
2 eggs, hard-boiled and sliced
Small can tuna or shrimp

2 cups cabbage, shredded
1/2 cup mayonnaise
2 tsp. mustard
2 Tbsp. vinegar

Chill cooked macaroni until cold. Add olives, eggs, tuna and cabbage. Toss lightly. In small bowl, combine mayonnaise, mustard, vinegar, salt and pepper. Mix well. Stir into salad until well coated. Chill.

Marshmallow Fruit Salad

8 large marshmallows
1/2 cup strawberries, quartered
2 bananas, mashed
1/2 cup crushed pineapple

1/2 cup peaches, cubed
1/2 cup whipping cream
1/4 cup mayonnaise

Melt marshmallows in pan over boiling water. Let cool. Add all fresh fruits. Stir in whipping cream and mayonnaise until well blended. Pour into baking pan and freeze. To serve, cut into quarters. Top with sliced marshmallows.

Sour Cream Fruit Salad

1 cup sour cream
1 cup shredded coconut

1 cup miniature marshmallows
2 cups any fresh fruit, cubed

Mix together. Chill for several hours before serving.

Easy Seven-Layer Salad

1 head lettuce, chopped
3 stalks celery, chopped
1 small white onion, chopped
1 large green pepper, chopped
1 large cucumber, chopped

10-oz. pkg. frozen peas, thawed
2 cups mayonnaise
2 Tbsp. granulated sugar
1 cup parmesan cheese
1/2 cup bacon, cooked and crumbled

Layer ingredients in a large bowl beginning with the lettuce and ending with peas. Spread mayonnaise over the top to the edges of the bowl. Sprinkle with sugar, cheese and bacon. Keep covered in the refrigerator.

Creamy Carrot Salad

1/2 cup mayonnaise
2 tsp. milk
1/2 cup mini-marshmallows

1/2 cup crushed pineapple
1/4 cup nuts, chopped
1 1/2 cups carrots, grated

Mix mayonnaise and milk until creamy. Fold in remaining ingredients. Chill for several hours before serving.

Favorite Ham Salad

1 cup ham, cooked and diced
1 cup peas, cooked

1 cup French dressing
1 hard-boiled egg, sliced

Marinate ham and peas in French dressing overnight. Drain. Serve on lettuce. Garnish with egg.

Tempting Turkey Salad

2 cups cooked turkey, diced
1/2 cup nuts, chopped
1/2 cup raisins
1/4 cup shredded coconut
2 Tbsp. onion, chopped

1/4 cup green pepper, chopped
1/2 cup mayonnaise
1 tsp. lemon juice
Salt and pepper

Combine turkey, nuts, raisins, coconut, onion and green pepper. Mix mayonnaise, lemon juice, salt and pepper. Stir into salad.

Cabbage-Apple Slaw

1/4 cup mayonnaise
3 tsp. granulated sugar
2 tsp. lemon juice
2 tsp. milk

1/2 tsp. salt
Dash of pepper
1/4 head of cabbage, shredded
1 apple, cored and chopped

In large bowl, mix mayonnaise, sugar, lemon juice, milk, salt and pepper until creamy. Toss with cabbage and chill for several hours. Just before serving, core and chop apple then fold pieces into salad until well distributed throughout.

Quick Cole Slaw

1/2 head cabbage, shredded
1 carrot, grated
1 green onion, minced
1/4 cup mayonnaise

2 Tbsp. milk
2 Tbsp. granulated sugar
2 tsp. vinegar

Combine cabbage, carrot and green onion. In small bowl, stir together mayonnaise, milk, sugar and vinegar until well blended. Stir into cabbage mixture until vegetables are well coated. Chill well and serve.

Grandma's Potato Salad

2 potatoes, cooked and cubed
1 Tbsp. parsley, chopped
2 Tbsp. onion, diced
1/2 tsp. salt

1 cup celery, chopped
2 hard-boiled eggs, diced
1/2 cup mayonnaise
3 radishes, sliced

In bowl, mix parsley, onion, salt, celery, eggs and mayonnaise. Mix until well blended. Fold in potatoes until well coated. Chill for several hours. Serve on lettuce leaves and garnish with slices of radish and hard-boiled egg slices, if desired.

Hot Dutch Potato Salad

2 slices bacon
1/2 cup onion, chopped
3 Tbsp. cider vinegar
1 Tbsp. water

2 Tbsp. granulated sugar
1/2 tsp. salt
Dash of pepper
2 potatoes, cooked and diced

Dice bacon into fine pieces and fry until crispy and brown. Add onion. Cook until browned. Add vinegar, water, sugar, salt and pepper. Bring to a boil. Add potatoes. Heat through. Serve hot.

Easy Chicken Salad

1 cup cooked chicken, diced
1/2 cup celery, chopped
1/4 cup green pepper, chopped
1/4 cup nuts, chopped

1/2 cup mayonnaise
1/4 tsp. salt
Dash of pepper
1/4 tsp. curry powder

Combine chicken, celery, green pepper and nuts. In a small bowl, mix together mayonnaise, salt, pepper and curry powder. Stir into salad. Blend well. Chill before serving with lettuce. This is good in a sandwich, as well.

Vegetable Garden Dip

1 cup sour cream
1/4 cup parmesan cheese

1/4 cup fresh spinach, chopped
1 pkg. dry onion soup mix

Combine all ingredients and mix until fluffy. Use as dip for cut-up cauliflower, broccoli, carrots, celery, cucumbers and zucchini.

French Dressing

3/4 cup salad oil
1/4 cup lemon juice or vinegar
1 Tbsp. sugar
3/4 tsp. salt

1/4 tsp. paprika
1/4 tsp. dry mustard
1/4 tsp. pepper
1/4 tsp. onion salt

Mix all ingredients well. Store covered in refrigerator.

Green Salad Dressing

1 cup mayonnaise or salad dressing
1 cup milk with 1 tsp. lemon juice

2 eggs, hard-boiled and minced

Combine ingredients and add the following spices to taste: garlic powder, onion salt, celery salt, dried parsley, salt and pepper.

Italian Dressing

1 cup cooking oil or olive oil
1/2 cup vinegar
1 tsp. granulated sugar
1/2 tsp. salt

1/2 tsp. celery salt
1/4 tsp. dry mustard
1/4 tsp. red pepper
1/4 tsp. garlic powder

Mix all ingredients well. Store covered in refrigerator.

Thousand Island Dressing

1 cup mayonnaise
2 Tbsp. ketchup
2 Tbsp. sweet pickle relish
1 Tbsp. green pepper, minced

1 Tbsp. onion, minced
1 hard-boiled egg, chopped
1/2 tsp. salt
Dash of pepper

Mix all ingredients well. Store covered in refrigerator.

Real Roquefort Dressing

2-oz. Roquefort cheese
1/2 cup buttermilk

1/2 cup mayonnaise
Salt and pepper

Mash cheese with fork. Beat in buttermilk and mayonnaise until smooth. Add salt and pepper to taste. Store covered in refrigerator.

Easy Fruit Dip

1/2 cup frozen whipped
    topping, partially thawed

1 cup fruit-flavored yogurt

Fold yogurt into whipped topping. Use as dip for cut-up fruit.

Easy Raspberry Cooler

1 cup applesauce
3-oz. pkg. raspberry gelatin

1 cup raspberries
1 cup nuts, chopped

Heat applesauce until it boils. Dissolve gelatin in it. Stir in raspberries. Fold in nuts. Chill until firm.

Cherry-Applesauce Salad

Two 3-oz. pkgs. cherry gelatin
2 cups boiling water
6-oz. can thawed orange juice

1 cup cold water
1 small can applesauce
1 cup apples, diced

Dissolve gelatin in boiling water. Stir in juice, water and applesauce. Pour into 9x13 glass pan. Top with diced apples. Chill until firm.

Fruity Emerald Salad

3-oz. pkg. lemon gelatin
3-oz. pkg. lime gelatin
1 1/2 cups pineapple juice
1 cup crushed pineapple

1 cup mayonnaise
1 cup cottage cheese
1 cup canned milk
1 cup fruit cocktail, drained

Heat pineapple juice. Dissolve gelatin in it. Chill until partially set. Fold in remaining ingredients. Chill until firm.

Homemade Mayonnaise

You'll need a mixer or blender for this!

1 egg
1/2 lemon, juiced
1 tsp. honey

1/2 tsp. salt
1 cup cooking oil

In bowl or blender, combine egg, lemon juice, honey and salt. While beating, add oil, one drop at a time, until desired consistency.

Easy Taco Salad

1 lb. ground beef
1/2 cup onion, chopped
2 Tbsp. fresh cilantro, chopped
1/2 tsp. garlic powder
1/2 tsp. ground cumin
Salt and pepper

8-oz. can pinto beans, drained
1/2 head lettuce, torn
2 cups corn chips, crushed
1 cup cheese, grated
1 tomato, chopped

Brown beef with onion, cilantro and spices. Drain grease. Drain and rinse beans. Add beans to meat. Heat through. For each serving, place lettuce on corn chips. Top with hot meat mixture, cheese and tomatoes. Salt and pepper to taste and serve with sour cream and salsa, if desired.

Authentic Guacamole

1 ripe avocado, mashed
1 tsp. lemon juice
1 tsp. salt
1/4 tsp. chili powder
1/4 tsp. garlic powder

1/4 tsp. ground cumin
2 tsp. fresh cilantro, chopped
1/4 cup sour cream (optional)
2 Tbsp. onion, minced
1 tomato chopped

Combine all ingredients. Store covered in refrigerator. For variation, add your favorite salsa, sour cream or chopped jalapeños for heat.

The Real Thing Salsa

3 large ripe tomatoes, chopped
1/2 cup tomato sauce
1/2 tsp. salt
1/4 tsp. pepper
1/4 tsp. ground cumin

1/4 tsp. garlic powder
1/4 tsp. chili powder
1/2 cup onion, chopped
1/4 cup green pepper, chopped
1/2 small jalapeño, minced

Combine all ingredients. Mix well. Add more seasonings to taste. For hot and spicy salsa, add jalapeño. Chill before serving.

MOM'S OLD Standbys

Mom's Old Standbys

Main Dishes

A Chicken Standing Up?
(One of Mom's Best Kept Secrets)

To get the tastiest and juiciest chicken ever, Mom likes to roast it standing on end. That is, placing the chicken in an upright position in the oven. What makes this possible? Mom endorses *The Original Spanek Vertical Roaster,* a vertical metal stand that keeps chicken standing upright inside a baking pan during the cooking process. Invented by a French woman and marketed by her son, the vertical roaster's unique Eiffel Tower design, made of tempered steel, cooks the chicken from the inside out.

Denis Spanek, who patented the first vertical roaster, says the heat of the simple device forces the juices outward while the heat of the oven forces the juices inward. Thus, the juices stay inside the bird, tenderizing and richly flavoring the meat. The Spanek family has developed various sizes of vertical roasters to accommodate all poultry including game hen, chicken, duck and turkey. With a vertical roaster, small and large poultry cooks about 30 percent faster because the metal frame, in contact with the bird's interior, conducts heat so efficiently. The outside of the chicken browns perfectly while the inside remains superbly moist.

How to Use a Vertical Roaster

The same easy method is used for all forms of poultry. For poultry other than chicken, the basic "roasting guide" that comes with the vertical roaster will give times and temperatures. A good rule of thumb is to cook the poultry for *15 minutes per pound in a 350-degree oven* until the meat is tender and juices run clear.

Preparing the meat: Wash and dry hands and preparation area before working with meat, especially poultry.

Step 1: Rinse and dry chicken inside and out. Season as desired. Place chicken on vertical roaster, rump side down. Push down gently until ring at top of vertical roaster comes through neck cavity with ease.

Step 2: Set prepared roaster upright in deep baking pan. Add one half to one cup liquid.

Carving the meat: *The Original Spanek Vertical Roaster* positions all poultry for easy carving. Cut any bird quickly and efficiently *while it is still on the roaster* in four steps:

Step 1: Remove leg and thigh from each side using a sharp, properly sized carving knife according to the size of the bird.

Step 2: Separate the leg from the thigh, again using the knife to make a clean cut through the skin, meat and joint.

Step 3: Make a "V" slice under the wishbone and remove the bone.

Step 4: Peel down the breast meat by placing knife on the top shoulder of the bird and pressing downward.

Extra tips: Save the bones for the stockpot to make a soup base. The pan juices can be poured over the carved bird for extra flavoring. Set the roasted bird *while it's still on the vertical roaster* in the middle of a large platter of cooked rice, then carve the bird over the rice to catch the delicious drippings.

Denis Spanek has cooked more than 30,000 birds during demonstrations and tests. His favorite recipe includes a bleu cheese and mushroom stuffing (on the next page). However, simply rubbing the entire bird, over the skin and inside the cavity with olive oil and your favorite fresh herbs and spices, will also produce great tasting meat.

Remember that placing spices and herbs under the skin will make the meat richer tasting. You can also marinate the bird before-hand or baste while roasting.

Stuffing the meat: Some recipes include preparation of stuffing that is to be placed between the chicken skin and meat before baking. Refer to these steps to loosen the skin:

Step 1: Thoroughly wash and dry the inside and outside of the bird. Wash and dry your hands. Place the chicken on its back on a clean dish cloth, cutting board or platter.

Step 2: Using your fingertips, break the skin membrane at the opening on each side of each breast. Work your fingers under the skin across both sides and along the thighs and legs. *Be careful not to break the skin attached at the center of the breastbone.*

Step 3: Spoon the stuffing under the skin, working over the breast, thigh and leg areas, smoothing it evenly over each side of the bird.

To find *The Original Spanek Vertical Roaster,* get on a computer and go to *www.spanek.com* on the Internet to order your very own. Or check at most large department stores and specialty gourmet cooking shops.

These recipes call for a special cooking device called a vertical roaster. Refer to information on how to use The Original Spanek Vertical Roaster on previous pages.

Bleu Chicken with Mushrooms

1 whole roasting chicken
2 cloves garlic, diced
1 cup mushrooms, diced
1 cup bleu cheese, crumbled

2 Tbsp. butter or margarine
1 Tbsp. white cooking wine
1/4 tsp. paprika

Preheat oven to 450 degrees. In a bowl, mix garlic, mushrooms (Shittake mushrooms taste best, but any mushrooms will do), bleu cheese and butter until mixture just holds together. Follow the instructions on the previous pages to loosen the skin, stuff with mushroom mixture and place the chicken on the vertical roaster. Set the roaster in an eight or nine inch cake pan and add a half cup of water to the pan.

In a small bowl, mix wine and paprika. Baste chicken with mixture. Cook for 15 minutes at 450 degrees, then lower the temperature to 350 degrees and continue cooking for 15 minutes per pound or until meat is tender and juices run clear. Baste the chicken throughout the cooking time as desired.

Roasted Citrus Chicken

1 whole roasting chicken
1/2 cup margarine or butter, softened
2 tsp. crushed basil
2 tsp. grated orange peel

1 tsp. lemon pepper
4 thin orange slices
4 thin onion slices

Preheat oven to 350 degrees. In a small bowl, combine margarine, basil, grated orange peel and lemon pepper. Follow the instructions on the previous pages to loosen the skin of the chicken. Using your fingers, spread half of the margarine mixture evenly under the skin of the chicken over each breast. Place two orange slices and two onion slices under the skin atop each breast.

Beginning at the rump end, gently press the chicken onto the vertical roaster so the metal ring at the top comes up through the neck cavity of the bird. Set the roaster in an eight or nine inch cake pan and add a half cup of water to the pan.

Spread some of the remaining margarine mixture over the outside of the chicken. Reserve the rest for basting. Place pan in preheated oven. Cook for 15 minutes per pound or until meat is tender and juices run clear. Baste the chicken with the margarine and basil mixture throughout the cooking time as desired.

Mom's Old Standbys

Easy Chicken Bake

1 can cream of chicken soup
1 can cream of mushroom soup
1/2 cup milk

1 cup instant rice, uncooked
1 pkg. dry onion soup mix
1 fryer chicken, cut up

Preheat oven to 325 degrees. Combine soups and milk. Stir until blended. Sprinkle rice in 9x13 greased baking pan. Arrange chicken pieces on rice. Pour soup mixture over chicken and rice. Sprinkle dry soup mix over chicken. Cover with foil tightly. Bake for two hours, or until chicken is cooked through.

Best Barbecued Chicken

2 Tbsp. Worcestershire sauce
1 Tbsp. vinegar
1 Tbsp. steak sauce

1 Tbsp. granulated sugar
1/4 cup ketchup
1 fryer chicken, cut up

Preheat oven to 350 degrees. Combine all ingredients except chicken. Mix well. Arrange chicken, skin side up, in greased baking dish. Brush with sauce. Bake uncovered for one hour.

Chicken Filled Dumplings

1 can cream of chicken soup
1 can golden mushroom soup
1 cup water
3 Tbsp. onion, chopped
2 cups chicken, cooked and cubed

1/4 cup celery, minced
2 Tbsp. onion, minced
1/4 tsp. salt
1/4 tsp. pepper
1 can refrigerated, country-style biscuits

In large saucepan, combine soups, water and onion. Heat to boiling. Reduce heat and simmer. In small bowl, combine chicken, celery, onion, salt and pepper. Stir to blend. Separate biscuits and roll each out until thin. Spoon chicken mixture into center of each. Wrap dough around mixture. Pinch to seal. Place dumplings on top of simmering soup. Spoon soup over dumplings. Simmer for 20 minutes or until dough is cooked through.

Creamy Chicken Divan

2 pkgs. frozen broccoli
3 cups chicken, cooked and cubed
2 cans cream of chicken soup
1 cup mayonnaise
1 tsp. lemon juice

1/2 tsp. curry powder
1 cup bread crumbs
2 Tbsp. butter or margarine
1 cup cheddar cheese, grated

Preheat oven to 350 degrees. Cook broccoli according to package directions. Drain. Arrange in bottom of 9x13 baking pan. Arrange chicken over broccoli. In large bowl, combine soup, mayonnaise, lemon juice and curry powder. Mix well. Pour over chicken. Combine bread crumbs and melted butter. Sprinkle over chicken. Bake for 25 to 30 minutes. Remove from oven and sprinkle with cheese. Return to oven until cheese melts.

Golden Chicken Bake

1 cup biscuit mix
1 tsp. salt
1 1/2 tsp. paprika

Dash of pepper
1 fryer chicken, cut up
1/2 cup butter or margarine

Preheat oven to 400 degrees. Combine biscuit mix, salt, paprika and pepper in a paper bag. One at a time, put chicken pieces in bag and shake to coat. Melt butter in baking dish, then arrange chicken pieces. Bake uncovered for one hour.

Herbed Lemon Chicken

4 boneless chicken breasts
1/2 can frozen lemonade drink, thawed
1/4 cup honey
1/2 tsp. sage

1/4 tsp. tarragon
1/4 tsp. thyme
1/4 tsp. ground mustard
1/4 tsp. parsley flakes

Preheat oven to 350 degrees. Place chicken in greased 9x13 baking pan. In bowl, combine lemonade, honey, sage, tarragon, thyme, mustard and parsley flakes. Pour half of mixture over chicken. Bake uncovered for 20 minutes. Turn chicken with tongs. Pour remaining sauce over chicken. Bake 20 minutes more or until chicken juices run clear and meat is no longer pink.

Tangy Skillet Chicken

1 fryer chicken, cut up
1/2 cup flour
1 tsp. salt
2 Tbsp. butter or margarine
1/2 cup celery, chopped

1 cup water
2 Tbsp. brown sugar, packed
1/2 tsp. pepper
1/2 cup onion, chopped
1 cup ketchup

Combine flour and salt. Coat chicken. Fry in oil until brown. In bowl, mix melted butter, celery, water, sugar, pepper, onion and ketchup. Pour over chicken. Simmer 30 minutes or until thick.

Tender Asparagus Chicken

2 lbs. fresh asparagus spears
4 boneless chicken breasts
2 Tbsp. cooking oil
1 can cream of mushroom soup
1/2 cup mayonnaise

1 tsp. lemon juice
1/2 tsp. curry powder
1/4 tsp. garlic powder
1/4 tsp. onion salt
1 cup colby-jack cheese, grated

Preheat oven to 375 degrees. Partially steam asparagus. Place asparagus in greased 9x13 baking pan. Set aside. In frying pan, brown chicken in oil. Place chicken over asparagus. In bowl, mix soup, mayonnaise, lemon juice, curry, garlic and onion spices. Pour over chicken. Cover and bake for 30 minutes. Remove and sprinkle with cheese. Bake uncovered for ten minutes or until chicken juices run clear.

Easy Chicken Pie

2 cups chicken, cooked
    and cubed
4 Tbsp. butter or margarine
4 Tbsp. flour
Salt and pepper
1 cup chicken broth

1 cup milk
1 cup carrots, cooked
1 can green beans, drained
1 potato, cooked and cubed
1 can refrigerator biscuits

Melt butter in pan. Stir in flour, salt and pepper. Stir broth into flour. Add milk, stirring until thick. Combine sauce with chicken, carrots, green beans and potato. Pour into baking pan. Arrange biscuits on top. Bake at 450 degrees for ten to 15 minutes.

Easy Hamburger Pie

1 lb. ground beef
1/2 cup onion, chopped
1 can cut green beans, drained

1 can cream of tomato soup
4 servings of mashed potatoes
1 1/4 cups cheese, grated

Preheat oven to 350 degrees. Brown meat and onions in skillet until cooked thoroughly. Drain fat. Stir in green beans and soup. Heat through. Pour into lightly greased baking dish. Top with mashed potatoes. Bake for 25 minutes. Spread cheese over top and bake ten minutes longer or until cheese melts.

Upside Down Meat Pie

1/2 lb. ground beef
1/4 cup celery, chopped
1/4 cup onion, chopped
1 small carrot, grated
1/4 cup green pepper, chopped

1/2 cup tomato sauce
1 tsp. mustard
1 cup biscuit mix
1/4 cup milk
4 slices cheddar cheese

Preheat oven to 450 degrees. In small skillet, brown beef, celery, onion, carrot, green pepper and tomato sauce. Cook until vegetables are tender. Stir in mustard. In small bowl, combine biscuit mix and milk. Knead and roll out into a circle. Spoon meat mixture into pie plate. Top with dough. Bake for ten to 15 minutes. Turn upside down on serving plate. Top with cheese slices.

Easiest Meat Loaf

1 lb. ground beef
1 cup dry bread crumbs
2 eggs, beaten
1/2 cup onion, minced

1/2 cup green pepper, diced
1 tsp. salt
1/4 tsp. pepper
2 cups tomato sauce

Preheat oven to 350 degrees. Combine ground beef, bread crumbs, eggs, onion, green pepper, salt, pepper and one cup tomato sauce. Knead mixture until combined. Shape into loaf and bake for 30 minutes. Pour remaining tomato sauce over loaf and bake 30 minutes longer.

Stove Top Meatloaf

1 lb. ground beef	1 egg, slightly beaten
1/4 cup cracker crumbs	1/2 tsp. salt
1/2 can tomato soup	1/8 tsp. pepper
4 Tbsp. onion, minced	1/8 cup water

Combine beef, crumbs, three tablespoons soup, onion, egg, salt and pepper. Mix thoroughly with hands. Mound in frying pan and cut into four sections. Brown each section on both sides. Cover and simmer for 20 to 25 minutes or until done. Spoon off fat. Combine rest of soup with water and pour into skillet over meat. Cook ten minutes.

Best Hamburger Stew

1 lb. ground beef	1 tsp. salt
1 small onion, chopped	1/2 tsp. pepper
1 small green pepper, chopped	1 can cream of mushroom soup
2 cups carrots, grated	1/2 cup water
2 cups potatoes, grated	3/4 cup potato chips, crushed

Preheat oven to 350 degrees. Brown ground beef, onion and green pepper. Add carrots, potatoes, salt and pepper. Pour into baking dish. Combine water and soup. Pour over meat, stirring to combine. Top with crushed chips. Bake for 35 to 40 minutes.

Simply Beef Stew

1 lb. stewing beef	1 1/2 cups water
1/2 cup flour	2 onions, sliced
1 tsp. salt	3 carrots, sliced
1/2 tsp. pepper	3 stalks celery, sliced
3 Tbsp. cooking oil	3 potatoes, cubed

Cut meat into bite-sized pieces. In paper sack, combine flour, salt and pepper. Shake meat in sack to coat. Cook meat in oil until browned. Add water. Cover and cook over low heat until tender, about 90 minutes. Add vegetables, continue cooking until tender, about 30 minutes. Thicken stew by mixing one tablespoon flour with two tablespoons water, then stirring it into the stew.

Ground Beef and Noodles

1 lb. ground beef
1/4 cup fresh parsley, chopped
1 cup carrots, chopped
1/2 cup celery, chopped

1 pkg. dry onion soup mix
4 cups hot water
1 cup noodles, uncooked
2 small tomatoes, chopped

Brown the ground beef and drain the grease. Stir in parsley, carrots, celery, soup mix and water. Bring to a boil. Reduce heat and simmer for ten to 15 minutes, stirring occasionally. Add noodles. Cover and cook until tender, about ten minutes. Add tomatoes and heat through.

Hamburger Stroganoff

1 lb. ground beef
1 small onion, chopped
1/2 cup mushrooms, sliced
1 can cream of mushroom soup
1/2 cup milk

2 cups noodles, cooked
2 Tbsp. butter or margarine
1 tsp. salt
1/4 tsp. pepper
1/2 cup sour cream

Brown beef, onions and mushrooms. Drain grease. Stir in soup, milk, noodles, butter, salt and pepper. Simmer covered about 15 minutes. Uncover and simmer ten more minutes. Remove from heat. Stir in sour cream. Heat through but do not boil.

Lazy Gravy
Gravy really is a cinch to make.

For basic gravy:
4 Tbsp. meat drippings
4 Tbsp. flour
2 cups hot water

Combine drippings and flour, stirring over medium heat until smooth. Stirring constantly, add hot water, salt, pepper to taste and/or onion, celery and garlic seasonings.

or instant gravy:
Boiled meat drippings
1 cup condensed cream soup
Water or milk

Drain off surplus fat. Add soup to meat drippings and stir over low heat. If needed, add water or milk for correct consistency.

To go with chicken, use cream of chicken soup. For beef or ham, use cream of mushroom soup. For pork, use cream of celery.

Easy Savory Meatballs

1/2 lb. ground beef	1/2 cup water
1 pkg. dry onion soup mix	1 Tbsp. flour
1/8 cup cracker crumbs	1/2 tsp. garlic powder
1 egg, beaten	1 small tomato, chopped
1 Tbsp. cooking oil	1/4 cup sour cream

Combine ground beef, half of the soup mix, cracker crumbs and egg. Form into meatballs. Brown in hot oil. In a bowl, combine remaining soup mix, water, flour, garlic powder, tomatoes and sour cream. Pour into pan over the meatballs. Cover and simmer for ten minutes.

Meatballs with Potatoes

1/2 lb. ground beef	2 Tbsp. flour
1/4 cup dry bread crumbs	1 onion, sliced and separated into rings
1/4 cup evaporated milk	2 large potatoes, sliced thin
1 egg, beaten	1/2 tsp. salt
1/2 tsp. salt	1/4 tsp. pepper
1/4 cup onion, minced	1/2 cup hot water

Combine beef, bread crumbs, milk, egg, salt and onion. Form into large meatballs. In paper sack, combine flour, salt and pepper. Shake meatballs separately in sack to coat. Brown meatballs in oil until cooked through. Brown onion rings. Layer sliced potatoes over meat and onions. Season with salt and pepper. Pour water into pan. Cover and simmer for 15 to 20 minutes or until potatoes are tender.

Porcupine Meatballs

1 lb. ground beef	1 tsp. salt
1/4 cup rice, uncooked	1/4 tsp. pepper
1 can cream of chicken soup	1 egg, beaten
1/4 cup onion, minced	1 cup water
1/4 cup green pepper, minced	

Combine ground beef, 1/4 cup of chicken soup, rice, onion, egg, salt and pepper. Mix well with hands. Shape into meatballs. Brown in frying pan. Mix remaining soup with water. Pour over meatballs. Cover and simmer for 30 to 40 minutes or until rice is tender.

Hamburger Cheese Patties

1/2 lb. ground beef
Salt and pepper

2 slices of cheese
1 small can tomato sauce

Combine beef, salt and pepper. Form into four patties and press thin. Put one slice of cheese between two patties each. Pinch edges to seal. Brown on both sides. Pour in tomato sauce. Simmer ten minutes.

Meat Patties in Sauce

1/2 lb. ground beef
1/4 cup quick-cooking oatmeal
1/2 tsp. salt
Dash of pepper
2 Tbsp. onion, minced

1 egg, beaten
1/4 cup milk
1/4 cup ketchup
1 Tbsp. brown sugar, packed
2 tsp. mustard

Combine ground beef, oatmeal, salt, pepper, onion, egg and milk. Mix thoroughly with hands and form into patties. Brown patties on both sides. In small bowl, mix ketchup, brown sugar and mustard. Put a spoonful on each patty. Cover. Simmer for 15 to 20 minutes until meat is cooked through.

Beef Rolls and Gravy

1/2 lb. ground beef
1/2 cup onion, chopped
1/4 cup ketchup
1 Tbsp. Worcestershire sauce
1/4 tsp. pepper

2 cups biscuit mix
2/3 cup milk
2 Tbsp. flour
3 cups hot water
2 beef bouillon cubes

Preheat oven to 475 degrees. Brown beef in frying pan. Add onions and cook until tender. Stir in ketchup, Worcestershire sauce and pepper. Take mixture out of pan. Set aside. In bowl, combine biscuit mix and milk. Knead and roll into rectangle. Spread with meat mixture. Roll up and pinch seams shut. Slice into 1-inch thick rounds. Arrange slices on cookie sheet. Bake for ten minutes. In pan drippings from cooked beef, stir in flour. Dissolve bouillon cubes in hot water and pour into pan. Cook, stirring constantly until thickened. Season with salt and pepper. Pour gravy over beef rolls. Serve immediately.

Easy Tamale Pie

1/2 lb. ground beef	6-oz. can whole-kernel corn
1/2 cup onion, minced	1/4 cup black olives, sliced
2 tsp. garlic powder	1/2 cup yellow cornmeal
8-oz. can tomato sauce	1 tsp. chili powder
1/2 cup milk	1 tsp. salt
1 egg, beaten	

Preheat oven to 350 degrees. Cook beef and onion with garlic powder. Combine tomato sauce, milk, egg, corn, olives, cornmeal, chili powder and salt. Pour into meat and mix well. Spoon into 8x8 baking pan. Bake for 40 to 45 minutes or until knife inserted in middle comes out clean. Cut into squares.

Best Beef Nachos

1/2 lb. ground beef	4 Tbsp. jalapeño pepper, diced
1/2 onion, minced	1 large tomato, chopped
1 cup refried beans	1 cup black olives, sliced
1 tsp. salt	1 pkg. lightly salted corn chips
1/4 tsp. pepper	1 1/2 cups cheese, grated
1 1/2 cups tomato sauce	

Cook beef and onion. Spoon off excess fat. Stir in refried beans, salt, pepper, tomato sauce and jalapeños. Heat through. Arrange corn chips on baking pan. Spoon beef mixture over chips. Top with tomato, olives and cheese. Place under broiler until cheese melts. Scoop servings onto plates with pancake turner.

Quick Quesadillas

1/2 cup cheddar cheese, grated	4 flour tortillas
1/2 cup Monterey Jack, grated	4 Tbsp. salsa
2 Tbsp. onion, minced	

In bowl, combine cheeses and onion. Place one tortilla in lightly greased pan. Top with half of cheese mixture and one or two tablespoons of salsa. Place another tortilla on top. Brown one side. Flip to brown other side until cheese melts. Repeat with remaining two tortillas. Garnish with sour cream and more salsa, if desired.

Extra-Tasty Enchiladas

1/2 lb. ground beef
1/4 cup onion, chopped
2 Tbsp. green chilis, chopped
1 small can tomato sauce
1/4 cup black olives, sliced

2 cups cheddar cheese, grated
1 can mild enchilada sauce
3 corn tortillas
1/2 cup sour cream
1/2 head lettuce, shredded

Preheat oven to 350 degrees. In large skillet, brown beef, onion and chilis. Stir in tomato sauce, olives and one cup cheese. In small skillet, warm enchilada sauce with small amount of cooking oil. Place tortillas separately in sauce and turn until pliable. Pull out with tongs. Place spoonful of meat on each tortilla. Roll tortilla and place in greased baking pan, seam side down. Pour enchilada sauce over tortillas. Top with remaining cheese. Bake for 20 to 25 minutes. Serve with sour cream on bed of lettuce.

Easiest-Ever Pizza

1 cup flour
1/2 tsp. salt
1/8 tsp. pepper
2 eggs, beaten
2/3 cup milk

1 lb. ground beef
4-oz. can mushrooms, drained
8-oz. can tomato sauce
1/2 tsp. oregano flakes
2 cups mozzarella cheese, grated

In bowl, beat flour, salt, pepper, eggs and milk. Pour into baking pan. Brown beef. Drain. Distribute beef over batter. Top with mushrooms then tomato sauce. Sprinkle with oregano flakes. Top with cheese. Bake at 425 degrees for 20 to 25 minutes.

Pizza Burger

1 lb. ground beef
1 tsp. salt
1/4 tsp. pepper
1 large tomato, chopped

1 cup mozzarella cheese, grated
1 Tbsp. onion, chopped
1/2 tsp. oregano flakes
1 pkg. hamburger buns

Preheat oven to 350 degrees. Thoroughly mix ground beef, salt and pepper. Pat into bottom of square baking pan. Top with tomatoes, cheese and onion. Sprinkle oregano over all. Bake for 25 to 30 minutes. Cut into squares. Serve on buns.

Spaghetti and Meatballs

1/2 lb. ground beef	8-oz. can tomato sauce
1/2 cup onion, minced	1/4 cup water
1/2 tsp. salt	4-oz. can mushrooms, drained
Dash of pepper	4 oz. dry spaghetti noodles
2 Tbsp. cooking oil	1/2 cup Parmesan cheese

In small bowl, combine ground beef, onion, salt and pepper. Shape into small meatballs. In large skillet, brown meatballs in cooking oil until done. Drain grease. Pour in tomato sauce, water and mushrooms. Stir to blend. Cover and simmer over low heat about ten to 15 minutes. In large pan, heat two quarts of salted water to boiling. Cook spaghetti noodles until tender. Rinse in hot water and drain well. Place noodles on plates. Top with sauce and cheese.

Swift and Spicy Spaghetti

1 small onion, chopped	1/4 tsp. hot sauce
1 tsp. garlic powder	1 tsp. Worcestershire sauce
1 Tbsp. cooking oil	1/2 can cream of tomato soup
1/2 lb. ground beef	1/2 can cream of mushroom soup
1/2 tsp. salt	4-oz. can mushrooms, drained
1/8 tsp. pepper	4 oz. dry spaghetti noodles
Dash of crushed red pepper	1/2 cup Parmesan cheese
1/4 tsp. chili powder	

Brown onion with garlic powder in oil. Add ground beef and cook until done. Spoon off excess fat. Add seasonings, soups and mushrooms. Cover and simmer for 20 to 30 minutes. Cook spaghetti noodles in boiling salted water. Drain and rinse with hot water. Arrange noodles on plates. Top with sauce and cheese.

Fast Chili Mac

1 lb. ground beef	1 can tomatoes, undrained
1 small onion, chopped	1/2 cup macaroni, uncooked

Brown ground beef and onions until meat is cooked and onion tender. Stir in tomatoes and macaroni. Cover and simmer until macaroni is tender, about 15 minutes. Salt and pepper to taste.

Beef with Chili Beans

1 cup onion, chopped	1/2 cup ketchup
1/4 cup green pepper, chopped	1/4 tsp. chili powder
1 Tbsp. cooking oil	2 Tbsp. sugar
1 lb. ground beef	1 Tbsp. vinegar
16-oz. can tomatoes	Dash of crushed red pepper
Two 16-oz. cans chili beans, drained	1/2 tsp. oregano flakes
1 tsp. salt	

Cook onions and green pepper in oil until tender. Add ground beef and brown thoroughly. Stir in tomatoes, beans, salt, ketchup, chili powder, sugar, vinegar, red pepper and oregano. Bring to boil. Reduce to low. Cover and simmer for 25 to 30 minutes or until thick. Garnish with grated cheese or chopped onion, if desired.

Cheeseburger Casserole

1/2 lb. ground beef	1/2 cup creamy cottage cheese
3 Tbsp. onion, minced	3 Tbsp. fresh parsley, chopped
8-oz. can tomato sauce	1/2 cup carrots, sliced into thin rounds
Salt and pepper	4 oz. macaroni, cooked
1 cup sour cream	

Preheat oven to 350 degrees. Brown beef and onions in large frying pan. Stir in tomato sauce, salt and pepper. Simmer uncovered five minutes. In bowl, combine sour cream, cottage cheese, parsley and carrots. Fold in noodles. In greased baking pan, layer half meat mixture and half sour cream mixture. Repeat layers. Top with cheese. Bake for 25 to 30 minutes or until bubbly.

Chinese Beef Casserole

1 lb. ground beef	1 can cream of mushroom soup
1 small onion, chopped	1 Tbsp. soy sauce
2 cups rice, cooked	1 can crunchy chow mein noodles
1 can cream of chicken soup	

Preheat oven to 350 degrees. Brown beef and onions. In bowl, combine rice, soups and soy sauce. In bottom of baking pan, distribute half the chow mein noodles. Spread meat mixture over noodles. Top with soup mixture and remaining noodles. Bake for ten to 15 minutes or until bubbly.

Oriental Beef Stir-Fry

1 lb. ground beef (or thinly sliced steak)	3 medium carrots, sliced
1 Tbsp. butter or margarine	1 green pepper, cut into strips
2 Tbsp. water	1/2 cup sliced onion
1 beef bouillon cube	1 Tbsp. soy sauce
2 zucchini squash, sliced	2 cups instant rice, cooked
1/4 lb. fresh mushrooms, sliced	

Brown beef until cooked through. Add water and dissolve bouillon cube. Add zucchini, mushrooms and carrots. Cook about three minutes. Add green pepper and onion. Cook about three more minutes or until vegetables are crispy-tender. Add soy sauce. Serve over rice.

Hamburger Rice Casserole

1/2 lb. ground beef	1 Tbsp. mustard
1/2 cup onion, chopped	1/4 tsp. salt
1 can vegetable soup	Dash of pepper
1 cup water	1 cup instant rice
1 Tbsp. ketchup	1/2 cup Monterey Jack cheese, grated

Brown ground beef and onion. Stir in soup, water, ketchup, mustard, salt, pepper and instant rice. Mix well. Bring to a boil. Reduce heat. Cover and simmer 15 minutes or until rice is tender. Pour into baking pan. Top with grated cheese. Place under broiler for three to five minutes or until bubbly and cheese melts.

Beefy Mushroom Casserole

1 lb. ground beef	1/2 cup onion, chopped
1 can cream of mushroom soup	1 cup sour cream
1/4 cup milk	4-oz. macaroni, cooked
1/2 cup mushrooms	

Brown ground beef until done. Drain grease. Stir in cream of mushroom soup, milk, mushrooms, onion, sour cream and macaroni. Cover and simmer five to eight minutes. Serve immediately.

Vegetable Beef Casserole

1 lb. ground beef
1/2 tsp. salt
1/4 tsp. pepper
10-oz. pkg. frozen peas
4 Tbsp. onion, chopped

1 cup celery, chopped
1 can cream of mushroom soup
3 Tbsp. evaporated milk
2 cups potato chips, crushed

Preheat oven to 350 degrees. In frying pan, brown ground beef with salt and pepper. Spread in bottom of baking pan. In large bowl, combine peas, onion, celery, soup and milk. Pour over beef. Top with potato chips. Bake for 30 minutes.

Tender Pot Roast

3-lb. beef roast
1/2 tsp. salt
1/4 tsp. pepper
1 pkg. dry onion soup mix
2 potatoes, quartered

1 onion, quartered
4 carrots, sliced lengthwise
2 stalks celery, quartered
1/2 cup hot water
3 Tbsp. flour

Wipe roast with clean, damp cloth to remove juices. Place in slow cooking pot or heavy skillet with lid. Sprinkle with salt, pepper and soup mix. Cover and cook on medium heat for two and a half hours. About one hour before serving, add vegetables. Keep covered. When done, move meat and vegetables to serving dish and keep warm in oven. Leave meat juices in pan. Combine hot water and flour in a small jar with screw-on lid. Shake to mix thoroughly. Pour into meat juices, stirring constantly until thickened to gravy consistency. Pour over meat and vegetables, or serve on the side.

Easy Foil Roast

3-lb. beef roast
1 pkg. dry onion soup mix

1 can cream of mushroom soup

Preheat oven to 350 degrees. In baking pan, place doubled sheet of foil twice the size of pan. Place roast on foil. In bowl, stir together soup and soup mix. Pour over roast. Fold foil over top and seal well. Bake in oven for 90 minutes.

Pepper Steak

3 Tbsp. soy sauce
1 1/2 Tbsp. sugar
1 lb. round steak, cut in strips

2 green peppers, cut in strips
2 medium tomatoes, chopped
3 cups rice, cooked

Make marinade by combining soy sauce and sugar. Marinate beef overnight in refrigerator. When ready to cook, brown beef in small amount of cooking oil. Remove from pan. Sauté green peppers quickly, until bright, stirring constantly. Add tomatoes and return beef and marinade to pan. Bring to a boil. Serve over rice.

Savory Swiss Steak

1 lb. steak
2 Tbsp. flour
1 tsp. salt
1/2 tsp. pepper
3 Tbsp. cooking oil
16 oz. can tomatoes, undrained

1 carrot, diced
1 stalk celery, diced
1/4 onion, chopped
1/4 cup green pepper, chopped
1 cup cheese, grated

Preheat oven to 375 degrees. Cut meat into serving pieces. In paper sack, combine flour, salt and pepper. Shake meat in sack to coat. Cook in oil. Put meat in baking pan. Add flour mixture to oil. Stir in tomatoes and vegetables. Bring to boil. Pour over meat. Bake covered for one and a half hours. Uncover and top with cheese. Bake ten more minutes or until cheese melts.

Corned Beef Potpourri

6 slices bacon, cooked and crumbled
12-oz. can corned beef, cubed
1/4 cup onion, chopped
1 can cream of chicken soup
1/4 cup milk

1 Tbsp. mustard
16-oz. can whole potatoes, drained
  and sliced
OR 3 boiled potatoes, sliced
8-oz. can green beans, drained

Cook corned beef and onion in two tablespoons bacon grease. In bowl, combine soup, milk and mustard. Stir until well blended. Stir soup mixture, potato slices and beans into corned beef. Heat through, stirring frequently. Garnish with bacon.

Easy Sloppy Joes

1/2 lb. ground beef
1/4 cup ketchup
2 Tbsp. onion, minced

1/2 can chicken vegetable soup
1 pkg. hamburger buns

Brown ground beef. Add ketchup, onion and soup. Cover and simmer ten to 15 minutes, stirring occasionally. Serve on buns.

Corned Beef Casserole

2 cups macaroni, cooked
7-oz. can corned beef, crumbled
1/4 cup onion, minced
1/4 cup celery, minced
1 can cream of mushroom soup

4-oz. can mushrooms, drained
1/2 cup evaporated milk
1 cup cheese, grated
1/2 cup bread crumbs

Preheat oven to 425 degrees. In large bowl, combine all ingredients and pour into lightly greased baking pan. Top with bread crumbs. Bake for ten to 15 minutes or until bubbly.

New England Cabbage Bake

3 small potatoes, sliced thin
1/2 cup onion, chopped
Salt and pepper
2 cups cabbage, shredded

1 can corned beef
1 can cream of celery soup
1 cup milk
1 1/2 tsp. mustard

Preheat oven to 375 degrees. Layer potatoes in greased baking pan. Sprinkle with onions, salt and pepper. Spread cabbage over potatoes. Crumble corned beef over cabbage. In bowl, combine soup, milk and mustard. Pour over casserole. Bake covered for one and a half hours or until potatoes are tender.

Easy Fried Fish

4 fish fillets
1 cup flour
2 tsp. salt
1/2 tsp. pepper

1/2 tsp. onion salt
1/2 tsp. paprika
3 Tbsp. butter or margarine
3 Tbsp. cooking oil

In paper sack, combine flour, salt, pepper, onion salt and paprika. Shake to mix. One at a time, place fish in bag and gently shake to coat. Heat butter and oil in frying pan. Cook fish until lightly browned, turning only once. Do not overcook.

Citrus Halibut Steaks

1/4 cup butter or margarine
3 Tbsp. onion, chopped
6-oz. frozen orange juice
2 Tbsp. fresh parsley, chopped

1/4 tsp. salt
2 halibut steaks, 1-inch thick
Salt and pepper
1 lemon, sliced

Sauté onion in butter until tender. Stir in orange juice, parsley and salt. Cook until heated through. Sprinkle halibut steaks with salt and pepper. Brush with orange juice mixture. Broil in oven about five minutes or until fish flakes easily with fork. Garnish with lemon slices. Serve with remaining orange sauce.

Penny-Wise Salmon Bake

1 large potato, diced
3 Tbsp. butter or margarine
3 Tbsp. flour
4 tsp. onion, minced
1 1/2 tsp. mustard

1/2 tsp. salt
1/8 tsp. pepper
1 1/2 cups milk
1 can pink salmon, drained

Preheat oven to 350 degrees. Cook potatoes in salted boiling water until tender, about ten minutes. Drain well. Set aside. Melt butter in saucepan then blend in flour, onions, mustard, salt and pepper. Gradually add milk, stirring constantly, until thickened. Bring to boil and cook one minute. Flake salmon, removing bones and skin. Stir salmon and potatoes into sauce. Spoon into greased baking pan. Bake for 15 minutes. Serve with peas.

Simple Salmon Patties

1/2 cup flaked salmon
2 Tbsp. butter or margarine
1 Tbsp. flour
1/4 cup milk

1/4 cup bread crumbs
1/4 tsp. lemon juice
1/8 tsp. salt
Dash of black pepper and red pepper

Drain salmon well. In small saucepan, melt butter and stir in flour. Gradually beat in milk, stirring constantly until thickened. Add salmon, bread crumbs, lemon juice, salt, pepper and red pepper. Let cool just enough to form into patties with hands. Sauté patties in melted butter or oil until lightly brown and heated through.

Scalloped Tuna and Potatoes

3 Tbsp. butter or margarine
3 Tbsp. onion, minced
1/2 tsp. salt
Dash of pepper
3 Tbsp. flour

2 cups milk
1 small can tuna, drained and flaked
3 large potatoes, thinly sliced
1/2 cup cheddar cheese, grated

Sauté onion in butter until tender. Stir in salt, pepper and flour. Whip in milk to make sauce. Continue cooking, stirring constantly until thickened. Add tuna and 1/4 cup cheese. Heat through. Layer potato slices in 8x8 baking pan. Pour tuna mixture over potatoes. Bake covered at 350 degrees for one hour. Uncover and bake 30 minutes longer, or until potatoes are tender. Spread remaining cheese over top and place under broiler until melted.

Crunchy Tuna Casserole

Small can of tuna, drained
1 1/2 cups frozen peas, thawed
1 can cream of mushroom soup
1 cup macaroni, cooked

1/4 cup bread crumbs
3 Tbsp. butter or margarine, softened
1/4 cup potato chips, crushed

Preheat oven to 375 degrees. Combine tuna, peas, soup and noodles. Spoon into lightly greased baking pan. Moisten bread crumbs with melted butter. Sprinkle over casserole. Top with crushed potato chips. Bake for 35 minutes or until bubbly hot.

Broccoli and Ham Noodles

1 1/2 cups cooked ham, chopped
2 cups broccoli, chopped
2 cups water

1 Tbsp. soy sauce
2 pkgs. oriental-flavored Ramen noodles
2 hard-boiled eggs

In saucepan, combine ham, broccoli, water, soy sauce and one flavor packet from noodles. Break noodles into small pieces. Add to saucepan. Simmer uncovered for about ten minutes until noodles are tender, stirring frequently. Top with egg slices. Serve warm.

Ham, Egg and Cheese Pie

4 Tbsp. butter or margarine
1/2 lb. mushrooms, sliced thin
1 small onion, thinly sliced and
    separated into rings
1 cup ham, cooked and cut into thin strips
1 cup Swiss cheese, grated

4 eggs, beaten well
1 cup evaporated milk
3 Tbsp. mustard
3/4 tsp. salt
Dash of pepper

Preheat oven to 425 degrees. Melt butter or margarine in large skillet. Sauté mushrooms until tender. Remove mushrooms from butter and layer them on bottom of lightly greased 9-inch pie plate. Sauté onion rings in butter until limp. Layer onions on top of mushrooms. Arrange strips of ham on top of onions. Sprinkle grated cheese over ham.

In bowl, beat together remaining melted butter, eggs, milk, mustard, salt, pepper and biscuit mix. Pour gently over meat and vegetables in pie plate. Bake for 15 to 20 minutes.

Ham and Scalloped Potatoes

3 medium potatoes, thinly sliced
2 medium onions, thinly sliced and
    separated into rings
1 tsp. salt
1/2 tsp. pepper

1/2 cup milk
3 Tbsp. flour
1 can cheddar cheese soup
1 1/2 cups cheese, grated
3 cups cooked ham, cubed

Preheat oven to 300 degrees. Layer half the potatoes and half the onions in baking pan. Sprinkle with salt and pepper. In jar with screw-on lid, combine milk and flour until completely blended. In small saucepan, cook milk and flour, stirring constantly, until thickened. Stir in soup and 1 cup cheese until melted.

Pour half of cheese mixture over potatoes and onions. Distribute half the ham over potatoes. Repeat layers. Top with remaining 1/2 cup cheese. Bake for two and a half hours or until potatoes are tender.

Quick Hawaiian Delight

2 slices cooked ham, 1/2-inch thick
2 Tbsp. mustard
1 cup milk
1 can pineapple rings, drained
1 small apple, cored and sliced into rings

1/4 cup granulated sugar
4 Tbsp. butter or margarine
1 1/2 tsp. cinnamon
1/2 cup water

Preheat oven to 350 degrees. Spread ham with mustard and place in shallow baking pan. Pour 1/2 cup milk over ham. Bake until milk has evaporated, about ten minutes. While ham is cooking, heat pineapple rings, apple slices, sugar, butter, cinnamon and water in small saucepan. Simmer until apples are tender. Pour remaining milk on ham and cover with simmered fruit. Cook an additional ten minutes.

Barbecued Hot Dog Beans

Two 16-oz. cans pork and beans
1/4 cup brown sugar, packed
1/2 cup ketchup
1 Tbsp. vinegar

1 Tbsp. Worcestershire sauce
1/4 tsp. hot sauce
4 hot dogs

Preheat oven to 350 degrees. In large bowl, combine beans, brown sugar, ketchup, vinegar, Worcestershire sauce and hot sauce. Pour into shallow baking pan. Arrange sliced hotdogs on top. Bake for 30 to 35 minutes or until bubbly hot.

Cheesy Pigs in Blankets

1 cup biscuit mix
1/4 cup milk
2 Tbsp. mustard

2 Tbsp. pickle relish
4 hot dogs
4 slices of cheese

Preheat oven to 400 degrees. Combine biscuit mix and milk. Turn onto lightly floured surface and knead until smooth. Roll into rectangle and cut into four pieces. Spread each piece with thin layers of mustard and pickle relish. Split each hot dog lengthwise. Place cheese slices in hot dogs. Wrap dough pieces around hot dogs. Pinch ends of dough to seal. Bake on greased cookie sheet for five to seven minutes or until dough turns golden brown.

Crunchy Corn Dogs

1/2 cup flour
3/4 tsp. baking powder
1/3 cup cornmeal
1 Tbsp. sugar
1/2 tsp. salt

1/2 cup milk
1 egg, beaten
1 Tbsp. cooking oil
4 to 6 hot dogs

Sift together flour, baking powder, cornmeal and sugar. Stir together milk, egg and oil. Beat in dry ingredients. Skewer each hot dog on wooden stick, if desired. Dip in batter. Fry in hot oil using sticks or tongs. Drain on paper towels.

Fast Franks and Potatoes

4 small potatoes, cooked and cubed
2 small onions, chopped
3 Tbsp. butter or margarine

4 hot dogs, cut up
1/2 cup cheddar cheese, grated

Brown potatoes and onions in butter. Add hot dogs. Heat through. Top with cheese, if desired.

Easy Corn and Franks

1 Tbsp. cooking oil
2 small potatoes, peeled
3 Tbsp. onion, chopped
5 hot dogs, sliced

Two 8-oz. cans whole-kernel corn
1/2 tsp. salt
Dash of pepper
1/2 tsp. chili powder

Dice then sauté potatoes in oil until tender. Add onion and hot dogs. Cook over medium heat until hot dogs begin to brown. Stir in corn, salt, pepper and chili powder. Heat through.

Hot Dog Potato Bake

6 hot dogs
6 Tbsp. tomato sauce

4 servings mashed potatoes
2 cups cheddar cheese, grated

Preheat oven to 375 degrees. Split each hot dog lengthwise. Place in baking pan. Spoon one tablespoon tomato sauce into each hot dog. Spoon mashed potatoes between hot dogs in pan. Top all with grated cheese. Bake for 25 minutes.

Stove Top Kielbasa and Rice

1 Tbsp. butter or margarine
2 cloves garlic, minced
1 can cream of mushroom soup
2 cups water
1/4 tsp. celery salt
1/4 tsp. onion powder

1 lb. smoked Kielbasa sausage, cut into
    bite-size pieces
1 cup long-grain rice, uncooked
1 small pkg. frozen corn
1/2 cup mushrooms, sliced
1 cup cheddar cheese, grated

In large frying pan, brown garlic in butter. Add soup ,water, celery salt and onion powder. Bring to boil. Add sausage and rice. Reduce heat. Cover and simmer for 20 minutes. Stir in corn and mushrooms. Cover and simmer 20 minutes longer or until rice is tender. Sprinkle with cheese. Cover until cheese melts.

Easy Pineapple Pork

1/2 cup flour
Salt and pepper

4 pork chops
4 slices pineapple

Preheat oven to 375 degrees. Combine flour, salt and pepper. Put chops in flour to coat both sides. Place in baking pan. Bake uncovered for 30 minutes. Lay a slice of pineapple on each chop. Return to oven for 15 minutes.

Chops and Cheesy Potatoes

4 pork chops
3 boiled potatoes, cubed
1 Tbsp. onion, minced

1 can cream of mushroom soup
1 can cheddar cheese soup

Preheat oven to 350 degrees. Put chops in baking pan. Mix potatoes, onion and soups. Pour over chops. Bake for one hour or until pork chops are cooked through.

Pepper Pork and Rice

1/2 cup flour
Salt and pepper
4 pork chops
1/2 cup rice, uncooked

2 cups stewed tomatoes
2 Tbsp. onion, chopped
2 Tbsp. green pepper, chopped
1 tsp. salt

Mix flour, salt and pepper. Roll chops in flour to coat. Brown in oil in frying pan. In a bowl, combine remaining ingredients. Pour over chops. Cover and simmer for 45 minutes until rice is tender.

Pork Tenders with Carrots

1 lb. pork tenderloin, cut into half-inch
   round slices
1/2 cup flour
Salt and pepper
Olive oil

2 cloves garlic, minced
1/2 cup water
1 cup carrots, sliced diagonally
2 Tbsp. fresh parsley, chopped
1/4 cup red onion, diced

Lightly cover pork pieces with flour, salt and pepper. Brown in olive oil over medium heat. Remove pork from pan. Add garlic, stirring until browned. Stir in water, carrots and parsley. Cook covered until carrots are tender. Add pork and cook five minutes or until flavors blend. Top with diced red onion, if desired.

Stuffed Pork Chops

2 cups soft bread crumbs
1/2 tsp. salt
2 Tbsp. green pepper, minced
2 Tbsp. onion, minced
2 Tbsp. butter, melted

1 egg, beaten
3/4 cup whole-kernel corn
4 pork chops, one-inch thick
1 can cream of mushroom soup

Preheat oven to 350 degrees. In bowl, combine bread, salt, green pepper, onion, butter, egg and corn for stuffing. Cut deep slit in each chop on side. Stuff. Put chops in baking pan. Pour soup over chops. Bake covered for one hour.

Mandarin Almond Pork

4 pork chops, 1/2-inch thick
1/2 cup slivered almonds
1 Tbsp. cooking oil
Small can mandarin oranges, undrained

1/2 tsp. ground cloves
1 Tbsp. cornstarch
1/4 cup cold water
2 cups rice, cooked

Cut pork off bone and into bite-sized pieces. In large frying pan, brown pork and almonds in oil. Top with oranges and mix mandarin orange juice with pork drippings. Mix in ground cloves. Cover and simmer for 15 to 20 minutes or until pork is tender. Mix cornstarch with cold water. Pour slowly into pan, stirring constantly until sauce thickens. Serve over cooked rice.

Mom's Old Standbys

Vegetarian Main Dishes

Barley Mushroom Stew

3 Tbsp. cooking oil
1/2 onion, minced
1/2 cup pearl barley
1 cup sliced mushrooms

2 cups hot water
2 vegetable bouillon cubes
1/8 tsp. pepper
2 carrots, thinly sliced

Sauté onion, barley and mushrooms. Dissolve bouillon cubes in hot water and add to barley mixture. Stir in pepper and carrots. Bring to a boil, reduce heat and simmer for 25 minutes.

Italian Barley Casserole

2 cups water
1/2 cup pearled barley
1/2 cup onion, diced
1/2 cup zucchini, diced
1/2 cup red pepper, diced
1 1/2 tsp. flour
1/4 tsp. salt
1/4 tsp. black pepper

3/4 cup milk
1 cup mozzarella cheese, grated
1 Tbsp. Dijon mustard
1/2 tsp. garlic powder
1/2 tsp. parsley, minced
1/4 tsp. basil
1/4 tsp. oregano flakes

To cook barley: Bring water to a boil in one-quart saucepan. Add barley and salt. Cover, reduce heat and simmer 45 minutes or until tender. Let stand covered for five minutes.

To finish casserole: Preheat oven to 375 degrees. In large frying pan, sauté onion, zucchini and red pepper about 10 minutes or until tender. Stir in flour, salt and pepper. Cook 2 minutes. Add milk, stirring constantly until mixture is thickened. Remove from heat. Add barley, 3/4 cup cheese, mustard and spices. Stir until cheese melts. Spread in even layers into 9x13 baking pan. Sprinkle with remaining cheese. Bake for 20 minutes or until hot. Broil until cheese is lightly brown.

Broccoli Ricotta Lasagna

12 lasagna noodles, cooked and drained
16-oz. fat-free ricotta cheese
3 eggs, beaten
1 tsp. basil
2 Tbsp. butter or margarine
1/2 cup onion, chopped

2 cloves garlic, chopped
1/4 cup flour
2 cups milk
1 cup mozzarella cheese, grated
1 small tomato, chopped
2 Tbsp. Parmesan cheese

To prepare: Cook lasagna noodles according to package directions until done but still firm. Set aside. In bowl, combine ricotta cheese, eggs and basil. Set aside. Preheat oven to 350 degrees. In large frying pan, sauté onion and garlic in butter or margarine. Stir in flour. Cook for one minute. Gradually stir in milk. Cook, stirring until mixture thickens and begins to boil. Remove from heat. Stir in broccoli and cheese.

To bake: In lightly greased 9x13 baking pan, place 4 lasagna noodles. Top with 1/3 ricotta-egg mixture and 1/3 broccoli-cheese mixture. Repeat layers two more times. Top with chopped tomatoes. Sprinkle with parmesan cheese. Bake for one hour or until set. lasagna stand for ten minutes before serving.

Double Cheese Linguine

1 pkg. linguine, cooked
2 Tbsp. butter or margarine
3 Tbsp. flour
Salt and pepper

1 1/2 cups milk
3/4 cup mozzarella, grated
1/4 cup Parmesan, grated
2 Tbsp. lemon juice

Cook linguine according to package directions. In frying pan, melt butter. Stir in flour, salt and pepper until smooth. Gradually stir in milk. Bring to boil and stir for two minutes, or until thickened. Remove from heat. Combine cheeses and toss with lemon juice. Add cheese mixture to sauce, stirring gently until cheese begins to melt. Toss linguine with cheese sauce until noodles are well coated.

Mushroom Penne Pasta

1 pkg. penne pasta
2 Tbsp. olive oil
2 cloves garlic, peeled and chopped

1 cup mushrooms
2 Tbsp. fresh parsley, chopped
Salt and pepper

Cook penne pasta according to package directions. Drain and set aside. In large frying pan, sauté garlic, mushrooms and parsley in olive oil. Add pasta, stirring to coat. Serve immediately.

Oven Macaroni and Cheese

3/4 cup evaporated milk
1/2 cup water
1 cup cheese, diced
1 1/2 Tbsp. butter or margarine
1 cup soft bread cubes

2 Tbsp. onion, diced
1/2 tsp. salt
Dash of pepper
2 eggs, beaten
2 cups macaroni, cooked

Preheat oven to 350 degrees. In frying pan, combine milk, water, cheese and butter. Heat to boil, stirring constantly. Stir in bread, onion, salt and pepper. Fold in eggs and macaroni. Pour into greased baking pan. Bake for 30 minutes.

Speedy Mexican Pizzas

4 flour tortillas
1 can refried beans
1 cup salsa
2 small tomatoes, diced
Small can green chilis, diced

1/4 cup onion, diced
1/4 black olives, sliced
1/2 cup cheddar cheese, grated
1/2 cup Monterey Jack cheese, grated

Preheat oven to 350 degrees. Place tortillas on ungreased cookie sheet. Spread with beans. Layer with salsa, tomatoes, chilis, onion, olives and cheeses. Bake for ten minutes.

Southwestern White Chili

2 cups white beans, cooked
    OR large can white beans
1/4 cup onion, chopped
1 Tbsp. cooking oil
Small can green chilis, diced
1/2 tsp. fresh cilantro, minced
1 tsp. garlic powder

1 tsp. cumin
1/2 tsp. oregano flakes
1/4 tsp. crushed red pepper
1 vegetable bouillon cube
1 cup hot water
Monterey Jack cheese, grated

Cook beans according to package directions. Set aside. In large frying pan, brown onions in oil until transparent. Add green chilis, cilantro, garlic powder, cumin, oregano and red pepper. Dissolve bouillon cube in hot water. Add bouillon to pan, mixing well. Add cooked beans to broth. Simmer covered for two hours. Garnish with grated Monterey Jack cheese, if desired.

Eggplant Spinach Rollups

2 eggplants, sliced lengthwise
2 Tbsp. lemon juice
2 tsp. olive oil
1/2 tsp. parsley flakes
1/4 tsp. garlic powder
20 spinach leaves
1/4 cup cream cheese
3 Tbsp. sour cream

1 green onion, minced
1 small tomato, minced
1 clove garlic, minced
1/4 tsp. oregano flakes
Salt and pepper
1 cup spaghetti sauce, warmed
1/2 cup grated parmesan cheese

To bake eggplant: Preheat oven to 425 degrees. Trim ends from eggplants. Cut lengthwise into 1/4-inch thick slices to make 16 to 20 slices. In small bowl, combine lemon juice, olive oil, parsley flakes and garlic powder. Brush over both sides off eggplant. Arrange in single layer on cookie sheet. Bake for 20 to 25 minutes or until tender and golden, turning once. Set aside.

To prepare rollups: Trim, wash and dry spinach leaves. Set aside. Stir together cream cheese, sour cream, onion, tomatoes, garlic, oregano, salt and pepper. Spread about one teaspoon cream cheese mixture evenly on top of each eggplant slice. Arrange spinach leaves on top of cream cheese mixture. Roll up beginning at small end. Lay rolls seam side down on serving platter. Pour warm spaghetti sauce over rolls. Sprinkle with parmesan cheese.

Eggplant Zucchini Bake

2 tsp. olive oil
1/2 cup onion, chopped
2 cloves garlic, minced
1 large can whole tomatoes
1 Tbsp. tomato paste
2 tsp. basil

1 tsp. oregano flakes
1 tsp. sugar
2 medium eggplants, peeled and chopped
2 cups zucchini, sliced
1 cup mushrooms, sliced
Grated parmesan or mozzarella cheese

Preheat oven to 350 degrees. Heat oil in large frying pan. Sauté onion and garlic until onion is transparent. Add tomatoes, tomato paste, basil, oregano and sugar. Cook about five minutes or until sauce thickens. Place eggplant, zucchini and mushrooms in 9-inch baking pan. Pour sauce over eggplant mixture. Cover and bake for 30 minutes. Top with cheese, if desired.

Little Italy Tomatoes

2 large ripe tomatoes
1 cup instant rice, cooked
1 tsp. basil
1 tsp. oregano flakes
1/2 tsp. salt

1/4 tsp. garlic powder
1 Tbsp. olive oil
1/4 cup fresh Parmesan cheese, grated
2 Tbsp. bread crumbs
1 Tbsp. parsley flakes

Preheat oven to 200 degrees. Cut tomatoes in half crosswise. Spoon out the soft inside pulp and seeds, leaving 4 tomato cups. Mix pulp with rice, basil, oregano, salt and garlic powder. Spoon 1/4 mixture into each tomato cup almost to tops. Combine olive oil, parmesan cheese, bread crumbs and parsley flakes. Top each tomato cup with bread crumb mixture. Place tomatoes on cookie sheet.Bake for ten to 15 minutes or until heated through. Broil two minutes or until topping is browned.

Tastiest Vegetarian Chili

1 Tbsp. cooking oil
2 cloves garlic, minced
2 cups mushrooms, sliced
1/2 cup red onion, chopped
1/2 cup red pepper, chopped

2 Tbsp. chili powder
1/4 tsp. ground cumin
1/4 tsp. oregano flakes
1 large can whole tomatoes
1 cup chili beans, cooked

Sauté garlic in oil. Add mushrooms, onion and pepper. Cook five minutes. Add spices. Add tomatoes and beans. Reduce heat and simmer 30 minutes, stirring occasionally.

Stuffed Zucchini Casserole

1/4 cup onion, chopped
4 cups zucchini, sliced
1 can cream of celery soup
8-oz. pkg. herb-seasoned stuffing mix

1/2 cup butter or margarine, melted
1 cup sour cream
1 cup cheddar cheese, grated

Preheat oven to 350 degrees. Boil onion and zucchini in water until tender, about five minutes. Drain. In bowl, combine soup, sour cream and cheese. In another bowl, make stuffing according to package. Stir in butter or margarine. Spread half the stuffing over bottom of baking pan. Spoon on zucchini and soup mixture. Top with remaining stuffing. Bake for 25 to 30 minutes.

Zucchini Mushroom Frittata

1 Tbsp. olive oil
1 medium zucchini, grated
1 medium tomato, chopped
1 can mushrooms, drained
6 eggs, beaten

1/2 cup Swiss cheese, grated
1/4 cup milk
1/2 tsp. garlic powder
1/4 tsp. black pepper

In frying pan, sauté zucchini, tomatoes and mushrooms in olive oil until tender. In mixing bowl, combine eggs, cheese, milk, garlic powder and pepper. Mix until well blended. Pour into frying pan, stirring well. Cover and cook over low heat for 15 minutes (or until cooked on bottom and almost set on top.) Remove lid and place pan under broiler of oven for three minutes or until done as desired.

What's That?

The names of these recipes may sound odd, but the outcome is great. Give them a try!

Gazpacho

(Cold Tomato Soup)

4 large ripe tomatoes, peeled and diced
1 cucumber, peeled and diced
1/2 sweet red pepper, diced
1/2 green bell pepper, diced
1/2 onion, minced
2 cloves garlic, minced
1/4 cup fresh parsley, minced

1 Tbsp. fresh chives, minced
1 tsp. fresh basil, minced
1 Tbsp. olive oil
3 Tbsp. lemon juice
2 cups tomato juice
Salt and pepper

Combine tomatoes, cucumber, peppers and onion, mixing well. Purée half the vegetable mixture with garlic, parsley, chives, basil, olive oil and lemon juice. Combine purée with chopped vegetables and tomato juice. Refrigerate for at least three hours. Salt and pepper to taste.

Hummus

(Middle Eastern Dip)

1 can chick peas, rinsed and drained
2 cloves garlic, peeled and minced
1/4 cup fresh parsley, chopped
2 Tbsp. lemon juice

2 Tbsp. olive oil
1/4 tsp. curry powder
1/4 tsp. ground cumin

Place all ingredients in blender and blend well. Serve with pita bread triangles or crackers.

Ratatouille

(French Vegetable Stew)

2 Tbsp. olive oil
2 cloves garlic, minced
1 small onion, sliced and separated
    into rings
1/2 green pepper, chopped
1/2 red pepper, chopped
2 tomatoes, cut into wedges
1/2 cup tomato juice

1 lemon, quartered
1 eggplant, cubed
1 celery stalk, chopped
1 small zucchini, thinly sliced
2 Tbsp. Parmesan cheese
1/4 tsp. oregano leaves
1/4 tsp. thyme
1 bay leaf

Sauté onions, garlic and peppers in oil. Cook for five minutes. Add tomatoes, tomato juice, lemon wedges and remaining ingredients. Bring to a boil and simmer for 30 minutes. Before serving, remove lemon wedges and bay leaf. (For Microwave: Combine all ingredients in two-quart microwavable dish. Cover. Microwave on high for ten minutes or until eggplant is translucent, stirring every two minutes.) Serve warm or cold.

Tabbouleh

(Middle Eastern Salad)

1 cup bulgur wheat
1/4 cup olive oil
2 tomatoes, chopped
1/2 cucumber, peeled and chopped
3 Tbsp. green onion, minced

3 Tbsp. fresh parsley, minced
6 mint leaves, minced
1 lemon, juiced
Salt and pepper

Cook bulgur wheat in saucepan with water. Bring to a boil then simmer for 15 minutes until tender. Drain. Allow to cool. In large serving boil, mix bulgur with olive oil, tomatoes, cucumber, green onions, parsley, mint and lemon juice. Salt and pepper to taste. Serve as side salad or as stuffing in pita bread. Top with crumbled feta cheese, if desired.

MOM'S OLD Standbys

Mom's Old Standbys

Side Dishes

Sweet and Tender Asparagus

4 cups fresh asparagus,
   cut into 4-inch pieces
3 Tbsp. butter or margarine

2 Tbsp. brown sugar
1 cup chicken broth

In frying pan, heat butter and brown sugar until sugar is dissolved. Add asparagus. Sauté for two minutes. Stir in broth and bring to boil. Reduce heat. Cover and simmer for ten minutes or until asparagus is tender. Remove asparagus to serving dish. Cook sauce in pan uncovered until reduced by half. Pour over asparagus.

Easy Baked Beans

28-oz. can pork and beans
6 strips bacon, chopped
1/2 cup onion, chopped
1/4 cup ketchup

1 tsp. prepared mustard
1 tsp. salt
1/2 cup brown sugar, packed

Cook bacon until crisp. Sauté onions in drippings. Drain. Stir in remaining ingredients. Cook for ten minutes.

Island Baked Beans

1 large can pork and beans
1 small can pineapple chunks
1 small green pepper, sliced in thin strips
1/4 cup onion, diced

1/4 cup brown sugar, packed
2 Tbsp. vinegar
3 Tbsp. soy sauce

Preheat oven to 350 degrees. Combine all ingredients in greased baking pan. Mix well. Bake for 35 minutes.

Green Bean Casserole

2 cans French-style green beans, drained
1 can cream of mushroom soup

1 can French fried onion rings

Preheat oven to 325 degrees. Stir beans and soup together. Spoon into greased baking pan. Top with onion rings. Bake for 20 minutes or until bubbly hot.

French Almond Green Beans

1 pkg. frozen French-style green beans
2 Tbsp. butter or margarine
1/4 tsp. rosemary

1/4 tsp. basil
1/2 cup fresh mushrooms, thickly sliced
Toasted, slivered almonds

Cook beans according to package directions. Drain. Set aside. In frying pan, sauté mushrooms with butter, rosemary and basil. Reduce heat. Add beans, stirring until coated. Stir in almonds.

Harvard Beets

1/4 cup cider vinegar
1/4 cup granulated sugar
1/4 tsp. salt
1/2 tsp. mustard

2 tsp. flour
1/2 Tbsp. butter or margarine
2 cups red beets, cooked and cubed

Combine cider vinegar, sugar, salt, mustard, flour and butter until well blended, stirring constantly until thickened. Add beets.

Cheesy Broccoli Bake

1 pkg. frozen broccoli
1/2 cup mayonnaise
1/2 cup cream of mushroom soup

1 egg, beaten
1 1/2 cups cheese, grated
1 cup crackers, crushed

Preheat oven to 325 degrees. Cook broccoli according to package. Drain. Combine mayonnaise, soup, egg and cheese. Stir in broccoli. Pour into greased baking pan. Sprinkle cracker crumbs on top. Bake for 30 minutes.

Cabbage with Bacon

3 slices bacon, chopped
1 large carrot, sliced diagonally
1 cup celery, sliced diagonally
1/2 green pepper, sliced

1/2 onion, chopped
2 cups cabbage, shredded
1 tsp. sugar

Brown bacon, add vegetables and stir fry for five to ten minutes. The last minute of cooking time sprinkle with sugar.

German Red Cabbage

1 small head red cabbage, shredded
4 strips bacon, chopped
1 small onion, diced
2 Tbsp. flour

1/2 cup brown sugar, packed
1/2 cup vinegar
1/2 cup water

Boil cabbage until tender. Drain. In large frying pan, fry bacon and sauté onion. Add cabbage. In saucepan, combine flour, brown sugar, vinegar and water. Cook, stirring constantly, until thickened. Stir sauce into cabbage, bacon and onion. Serve immediately.

Minted Carrots and Snow Peas

1 Tbsp. butter or margarine
3 carrots, thinly sliced diagonally
1/2 lb. fresh snow peas
2 Tbsp. sugar

1 Tbsp. lemon juice
1 Tbsp. fresh mint leaves, chopped
OR 1 tsp. dried mint

Trim snow peas of tips and hard outer edge. In large frying pan, melt butter or margarine. Add carrots. Cook and stir three to five minutes. Add peas, sugar, lemon juice and mint. Cook and stir three to five minutes or until vegetables are glazed and tender.

Golden Onion Rings

1/2 cup flour
1/2 tsp. baking powder
1/4 tsp. salt
1 egg, beaten

1/2 cup milk
1 Tbsp. cooking oil
2 onions, sliced and separated into rings
Cooking oil for frying

Blend flour, baking powder and salt. Beat together egg, milk and oil. Stir into flour mixture until well blended. Heat frying oil in a deep pan to about 375 degrees. (Use instant-read thermometer.) Dip onion rings, a few at a time, into batter. Drop into hot oil. Turn over with tongs when golden. Drain on paper towels.

Zucchini Bacon Fry

3 slices bacon, chopped
1/4 cup onion, diced

2 cups zucchini, peeled and cubed

Fry bacon. Add onions. Cook until transparent. Add zucchini. Salt and pepper to taste. Cover and cook for 15 to 20 minutes.

Baked Cheese Fries

5 potatoes, peeled
3 Tbsp. butter or margarine
1 1/2 tsp. salt
Dash of pepper

3/4 cup cheddar cheese, grated
1/2 cup half and half cream
1/4 cup milk

Preheat oven to 350 degrees. Place long piece of foil in baking pan. Cut potatoes into strips. Place in center of foil. Dot with butter. Sprinkle with salt and pepper. Top with cheese. Fold up edges of foil to hold liquid. Add cream and milk. Fold foil over and seal edges. Bake for about one hour.

Creamed Potatoes and Peas

8 small red potatoes, boiled
1/4 cup butter or margarine
3 Tbsp. flour
1 1/2 tsp. salt
1/4 tsp. pepper

1 1/2 cups milk
1 cup evaporated milk
10-oz. pkg. frozen peas
1/2 cup onion, diced
4 slices bacon, cooked and crumbled

Preheat oven to 325 degrees. Cut potatoes in half and place on greased baking pan. Sprinkle peas over potatoes. In saucepan, melt butter or margarine. Stir in flour, salt and pepper. Add milk, stirring constantly until thickened. Pour sauce over vegetables. Top with crisp bacon. Bake for 20 minutes.

Ranchero Potatoes

4 potatoes, boiled and sliced
1/4 cup butter or margarine
2 Tbsp. flour
1 cup milk
1/2 tsp. salt

1/4 tsp. pepper
1/2 cup onion, diced
1/4 cup green pepper, diced
1/4 cup barbeque sauce
1 cup cheddar cheese, grated

Preheat oven to 350 degrees. Layer half of potatoes in 8x8 baking pan. In saucepan, melt butter or margarine. Stir in flour. Add milk gradually, stirring constantly until thickened. Remove from heat. Stir in salt, pepper, onions, green peppers and barbecue sauce. Stir in cheese until melted. Pour half of sauce over potatoes. Repeat layers. Bake for 25 minutes or until bubbly and brown.

Easiest-Ever Scalloped Potatoes

2 large potatoes, sliced
4 slices bacon, chopped and cooked
1 large onion, minced

1 can cream of mushroom soup
1 cup cheddar cheese, grated

Boil potatoes in salted water until tender but still firm. Drain and set aside. Cut bacon and cook with onions. Set aside. Combine soup and 1/2 cup cheese in saucepan. Simmer until cheese melts. Add potatoes, bacon and onions. Heat through. Pour into baking dish. Top with remaining grated cheese. Place under broiler until cheese bubbles, about two to three minutes.

Skillet Scalloped Potatoes

2 potatoes, peeled and thinly sliced
2 Tbsp. cooking oil
1/4 tsp. salt
Dash of pepper

2 slices bacon, cooked and crumbled
1 can evaporated milk
1/2 cup cheese, grated

Brown potatoes in frying pan with small amount of cooking oil. When tender, sprinkle with salt and pepper. Add milk, bacon and cheese. Cover and simmer over low heat for ten minutes or until milk has formed a sauce. Serve immediately.

Seasoned Sliced Potatoes

2 potatoes, unpeeled and thinly sliced
Cooking oil

Garlic powder
Onion salt

Lay potatoes in greased baking pan. Brush tops with oil. Sprinkle with garlic powder and onion salt. Place under broiler until brown on one side. Flip with pancake turner and brown other side. If you want to cut down on bad fat, use olive oil or cooking spray.

Zesty Zucchini Bake

2 zucchini, peeled and cubed
2 eggs, beaten
1/4 cup milk
1 tsp. baking powder

2 Tbsp. flour
1/2 lb. cheese, cubed
1/4 cup onion, diced
1/4 cup green pepper, diced

Preheat oven to 350 degrees. Cook zucchini in small amount of boiling water until almost tender, about five minutes. Drain and let cool. Combine eggs, milk, baking powder, cheese, onion and green pepper. Stir in zucchini. Bake in greased baking pan for 35 minutes. Let stand for ten minutes before serving.

Swiss Baked Vegetables

1 cup red potatoes, unpeeled and cubed
2 cups broccoli florets
1 cup cauliflower florets
1/2 cup carrots, thinly sliced diagonally
2 tsp. butter or margarine
1 cup fresh mushrooms, sliced
1 cup milk

1/2 cup Swiss cheese, grated
1/2 tsp. salt
1/4 tsp. black pepper
1/4 tsp. hot pepper sauce
1/8 tsp. nutmeg
1/4 cup parmesan cheese, grated

In saucepan, bring potatoes to boil. Reduce heat. Cover and simmer for ten minutes. Add broccoli, cauliflower and carrots. Cover and cook five to eight minutes or until all vegetables are tender. Drain and set aside. Melt butter or margarine in saucepan. Add mushrooms. Cook and stir for two minutes. Stir in flour. Gradually stir in milk until thickened. Remove from heat. Add Swiss cheese, stirring until melted. Stir in salt, pepper, hot sauce and nutmeg. Preheat broiler. Place vegetables in greased baking pan. Pour sauce over vegetables. Top with parmesan cheese. Place under boiler until cheese browns.

Perfect Rice

To cook perfect rice, pour desired amount of rice into saucepan. Fill saucepan slowly with hot water until it is one knuckle deep above rice. Cook, uncovered, over medium heat until "pocks" form in rice. Remove from heat. Cover with tight lid and let stand ten to 15 minutes. Rice will be tender and perfectly steamed. If you are in a hurry to eat, buy and prepare instant rice, or purchase an electric rice cooker for no-fail rice every time.

Chinese Fried Rice

1 Tbsp. cooking oil
1/2 cup onion, chopped
1 cup cold rice, cooked
1 egg, beaten

1 Tbsp. soy sauce
1/4 tsp. salt
1 cup chopped vegetables

Heat oil in frying pan. Cook onion until transparent, stirring constantly. Add rice and sauté. (Rice must be cold before you begin.) Beat egg, soy sauce and salt. Add to rice mixture, stirring constantly. Add vegetables. Cook until vegetables are tender.

Mexican Rice and Beans

1 cup short-grain rice, uncooked
2 Tbsp. oil
2 cups water
1 cube Mexican tomato-chicken bouillon
1/4 cup onion, diced
2 Tbsp. canned green chilis

2 Tbsp. fresh cilantro, diced
1/4 tsp. cumin
1/4 tsp. chili powder
1 can pinto beans, undrained
1/2 cup cheddar cheese, grated

Cook rice in oil, stirring constantly until grains are slightly broken. Set aside. In saucepan, dissolve bouillon in water. Add onion, chilis, cilantro, cumin and chili powder. Bring to boil. Add rice. Boil for ten minutes. Cover and simmer for 15 to 20 minutes or until tender. Pour pinto beans into another saucepan. Mash about half of beans with fork. Warm through. Top with grated cheese.

Rice Is More Than Nice

Rice is nutritional, inexpensive and goes with many dishes. In a casserole, rice can make two servings of meat and vegetables stretch into six servings. It's also a great side dish.

Long-grain rice is most common in the United States. Since grains stay separated in cooking, the rice turns out fluffy. Long-grain rice works well in casseroles, soups and stews, and as a side dish.

Medium-grain rice is slightly less fluffy. It's higher stickiness makes it ideal for desserts and rice rings.

Short-grain rice, most common in the Orient, is sticky and best for pudding. Instant rice cooks quickest but costs more. White rice is economical, but you might want to choose brown rice for its nutritional value.

Brown rice has only the outer hull removed while white rice is stripped to the grain. The bran provides fiber, protein, vitamin B-12, calcium, phosphorus, niacin and potassium.

Brown rice can't be stored as long as white rice. The outside layer starts to deteriorate in climates with high humidity. If you plan to store brown rice for a long period, put it in the refrigerator.

The bran adds more fiber and oil, which increases cooking time. Cooked brown rice will have a different texture. The inside grain will be tender, while the outside bran layer will cling to the grain providing a crunchy texture and nut-like taste.

You will need more water to cook brown rice. If package doesn't provide directions, use this formula:

Combine one cup brown rice, 2 1/2 cups water, 1/2 tsp. salt, and 2 tsp. oil. Place all in a saucepan with tight lid. Bring to boil, then reduce heat and simmer 45 to 55 minutes or until liquid is absorbed and rice is tender.

TIP: If you plan to cook white or brown rice often, invest in an electric rice cooker for no-fuss, perfect rice every time.

Mom's Old Standbys

....

....
....
....
....
....
....
....
....
....
....
....
....
....
....
....
....
....
....
....
....
....
....
....
....
....
....
....
....
....

MOM'S OLD Standbys

Breads

Yeast breads take some patience while waiting for the dough to rise. If you begin early in the morning, you can have fresh baked goods by breakfast or brunch. The warm, delicious aroma of bread baking and the rich, homemade taste is more than worth the extra effort and wait. If you have no patience, try the recipes for sweet breads and muffins, or those using biscuit mix or frozen bread dough.

Universal Dough

Use this for scones, dinner rolls or cinnamon rolls!

1/2 cup cooking oil	1 pkg. yeast
2 tsp. salt	2 eggs, beaten
1/2 cup granulated sugar	5 cups flour
1 cup evaporated milk	Shortening for greasing bowl and pans

In large bowl, combine oil, salt and sugar. Add milk. Add yeast and let stand 15 minutes. Add eggs and flour. Mix well. Cover bowl with clean damp kitchen cloth. Let dough rise for two to three hours or until doubled in size. Dough should be light.

For scones: Roll out dough and cut into pieces. Fry in hot oil until golden on both sides. Dust with powdered sugar, if desired.

For bread or rolls: Form dough into loaves for bread or balls for rolls. Place in well-greased loaf pans or muffin tins. Grease tops of dough. Cover with kitchen cloth and allow to rise until just above lip of pan. Preheat oven to 425 degrees. Bake for ten to 15 minutes or until golden brown. Let bread cool in pan for five minutes. Remove bread from pan and finish cooling on wire rack.

For cinnamon rolls: Roll dough into wide rectangle 1/4-inch thick. Cream together one stick butter with 1/2 cup brown sugar. Spread over dough. Sprinkle well with cinnamon. Roll dough jelly-roll fashion. Cut into 1-inch thick slices. Place on greased cookie sheet. Preheat oven to 350 degrees. Bake for ten to 15 minutes or until golden brown.

Basic Rolls

1 pkg. yeast
1/4 cup warm water
1 cup milk, scalded
1/4 cup shortening

2 eggs, beaten
1 tsp. salt
1/3 cup sugar
4 1/2 cups flour

Dissolve yeast in water. Set aside until bubbly. Pour warm milk over sugar, salt and shortening. Stir until well blended. Add yeast mixture, stir to blend. Add eggs, mix well. Cool. Stir in flour and place dough in a greased bowl. Cover with clean kitchen cloth and let rise until doubled in size, about 1 hour. Punch dough down and form into rolls of desired shape. Place rolls on greased cookie sheet or in greased muffin tins. Cover and let rise until doubled again, about 1 hour. Preheat oven to 375 degrees. Bake rolls for 15 to 18 minutes or until golden brown. Remove from oven and brush tops of rolls with melted butter or margarine, if desired.

Cinnamon Puffs

1 pkg. yeast
1/4 cup warm water
1/2 cup milk, scalded and cooled
1/8 cup granulated sugar
1/4 tsp. salt
1/4 cup cooking oil

1 egg, beaten
2 cups flour
1 1/2 tsp. vanilla extract
1/4 cup butter or margarine, melted
1/2 cup granulated sugar
1 Tbsp. cinnamon

In large bowl, dissolve yeast in warm water. Set aside for ten minutes. Stir in milk, sugar, salt, oil, egg and one cup flour. Mix well. Beat in additional flour and vanilla until dough is sticky. Spoon dough into greased muffin tins. Let rise until doubled in size, about 45 minutes. Preheat oven to 375 degrees. Bake for 15 to 18 minutes or until golden brown. Place melted butter or margarine in small bowl. Mix sugar and cinnamon in another small bowl. Remove rolls from muffin tin. Dip in melted butter then in cinnamon-sugar.

Easy Cheese Puffs

1/4 cup butter or margarine, softened
1/2 cup flour

1/4 lb. cheese, grated

Preheat oven to 350 degrees. Mix all ingredients well. Roll into small balls about the size of large marbles. Bake on an ungreased cookie sheet for 15 to 20 minutes.

30-Minute Hamburger Buns

1 3/4 cups warm water
1/4 cup honey
1/2 cup cooking oil
3 pkgs. yeast

1 1/2 tsp. salt
2 eggs, beaten
5 cups flour

In large bowl, combine water, honey, oil and yeast. Let stand about ten minutes. Stir in salt, eggs and flour. Mix well. Shape dough into size of hamburger patties. Place buns on greased cookie sheet and let rise for ten minutes. Preheat oven to 425 degrees. Bake buns for ten minutes or until golden. Let cool. Split with knife.

60-Minute Wheat Bread

2 pkgs. yeast
2 cups warm water
1/4 cup granulated sugar

2 tsp. salt
4 cups whole-wheat flour
Shortening for greasing pans

Dissolve yeast in warm water. Let stand for ten minutes or until bubbly. Stir in sugar, salt and flour. Mix well. Spoon into two greased loaf pans. Lightly oil tops of loaves. Let rise until loaves reach top of pans, about 20 minutes. Preheat oven to 400 degrees. Bake bread for 30 minutes or until golden brown. Let cool in pans for a few minutes, then remove bread. Finish cooling on wire rack.

90-Minute White Bread

1/2 cup warm water
2 pkgs. yeast
1 1/2 cups warm water
2 Tbsp. cooking oil

2 Tbsp. granulated sugar
2 1/2 tsp. salt
4 1/2 cup flour

Dissolve yeast in warm water. Let stand for ten to 15 minutes. In large bowl, combine yeast, additional water, oil, sugar, salt and enough flour to make sticky dough. Mix well. Let stand for 15 minutes. Add more flour to make dough pliable. Turn dough onto floured surface. Knead until firm and elastic. Shape into loaves and put in greased pans. Let rise for 30 minutes. Bake at 375 degrees for 30 minutes. Remove from pans and cool on wire rack.

Simple Corn Bread

1 cup yellow cornmeal
1 cup flour
1/4 cup granulated sugar
4 tsp. baking powder

1/2 tsp. salt
1 egg, beaten
1 cup milk
1/4 cup cooking oil

Preheat oven to 425 degrees. Mix all ingredients until well blended. Pour into greased 8x8 baking pan. Bake for 20 minutes or until light golden color. Knife inserted into center should come out clean when done.

Bran Banana Bread

1/3 cup shortening
3/4 cup granulated sugar
1 egg, beaten
2 cups bran flakes cereal
1 1/2 cups flour
2 tsp. baking powder

1/2 tsp. salt
1/2 tsp. baking soda
3/4 cup nuts, chopped
2 cups bananas, mashed
2 Tbsp. water
1 tsp. vanilla extract

Preheat oven to 350 degrees. In large bowl, cream shortening and sugar. Beat in egg. Stir in bran flakes. In another bowl, sift together flour, baking powder, salt and baking soda. Stir into bran flake mixture. Combine bananas and water. Stir in vanilla. Add to flour mixture and mix well. Fold in nuts. Bake in greased loaf pan for one hour.

Soft Zucchini Bread

3 eggs, beaten
1 cup cooking oil
2 cups granulated sugar
2 cups zucchini squash, grated
1 tsp. vanilla extract

3 cups flour
1 tsp. salt
3 tsp. cinnamon
1/4 tsp. baking powder
1 tsp. baking soda

Preheat oven to 350 degrees. Combine eggs, oil and sugar. Stir in zucchini and vanilla. In separate bowl, sift flour, salt, cinnamon, baking powder and baking soda. Stir flour mixture into zucchini mixture. Bake in greased loaf pan for one hour.

Pizza Dough

1/2 cup warm water
1 Tbsp. yeast
1/3 cup cooking oil

1 cup flour
1 tsp. garlic salt
1/2 cup cornmeal

Preheat oven to 425 degrees. Dissolve yeast in water. Let stand for ten minutes. Add oil. Mix in flour, garlic salt and cornmeal. Mix until combined but soft, not stiff. Form into ball and roll out. Place on greased pizza pan or pie pan. Gently pull dough out to edges. Poke with fork randomly. Bake crust for about ten minutes. Spread on sauce and favorite toppings. (Meat should already be cooked if used as topping.) Top with cheese. Place in oven for about ten minutes longer or until done.

Pizza Wheat Crust

1 egg, beaten
1/4 cup cooking oil
2/3 cup warm water
1 1/2 cups whole-wheat flour

1/2 cup cornmeal
1 tsp. baking powder
1 tsp. salt
2 tsp. garlic powder

Preheat oven to 425 degrees. Mix egg, oil and water. Set aside. In large bowl, combine flour, cornmeal, baking powder, salt and garlic powder. Pour liquid mixture into flour mixture. Blend well with hands. Form into ball. Press onto greased pizza pan. Bake for ten minutes, or top with sauce, toppings and cheese, then cook in oven for ten to 20 minutes or until done through.

Early American Brown Bread

2 cups whole-wheat flour
3/4 cup white flour
1 cup brown sugar, packed
2 tsp. baking soda

1/2 tsp. salt
2 cups milk
4 tsp. juice or vinegar

In a large bowl, mix wheat flour, white flour, brown sugar, baking soda and salt. In a small bowl, combine milk and lemon juice or vinegar. Let stand ten minutes. Stir milk mixture gradually into flour mixture until well blended. Spoon batter into greased loaf pan. Preheat oven to 350 degrees. Bake for one hour.

Basic Muffin Mix

2 cups flour, sifted
1 Tbsp. baking powder
1/2 tsp. salt
3 Tbsp. sugar

1 egg, beaten
1 cup milk
3 Tbsp. cooking oil or melted shortening

Preheat oven to 450 degrees. Sift together flour, baking powder, salt and sugar. Combine egg, milk and oil. Pour into dry ingredients. Stir only until moist. Do not over-mix. Spoon batter into greased muffin tins, filling cups about two-thirds full. Bake at 450 degrees for 20 to 25 minutes. Try the delicious variations below.

Muffin Mix Variations:

Apple-Nutmeg. Peel and dice one medium apple. Sprinkle with one teaspoon nutmeg and two tablespoons of sugar. Stir into batter.

Apricot-Nut. Drain 1/2 cup cooked, pitted and finely chopped apricots. Combine with 1/2 cup chopped walnuts. Stir into batter.

Cheese-Garlic. Combine one cup grated cheese with 1/8 teaspoon garlic salt. Stir well into dry ingredients then add egg, milk and oil. Bake 20 to 25 minutes.

Lemon-Sugar. Combine 1/2 cup sugar with two tablespoons grated lemon peel. Fill tins to one-fourth full with batter. Sprinkle with sugar mixture, then top with another layer of batter to fill two-thirds full.

Berries. Drain 3/4 cup canned or freshly washed berries. Add 1/4 cup granulated sugar and 1/8 teaspoon cinnamon. Gently fold into muffin batter.

Carrots. Add 1/2 cup of shredded carrots to dry ingredients.

Jam or Preserves. Fill muffin tins half-full of basic muffin mix batter. Put 1 teaspoon of jam in middle of each. Top with batter so cups are two-thirds full.

Orange. Use only 3/4 cup milk and add 1/4 cup orange juice. Grate one tablespoon of orange peel and stir into liquid ingredients. Mix in dry ingredients.

Pineapple. Drain one cup crushed pineapple. Stir into batter just until well mixed.

Buttermilk Oatmeal Muffins

1 cup milk
2 tsp. lemon juice or vinegar
1 cup quick-cooking oatmeal
1/3 cup butter or margarine
1/2 cup brown sugar, packed
1 egg, beaten

1 cup flour
1 tsp. baking powder
1/2 tsp. baking soda
1 tsp. salt
3/4 cup raisins
1/2 cup nuts, chopped

Preheat oven to 400 degrees. Combine milk and lemon juice or vinegar. Soak oatmeal in milk for 30 minutes. Cream butter or margarine, sugar and egg. Sift together flour, baking powder, baking soda and salt. Stir into creamed mixture. Stir in raisins and nuts just until moistened. Stir in oatmeal. Spoon into greased muffin tins. Bake for 20 minutes.

Spiced Pumpkin Bread

1 3/4 cups flour
1/4 tsp. salt
1 tsp. baking soda
1/2 tsp. cinnamon
1/2 tsp. nutmeg
1 cup cooked pumpkin

1 1/2 cups granulated sugar
2 eggs, beaten
1/2 cup cooking oil
1/2 cup water
1/2 cup nuts, chopped
1 cup raisins or chocolate chips

Preheat oven to 350 degrees. In bowl, sift flour, salt, baking soda, cinnamon and nutmeg. In another bowl, combine pumpkin, sugar, eggs, oil and water. Beat into flour mixture. Fold in nuts, raisins or chocolate chips. Pour into greased loaf pan. Bake for one hour.

Zesty Lemon Bread

1/3 cup butter or margarine
1 cup granulated sugar
2 eggs
1/4 tsp. almond extract
1 1/2 cups flour
1 tsp. salt

1 1/2 tsp. baking powder
1/2 cup milk
1 Tbsp. lemon peel grated
1/2 cup nuts, chopped
3 Tbsp. lemon juice
1/4 cup granulated sugar

Preheat oven to 325 degrees. Cream butter and sugar. Beat in eggs and extract. Sift flour, salt and baking powder. Add to egg mixture alternately with milk. Fold in lemon peel and nuts. Pour into loaf pan. Bake for one hour and ten minutes. Mix lemon juice and 1/4 cup sugar. Spoon over hot bread.

Simple Cinnamon Rolls

2 1/4 cups biscuit mix
2/3 cup milk
1/4 cup sugar
1 1/2 tsp. cinnamon

1/4 cup butter or margarine, melted
1/2 cup nuts, chopped
1/2 cup raisins

Preheat oven to 425 degrees. Beat biscuit mix and milk together until dough is stiff. Knead on flour surface until dough is smooth. Roll out into rectangle. Spread top with half of the melted butter. Sprinkle with sugar, cinnamon, nuts and raisins. Roll dough up tightly and press to seal. Cut into ten slices. Place rolls close together on greased cookie sheet. Brush with remaining melted butter. Bake for ten to twelve minutes or until golden.

Quick and Easy Donuts

2 cups biscuit mix
1/3 cup granulated sugar
1/3 cup milk
1 tsp. vanilla extract

1 egg, beaten
1/2 tsp. cinnamon
1/4 tsp. nutmeg

Mix all ingredients until well blended. Turn onto floured surface and knead until smooth. Roll out into a rectangle 1/2-inch thick. Cut into donuts with cookie cutter. Drop into hot oil and fry on each side until golden. Remove with tongs. Drain on paper towels. Roll donuts in powdered or granulated sugar.

Caramel Pecan Rolls

1 loaf frozen bread dough
Cooking oil
1/4 cup butter or margarine
1/2 cup brown sugar, packed
3/4 cup pecan halves

2 Tbsp. light corn syrup
4 Tbsp. butter or margarine, melted
1/4 cup granulated sugar
2 tsp. cinnamon

Preheat oven to 375 degrees. Brush frozen loaf with oil. Cover with clean cloth and thaw, about 3 hours. Melt 1/4 cup butter in saucepan. Stir in brown sugar, pecans and corn syrup. Spread in bottom of 9x13 baking pan. Set aside. Roll dough into rectangle. Brush with four tablespoons melted butter. Sprinkle with sugar and cinnamon. Roll up tightly and pinch to seal. Cut into twelve slices. Place slightly apart in baking pan. Let rise until doubled, about 1 hour. Bake for 15 to 20 minutes. Turn pan over onto large tray. Leave pan on top of rolls for a moment so that caramel drizzles down.

Healthy Carrot Muffins

1 cup white flour
2 cups whole-wheat flour
2 tsp. baking powder
1 cup carrots, grated
1/4 cup honey
2 eggs, beaten

1 tsp. baking soda
1/2 tsp. salt
1 tsp. cinnamon
1/3 cup cooking oil
1 1/2 cups milk

Preheat oven to 400 degrees. Sift together dry ingredients. Stir in remaining ingredients, until moist; do not over-mix. Fill greased muffin tins about 2/3 full. Bake for 20 minutes.

Baking Soda Drop Biscuits

2 cups flour
3/4 tsp. baking soda
1/2 tsp. salt

1/2 cup shortening
1/4 cup vinegar
1/2 cup milk

Preheat oven to 450 degrees. Sift together flour, baking soda and salt. Cut in shortening. Stir in vinegar and milk until dough is sticky. Spoon onto greased cookie sheet. Bake for twelve to 15 minutes, or until light golden brown.

Rich Buttermilk Biscuits

1 cup flour
1/2 tsp. salt
2 tsp. baking powder
1/8 tsp. baking soda

1/8 cup shortening
1/2 cup milk
1 tsp. lemon juice or vinegar

Preheat oven to 450 degrees. Sift flour, salt, baking powder and baking soda. Cut in shortening. Combine milk and lemon juice or vinegar. Stir into flour mixture to make soft dough. Turn dough onto floured surface. Knead until soft and elastic. Roll into rectangle about 1/2-inch thick. Cut into biscuits. Place on ungreased cookie sheet. Bake for eight to ten minutes.

Simple Pretzels

1 loaf frozen bread dough
1 egg white, slightly beaten

1 Tbsp. water
Coarse salt

Thaw bread completely. On floured surface, roll into square. Cut dough into 30 strips. Roll each strip between palms into long rope. Shape into pretzels by tying in a loose knot and looping ends through. Pinch to seal. Let stand for 30 minutes. Mix egg white and water. Brush mixture on pretzels and sprinkle with coarse salt. Bake on greased cookie sheet at 350 degrees for 15 to 18 minutes or until pretzels are golden brown.

Easy Bread Sticks

2 hard hot dog buns
melted butter or margarine

Parmesan cheese

Preheat oven to 350 degrees. Cut each bun lengthwise into 4 sticks. Brush with melted butter. Sprinkle with parmesan cheese. Bake on lightly greased cookie sheet for ten minutes or until sticks begin to turn golden brown. Serve while still warm.

MOM'S OLD Standbys

Mom's Old Standbys

MOM'S OLD Standbys

Mom's Old Standbys

Beverages

Bubbly Grapefruit Ice

1 can grapefruit sections
1 cup granulated sugar
1 lemon, juiced

2 cups water
6 cups ginger ale

Drain grapefruit sections. Set aside juice. Beat together grapefruit sections and sugar. Add grapefruit juice, lemon juice and water. Mix well. Freeze in bowl. When ready to serve, let mixture thaw slightly, then scoop into glasses. Fill glasses with ginger ale. Garnish with mint leaf, if desired.

Fresh Lemonade

1/4 cup granulated sugar
1/2 cup hot water
Peel of 1 lemon, grated

2 lemons, juiced
2 cups cold water

Dissolve sugar in hot water. Add grated lemon peel. Let cool. Add lemon juice and cold water. Stir until well mixed. Strain, if desired. Serve over ice. Garnish with slice of lemon.

Limeade Zing

1 can frozen limeade
3 cups sugar

8 cups water
2 quarts lemon-lime carbonated beverage

Make limeade according to can. Combine sugar and water, stirring until sugar is dissolved. Add limeade. Freeze in large bowl. Two hours before serving, remove from freezer and allow to thaw in punch bowl. One hour before serving, pour carbonated beverage over slush. To make by glass, put in 1/3 glass of slush and fill with carbonated beverage.

Sweet Cherry-Apple Punch

1 pkg. unsweetened cherry drink mix
6-oz. can frozen lemonade
2 cups unsweetened apple juice

1 quart cold water
1/4 cup granulated sugar

Combine all ingredients, stirring until sugar is dissolved. Place in glasses over ice cubes. Enjoy!

Orange Slush

2 cups cold water
2 cups granulated sugar

6-oz. can frozen orange juice
Ginger ale

Combine water and sugar in saucepan. Heat to boiling. Boil for two minutes. Remove from heat. Stir in orange juice. Freeze. When ready to serve, spoon slush into glasses and fill with ginger ale. For variation, instead of orange juice substitute a 6-oz. can of any frozen juice or cocktail concentrate.

Tangy Citrus Punch

1 pkg. unsweetened orange drink mix
1 pkg. unsweetened lime drink mix
1 pkg. unsweetened lemonade mix

1 1/2 cups granulated sugar
9 cups water
Ginger ale

Mix each of the unsweetened drink mixes separately with 1/2 cup sugar and 3 cups water until sugar is dissolved. Pour each into separate ice cube trays and freeze. When ready to serve, put a cube of each flavor into glass and fill with ginger ale. Stir until slightly thawed. Garnish with lemon or lime slice, if desired. For a creamy treat, add a scoop of sherbet to glasses before ginger ale.

Triple Fruit Punch

2 quarts unsweetened apple juice
2 cups cranberry juice

2 cups orange juice
16-oz. bottle ginger ale

Mix all ingredients well. Serve chilled over ice.

Orange Jubilee

2 cups milk
1/2 cup frozen orange juice
2 eggs, beaten

2 Tbsp. granulated sugar
2 tsp. vanilla extract

Place all ingredients in jar with screw-on lid. Shake vigorously.

Sweet Banana Shake

1 cup instant dry milk
2 cups cold water

3 Tbsp. honey
3 ripe bananas, mashed

Stir dry milk into water. Place in jar with screw-on lid. Shake until smooth. Add honey and bananas. Cover and shake vigorously.

Creamy Berry Floats

2 scoops vanilla ice cream
1 cup berries

1 12-oz. bottle ginger ale

Put scoop of ice cream in each of two glasses. Spoon half the berries over each. Fill glasses with ginger ale. Stir gently. Serve.

Pineapple Floats

2 cups pineapple juice
2 cups ginger ale

4 scoops of sherbet

Fill two glasses each halfway with pineapple juice. Drop two scoops of sherbet into each one. Fill to top with ginger ale. Stir until mixed. Serve immediately.

Jiffy Hot Chocolate

2 tsp. cocoa
1 Tbsp. corn syrup
Dash of salt

3/4 cup boiling water
Milk or light cream

Mix the cocoa, corn syrup and salt in a mug or cup. Add boiling water. Stir to completely dissolve. Dilute to taste with milk or light cream. Add miniature marshmallows, if desired.

Steaming Autumn Treat

3 quarts orange juice
3 oz. can pre-sweetened lemonade mix
1/3 cup sugar

1 tsp. cinnamon
1/2 tsp. ground cloves

Mix all ingredients together in large pan. Add water to taste. Bring to boil. Simmer. Serve warm.

Winter Wassail

1 gallon apple cider
2 quarts orange juice
1 cup granulated sugar

1/2 tsp. salt
3 cinnamon sticks
1/2 tsp. whole cloves

Mix all ingredients in large pan. Simmer over low heat for three hours. Strain and serve hot. Garnish with cinnamon stick, if desired.

Traditional Eggnog

3 eggs, slightly beaten
1/2 cup granulated sugar
1/4 tsp. salt
3 cups milk

1 1/2 cups evaporated milk
1/2 tsp. vanilla extract
Dash of nutmeg and cinnamon

In small saucepan, combine eggs, sugar and salt. Stir in milk and canned milk. Cook over boiling water (in double boiler) until mixture coats spoon, about ten minutes. Stir constantly to prevent scorching. Remove from heat. When cool, stir in vanilla. Chill. Strain, if needed. Beat until frothy. Add a dash of cinnamon and nutmeg to each serving.

No-Cook Eggnog

5 eggs, well beaten
1/2 cup evaporated milk
1 pkg. instant vanilla pudding mix
3/4 cup granulated sugar

7 cups milk
1/2 tsp. vanilla extract
Dash of nutmeg and cinnamon

Beat eggs with canned milk and instant pudding mix. Stir in sugar until well dissolved. Add milk and vanilla. Stir well. Sprinkle with dash of cinnamon and nutmeg in each glass at serving time.

Easy Strawberry Soda

1 Tbsp. strawberry jam
1/2 cup vanilla ice cream

Ginger ale

Spoon strawberry jam into bottom of tall glass. Drop in scoop of ice cream. Fill glass with ginger ale. Stir gently. Serve.

Cherry Soda

1 pkg. unsweetened cherry drink mix
1 cup granulated sugar
2 cups cold milk

Vanilla ice cream
Ginger ale

Combine drink mix, sugar and milk until well blended. Pour into six glasses. Add scoop of vanilla ice cream to each glass. Fill glasses with ginger ale.

Spiced Grape Juice

4 cups water
3/4 cup sugar
2 cinnamon sticks
8 whole cloves

4 cups grape juice
2 cups orange juice
Lemon slices

Combine water, sugar and spices. Boil for ten minutes. Strain. Add fruit juices to spiced water. Heat. Serve hot with lemon slices.

Hot Cider Punch

4 cups water
4 cups apple juice
1 cup raspberry powdered punch drink

1/8 tsp. ground cloves
1/4 tsp. cinnamon
1/8 tsp. nutmeg

Mix all ingredients in large pan. Simmer over low heat. Serve hot. Garnish with cinnamon stick and mint leaf, if desired.

Mexican Hot Chocolate

1 pkg. IBARRA Mexican-style sweet
  chocolate wedges
1 or 2 gallons 2% milk

Cinnamon sticks
Mini candy canes

Find IBARRA chocolate in the Mexican food section of the grocery store. The box comes with three discs, eight wedges per disc. Break wedges apart using a tablespoon and kitchen mallet. In blender, place two or three chocolate wedges per cup of cold milk. Let stand about 15 minutes to soften wedges. Blend well.

Pour cold mixture into large pan. Heat on stove slowly until warm. Do not boil. Place cinnamon stick and candy cane in each cup. Fill with hot chocolate and let cool to warm. Serve warm.

Mom's Old Standbys

MOM'S OLD Standbys

Mom's Old Standbys

Cakes, Pies & Puddings

Applesauce Cake

2 cups flour
1 tsp. cinnamon
1 tsp. baking powder
1/2 tsp. nutmeg
1/2 tsp. cloves

1 cup granulated sugar
1 Tbsp. cocoa
1 cup applesauce
1/2 cup cooking oil

Preheat oven to 350 degrees. Mix all ingredients until well blended. Pour into a 9-inch cake pan. Bake for 35 minutes.

Carrot Cake

1 cup cooking oil
2 cups granulated sugar
3 eggs, beaten
2 cups carrots, grated
1 small can crushed pineapple
3 cups flour

1 tsp. cinnamon
1 tsp. baking soda
1 1/2 cups nuts, chopped
1 1/2 cups raisins
1 tsp. vanilla extract

Preheat oven to 350 degrees. Combine oil and sugar. Add eggs, carrots and pineapple. Sift together flour, cinnamon and soda. Stir into batter and blend well. Stir in vanilla, nuts and raisins. Spread batter into greased 9x13 pan. Bake for 45 to 50 minutes or until center springs back when lightly touched.

Chocolate-Mayonnaise Surprise

2 cups flour
2 tsp. baking soda
4 Tbsp. cocoa
1 cup water

1 cup granulated sugar
1 cup mayonnaise
2 tsp. vanilla

Preheat oven to 350 degrees. Sift flour, baking soda and cocoa. Set aside. In large bowl, beat sugar, mayonnaise, water and vanilla. Stir in flour mixture until well blended. Pour batter into two greased and floured layer cake pans or one greased and floured 9x13 cake pan. Bake for 30 to 35 minutes for layer pans or 30 minutes for an oblong pan. Let cool thoroughly, then frost.

Dump-It Cake

Preheat oven to 350 degrees. Grease 9x13 cake pan.
Dump 1 can applesauce into pan.
Dump 1 can crushed pineapple on top of that.
Spread 1 pkg. dry yellow cake mix over pineapple.
Melt 1 cup butter or margarine. Pour on top of cake mix.
Sprinkle 1 1/2 cups nuts over melted butter.
Do not stir. Bake for one hour.
Top with whipped cream, if desired.

Easy Lemon Cake

1 pkg. white cake mix	3 eggs
3-oz. pkg. lemon gelatin	1 cup cold water
1/2 cup cooking oil	

Preheat oven to 375 degrees. Stir cake mix and gelatin until blended. Beat in oil, eggs and 1/2 cup water until smooth. Add another 1/2 cup water and beat one minute. Pour into greased and floured 9x13 cake pan. Bake for 30 to 35 minutes.

Any-Fruit Cobbler

1/2 cup butter or margarine	3/4 cup milk
1 cup flour	1/4 tsp. salt
1 cup granulated sugar	1 can fruit pie filling
2 tsp. baking powder	

Preheat oven to 350 degrees. Melt butter in baking pan. Stir in flour, sugar, baking powder, milk and salt until smooth. Dump fruit on top. Don't stir. Bake for one hour.

Easy Butter Frosting

1/2 cup butter or margarine	3 1/2 cups powdered sugar
2 egg whites or 1 egg, beaten	1 1/2 tsp. vanilla extract

Cream butter and eggs until fluffy. Add sugar and vanilla, beat until fluffy. Add a few drops of milk if frosting is too thick.

Creamy Caramel Frosting

1/2 cup butter or margarine
1/4 cup milk
1 cup brown sugar, packed

2 cups powdered sugar
1 1/2 tsp. vanilla extract

In saucepan, combine butter, milk and brown sugar. Heat to boiling. Cook for two minutes, stirring frequently to prevent scorching. Cool. Stir in powdered sugar and beat until smooth. Add vanilla and beat until well blended.

Simple Chocolate Frosting

1 pkg. chocolate pudding mix
   (not instant)
1 1/4 cups cold milk
1/2 cup butter or margarine

1/2 cup shortening
1 cup powdered sugar
1 tsp. vanilla
1/4 tsp. salt

Cook pudding with milk according to package directions. Set aside. Cream butter, shortening and sugar until fluffy. Stir in vanilla and salt. Gradually add pudding, beating well.

Nutty Coconut Frosting

1 1/2 cups granulated sugar
1/2 can sweetened condensed milk
1/4 cup butter or margarine

1 cup shredded coconut
1/2 cup nuts, chopped

Combine sugar, milk and butter in saucepan. Bring to a boil. Boil for three minutes, stirring constantly to prevent scorching. Remove from heat. Stir in coconut and nuts.

Lemon Glaze

1/2 cup boiling water
1 cup powdered sugar, sifted
1 Tbsp. canned milk

1 tsp. lemon juice
1/2 tsp. lemon peel, grated

Combine boiling water and sugar until smooth. Stir in milk, lemon juice and lemon peel. Pour immediately over cake.

Easy Apple Pie

3 cups apples, sliced
1 cup water
1 cup granulated sugar

2 Tbsp. butter or margarine
2 Tbsp. cornstarch
1 tsp. cinnamon

Preheat oven to 350 degrees. Combine all ingredients in a saucepan. Boil for three minutes. Remove from heat. Cool to lukewarm. Pour into pie crust. Bake for 50 minutes.

Fresh Peach Pie

1 cup peaches, mashed
3/4 cup water
1 cup granulated sugar

3 Tbsp. cornstarch
1 tsp. cinnamon
3 cups sliced peaches

In saucepan, combine mashed peaches with water, sugar and cornstarch. Bring to boil. Reduce heat and simmer for five minutes, stirring constantly. Stir in cinnamon. Arrange sliced peaches in prebaked pie shell. Pour peach mixture over sliced peaches. Chill in refrigerator until set. Top with whipped cream, if desired.

Strawberry-Banana Pie

1/2 cup strawberries, mashed
1 cup granulated sugar
3 Tbsp. cornstarch

1 Tbsp. lemon juice
2 cups strawberries, sliced
2 bananas, sliced

Add enough water to mashed berries to make one cup. In saucepan, combine berries, sugar, cornstarch and lemon juice. Cook over medium heat until thick. Fill 8-inch prebaked pie shell with sliced strawberries and bananas. Pour glaze over top. Chill and serve.

No-Bake Pumpkin Pie

1 pkg. instant vanilla pudding
1/2 cup milk

1 cup cooked pumpkin
3/4 tsp. pumpkin pie spice

Combine all ingredients in large bowl. Beat until well-blended. Pour into prebaked pie shell. Chill for about two hours.

Incredible Coconut Pie

1/2 cup flour
1 cup granulated sugar
1/4 cup butter or margarine, melted
4 eggs, beaten

2 cups milk
1 tsp. vanilla extract
7-oz. pkg. shredded coconut

(No pie shell needed.) In large bowl, combine flour and sugar. Add butter, eggs, milk and vanilla until well blended. Stir in coconut. Pour into buttered 10-inch pie plate. Put in cold oven. Heat to 350 degrees. Bake for 45 minutes. Cool.

Lemon Cream Pie

1 can frozen lemonade concentrate
1 9-oz. container frozen whipped
   topping, thawed

1 can sweetened condensed milk
1 graham cracker crust

Combine lemonade, whipped topping and milk. Beat until creamy. Pour into crust. Chill until firm.

Graham Cracker Crust

1/4 cup butter or margarine, melted
1 1/2 cups graham cracker crumbs
2 Tbsp. brown sugar, packed

1/4 tsp. cinnamon
1/8 tsp. nutmeg

Combine all ingredients until well blended. Press into 9-inch pie plate. Bake at 350 degrees for eight minutes.

Easiest-Ever Pie Crust

1 1/2 cups flour, white or whole-wheat
1/2 cups cooking oil
3/4 tsp. salt

2 Tbsp. granulated sugar
2 Tbsp. cold water or milk

Dump flour in an ungreased pie plate. Add oil, salt, sugar and stir well. Pour in water or milk. Mix with fork into stiff dough. Press into shape in pie plate. Bake at 350 degrees for ten to twelve minutes or until pie crust is lightly browned.

Never-Fail Pie Crust

3/4 cup shortening
1 1/2 cups flour
1/4 tsp. salt

2 1/2 Tbsp. cold water
1 1/2 tsp. vinegar
1 egg, beaten

Use pastry blender or two knives to cut shortening into flour and salt until crumbly. Combine water, vinegar and egg. Blend well into flour mixture. Shape dough into two balls. The ball of dough can be used immediately or wrapped and frozen for later use. To use, flatten ball. Using a flour-dusted rolling pin, roll dough into circle about two inches larger than rim of pie plate. Put dough in plate, prick bottom with fork and moisten the rim slightly. Bake at 475 degrees for eight minutes or until lightly browned. Let cool.

Apple Banana Pudding

2 1/2 cups apple juice
2 bananas

5 Tbsp. cornstarch

Blend bananas and apple juice in blender. Add cornstarch and mix until well blended. Cook over medium heat until thickened, stirring constantly. Arrange sliced bananas in bottom of serving dish. Pour hot mixture over bananas. Chill until set.

One-Pan Rice Pudding

1/2 cup long-grain rice
1 cup water, slightly salted
1 quart milk
1/4 cup butter
3 eggs

1/2 cup sugar
1 cup raisins
1/2 tsp. vanilla extract
3 Tbsp. sugar
1 Tbsp. cinnamon

Pour rice slowly into boiling water. Cover and cook seven to ten minutes. Add milk and butter. Stir and bring to boil Cover and turn to low. Cook for one hour. Meanwhile, beat eggs, add sugar, raisins and vanilla. Pour mixture into rice, stirring slowly until rice starts thicken and bubble. Serve with cinnamon-sugar on top.

MOM'S OLD Standbys

Mom's Old Standbys

Cookies & Bars

Classic Chocolate Chip Cookies

1 cup shortening
1 cup granulated sugar
1/2 cup brown sugar, packed
2 eggs, beaten
1 tsp. vanilla extract
1 tsp. baking soda

2 Tbsp. warm water
1/2 tsp. salt
3 cups flour
1 cup nuts, chopped
12-oz. pkg. chocolate chips

Preheat oven to 375 degrees. Cream together shortening, sugars, eggs and vanilla. Add remaining ingredients. Bake for eight to ten minutes. Do not overbake. Cool on wire rack.

Chewy Oatmeal Cookies

3/4 cup shortening
1 cup brown sugar
1/2 cup granulated sugar
1/4 cup water
1 egg

1 tsp. vanilla extract
1 cup flour
1/2 tsp. baking soda
1 tsp. salt
3 cups quick-cooking oatmeal

Preheat oven to 350 degrees. Cream together shortening, sugars, water, egg and vanilla. Sift together flour, baking soda and salt. Add to creamed mixture. Stir in oatmeal until well blended. Fold in nuts and raisins, if desired. Drop by spoonfuls onto greased cookie sheets. Bake for twelve to 15 minutes.

Peanut Butter Cookies

1 1/4 tsp. flour
1/4 tsp. salt
1/4 tsp. baking soda
1/2 cup butter or margarine

1/2 cup peanut butter
1/2 cup granulated sugar
1/2 cup brown sugar
1 egg

Preheat oven to 375 degrees. Combine flour, salt and baking soda. Set aside. In large bowl, mix butter and peanut butter. Add sugars, mixing well. Beat in egg. Stir flour mixture into peanut butter mixture. Blend well. Drop by spoonfuls onto greased cookie sheet. Flatten with fork. Bake for ten to 15 minutes.

Moist Sugar Cookies

1/2 cup butter or margarine
1/2 cup granulated sugar
1 egg
1/2 cup cooking oil

1/2 cup powdered sugar
1/2 tsp. cream of tartar
1/2 tsp. baking soda
2 cups flour

Preheat oven to 350 degrees. Cream butter and sugar. Add remaining ingredients. Drop by small spoonfuls onto ungreased cookie sheet. Dip bottom of glass in granulated sugar and press cookies slightly. Bake for seven minutes.

Applesauce Cookies

1 cup granulated sugar
1/2 cup shortening
1 egg
1 cup applesauce
1 tsp. baking soda
1 3/4 cups flour

1/2 tsp. salt
1 tsp. nutmeg
1 tsp. cinnamon
1 cup quick-cooking oatmeal
1 cup raisins
1 cup nuts, chopped

Preheat oven to 425 degrees. Cream sugar and shortening until fluffy. Beat in egg. Combine applesauce and baking soda. Add to mixture. Set aside. In large bowl, sift together flour, salt, nutmeg and cinnamon. Stir in egg mixture and blend well. Add oatmeal, raisins and nuts. Stir until well moistened. Drop by spoonfuls onto greased cookie sheet. Bake for ten minutes.

Carrot Cookies

1/4 cup butter or margarine
1/2 cup granulated sugar
1 egg, beaten
1/2 tsp. vanilla extract
1/2 tsp. lemon extract

1 cup sifted flour
1 tsp. baking powder
Pinch of salt
1/2 cup carrots, grated

Preheat oven to 375 degrees. Cream butter and sugar. Stir in egg. Add vanilla and lemon extracts. Sift together flour, baking powder and salt. Stir into creamed mixture until moistened. Beat in grated carrots until well blended. Drop by spoonfuls on greased cookie sheet. Bake for ten to 13 minutes.

Orange Cookies

1 pkg. chocolate cake mix
1 orange peel, grated
1 cup nuts, chopped

2 cups quick-cooking oatmeal
2 eggs
3/4 cup cooking oil

Preheat oven to 375 degrees. Stir together cake mix, orange peel, nuts and oatmeal. Set aside. In a small bowl, beat eggs and oil. Add to the flour mixture. Blend well. Drop by spoonfuls onto greased cookie sheet. Bake for twelve minutes. Cool on wire rack.

Pumpkin Cookies

1 1/4 cups flour
2 tsp. baking powder
1/2 cups shortening
1/2 cup granulated sugar
1 egg, beaten

1/2 cup pumpkin, cooked
1/2 tsp. vanilla extract
1/2 cup nuts, chopped
1/2 tsp. lemon extract
1/2 cup raisins

Preheat oven to 350 degrees. Sift flour and baking powder together. Set aside. Cream shortening and sugar until well-blended. Stir in flour mixture until moistened. Stir in egg, pumpkin, vanilla, nuts, lemon extract and raisins. Drop by spoonfuls onto cookie sheet covered with foil. Bake for 15 minutes.

Soft Zucchini Cookies

1/2 cup shortening
1/2 cup granulated sugar
1 cup brown sugar
2 eggs, beaten
3 cups zucchini, grated
2 1/2 cup flour
1 tsp. baking powder

1/2 tsp. baking soda
1 tsp. cinnamon
1/2 tsp. salt
2 cups quick-cooking oatmeal
1 cut nuts, chopped
1 cup raisins

Preheat oven to 375 degrees. Cream together shortening, sugars and eggs until light and fluffy. Stir in grated zucchini. Sift together flour, baking powder, baking soda, cinnamon and salt. Add to zucchini mixture. Stir in oatmeal until well blended. Add nuts and raisins. Drop by spoonfuls onto greased cookie sheet. Bake for twelve to 15 minutes.

Chocolate Chip Bars

2 3/4 cup flour
2 1/2 tsp. baking powder
1/2 tsp. salt
2/3 cup shortening

1 lb. pkg. brown sugar
3 eggs, slightly beaten
12-oz. pkg. chocolate chips
1 cup nuts, chopped

Preheat oven to 350 degrees. Sift together flour, baking powder and salt. Set aside. Cream shortening and brown sugar. Add eggs until well-blended. Add flour mixture. Stir to moisten. Stir in chocolate chips and nuts. Spread batter in greased 9x13 baking pan. Bake for 25 minutes.

English Toffee Bars

1/4 cup granulated sugar
1/4 cup brown sugar
1 cup flour, sifted
1/4 cup nuts, chopped

1/2 cup butter or margarine
1 egg yolk
1/2 tsp. vanilla extract
6-oz. pkg. chocolate chips

Preheat oven to 250 degrees. Cream together sugars and butter until smooth. Add egg yolk and vanilla, stirring until well-blended. Mix in flour. Spread evenly in greased 8 x 8 pan. Bake for 15 minutes. Remove from oven. Immediately sprinkle chocolate chips over surface. When chips melt completely, spread them evenly over surface. Sprinkle with nuts.

Lemon Drifts

1 cup butter or margarine
1/2 cup powdered sugar
2 cups flour
4 eggs, beaten

2 cups granulated sugar
1/2 cups lemon juice
5 Tbsp. flour
1 tsp. baking powder

Preheat oven to 350 degrees. Beat butter, powdered sugar and two cups flour together until smooth. Spread into greased 9x13 pan. Bake for 20 minutes. Beat together eggs, granulated sugar, lemon juice, five tablespoons flour and baking powder until well blended. The mixture will be thin. Pour over top of baked crust. Continue baking for 25 minutes. Sprinkle with powdered sugar. Cool and cut into bars.

Spicy Nut Bars

1/2 pkg. spice cake mix
1 egg
1/2 cup cooking oil
1 cup quick-cooking oatmeal

1/2 cup raisins
1/2 cup nuts, chopped
1/2 cup plain yogurt

Preheat oven to 375 degrees. Combine all ingredients until well blended. Spread mixture in greased 8 x 8 baking pan. Bake for 15 minutes. Cool and cut into bars.

Easy Brownies

1/2 cup butter or margarine
1 cup granulated sugar
1 tsp. vanilla extract
2 eggs

1/4 cup cocoa
3/4 cup flour
1/2 cup nuts, chopped

Preheat oven to 350 degrees. Melt butter and let cool. Stir in sugar and vanilla. Beat in eggs. Stir cocoa and flour together. Blend into creamed mixture. Fold in nuts. Press into greased, floured 8 x 8 baking pan. Bake for 25 to 30 minutes. Do not overbake. Cool pan on wire rack before cutting into squares.

Applesauce Brownies

1 cup shortening
3 squares baking chocolate
2 cups granulated sugar
4 eggs, beaten
1 cup applesauce
2 tsp. vanilla extract

2 cups flour
1 tsp. baking powder
1/2 tsp. baking soda
1/2 tsp. salt
1 cup nuts, chopped

Preheat oven to 350 degrees. Melt shortening and chocolate together in top of double boiler. Blend in sugar, eggs, applesauce and vanilla. Sift together flour, baking powder, baking soda and salt. Add to chocolate mixture. Stir in nuts. Spread in greased and floured 9x13 baking pan. Bake for 30 minutes. Cool in pan. Cut into squares. Sprinkle with powdered sugar.

Chewy Chocolate Brownies

1 large pkg. chocolate pudding mix
  (not instant)
1 cup flour
1/2 tsp. baking powder
2/3 cup butter or margarine

1 1/3 cup granulated sugar
4 eggs
2 tsp. vanilla extract
1 cup nuts, chopped

Preheat oven to 350 degrees. Stir together pudding mix, flour and baking powder until well blended. Set aside. Melt butter in saucepan. Remove from heat. Stir in sugar until well blended. Beat in eggs one at a time. Blend in vanilla and pudding mixture. Stir in nuts. Spread in greased 9x13 baking pan. Bake for 20 to 25 minutes. Do not overbake. Cool and cut into bars.

Peanut Butter Brownies

2 eggs
3/4 cup granulated sugar
1/3 cup brown sugar, packed
1/4 cup peanut butter
1/8 cup shortening

1 1/2 tsp. vanilla extract
1 cup flour
1 1/2 tsp. baking powder
1 1/2 tsp. salt
1/2 cup peanuts, chopped

Preheat oven to 325 degrees. Cream eggs, granulated sugar, brown sugar, peanut butter, shortening and vanilla until fluffy. Add flour, baking powder and salt, stirring only until moistened. Stir in peanuts. Spread into lightly greased 9x13 baking pan. Bake for 25 minutes. Cool and cut into squares.

No-Bake Caramel Drops

1 Tbsp. butter
6 Tbsp. canned milk
24 caramel candies

3 cups crispy rice cereal
2 cups corn flakes cereal
1 cup nuts, chopped

Melt butter and caramels over low heat, stirring frequently. Stir in milk. Stir together rice cereal, cornflakes and nuts in large bowl. Pour caramel mixture over cereals. Lightly butter hands. Mix and form into small balls. Chill in refrigerator.

MOM'S OLD Standbys

Mom's Old Standbys

....

....
....
....
....
....
....
....
....
....
....
....
....
....
....
....
....
....
....
....
....
....
....
....
....
....
....
....
....

Mom's Old Standbys

Candies & Sweet Treats

Caramel Corn

1 can sweetened condensed milk
2 cups brown sugar, packed
1/2 cup butter or margarine

1 cup light corn syrup
Dash of salt

Cook all ingredients in heavy saucepan to soft-ball stage (when a small amount dropped in cold water forms a soft ball.) Pour over popcorn until evenly coated. Form into balls. Store in covered container.

Raspberry Popcorn Balls

1 cup light corn syrup
3-oz. pkg. raspberry gelatin

1 cup granulated sugar
6 quarts popped popcorn

Stir together corn syrup and gelatin. Stir in sugar. Cook over low heat until sugar dissolves. Pour over popcorn. Form into balls. Store in covered container or wrap balls in plastic wrap.

Marshmallow Squares

1/4 cup butter or margarine
4 cups miniature marshmallows

1/4 cup peanut butter
5 cups crispy rice cereal

Melt butter in heavy saucepan. Add marshmallows. Cook until marshmallows melt. Stir in peanut butter. Remove from heat. Stir in cereal until well-coated. Press into buttered 9x13 pan. Cool and cut into squares.

Mixed-Up Candy

2 cups corn flakes
2 cups crispy rice cereal
1/2 cup salted peanuts
1/2 cup shredded coconut

1/2 cup dark corn syrup
1/2 cup granulated sugar
1/4 cup milk
1/4 tsp. vanilla extract

Mix cereals and peanuts in bowl. Stir to blend. Cook corn syrup, sugar and milk in saucepan, stirring constantly. Remove from heat. Add vanilla. Pour over cereal and nut mixture. Mix thoroughly, stirring in coconut. Spread on buttered cookie sheet. Let cool.

Puffed Rice Balls

1/2 cup peanut butter
1/2 cup honey

1/4 cup granulated sugar
Puffed rice cereal

Simmer peanut butter, honey and sugar until smooth. Pour over puffed rice cereal. Form into balls.

Butterscotch Freeze

1 pkg. instant butterscotch pudding mix
1 cup cold root beer

1 1/2 cups cold water

Make pudding. Beat in root beer and water. Pour into pan and freeze. Cut into squares. Roll in nuts or shredded coconut.

Eggnogsicles

2 cups vanilla ice cream
1 can frozen orange juice concentrate,
    thawed

1 egg
1 1/2 cups cold milk
Shredded coconut

Combine ice cream, orange juice concentrate and egg in large bowl. Beat until smooth. Gradually add milk, beating constantly. Pour into pan and freeze. Cut into squares. Roll in shredded coconut.

Fudgesicles

1 pkg. chocolate pudding mix
    (not instant)
2 cups milk

1 cup canned milk
1/4 cup granulated sugar

In a saucepan, combine the pudding mix, milks and sugar. Cook until thick, stirring constantly. Pour the mixture into a pan. Put in the freezer until partially frozen. Stir and spoon into paper cups. Insert wooden sticks or toothpicks for handles. Freeze until completely frozen.

Five-Minute Fudge

2/3 cup sweetened condensed milk
2 Tbsp. butter or margarine
1 2/3 cups granulated sugar
1/2 tsp. salt

2 cups miniature marshmallows
1 1/2 cups semisweet chocolate chips
1 cup nuts, chopped
1 tsp. vanilla extract

In a saucepan over medium beat, combine milk, butter, sugar and salt. Bring to boil. Cook for five minutes. Stir constantly during cooking. Remove from heat. Stir in marshmallows, chocolate chips, nuts and vanilla. Stir vigorously until marshmallows and chocolate chips are completely melted. Pour into buttered 8 x 8 square pan. Cool and cut into squares.

Rocky Road Fudge

12-oz. pkg. butterscotch chips
2 Tbsp. shortening
1 pkg. miniature marshmallows

2 cups nuts, chopped
12-oz. pkg. chocolate chips
2 Tbsp. shortening

Melt butterscotch chips and two tablespoons shortening in top of double boiler. Pour into greased 9x13 baking pan. Combine marshmallows and nuts. Spread over top and press slightly. Melt chocolate chips and two tablespoons shortening over double boiler. Pour over top and smooth with spatula. Refrigerate until firm. Cut into squares.

Peanut Brittle

2 cups granulated sugar
1/2 cup light corn syrup
1 cup water

2 1/4 cups salted peanuts
1 tsp. butter or margarine
1/4 tsp. baking soda

Spread peanuts evenly over a well-buttered cookie sheet. Set aside. Combine sugar, corn syrup and water in saucepan. Cook until color of a brown paper bag, stirring frequently, about 30 minutes. Remove from heat. Stir in butter and baking soda. Pour immediately over peanuts. Cool. Break into pieces with a wooden spoon.

Chewy Corn Flake Clusters

3/4 cup granulated sugar
Dash of salt
1/2 cup light corn syrup
1/8 cup butter or margarine

3/8 cup water
1 tsp. vanilla extract
1/4 cup chunky peanut butter
4 1/2 cups corn flakes

Combine sugar, salt, corn syrup, butter and water in a saucepan. Bring to a boil, then reduce to medium heat and cook to 236 degrees. Use candy thermometer to test temperature. Remove from heat. Stir in vanilla and peanut butter. Put corn flakes in a large buttered bowl. Pour cooked mixture over corn flakes until all are well coated. Drop by spoonfuls onto waxed paper. Cool.

Holiday Candy Logs

Make these and give as Christmas gifts!

1 pkg. graham crackers
1 egg
1 cup powdered sugar, sifted

2 Tbsp. butter or margarine
6-oz. pkg. chocolate chips
1 pkg. miniature marshmallows

Crush graham crackers and set aside. Mix egg and powdered sugar. Beat until well blended. Melt butter and chocolate chips over low heat. Stir into powdered sugar mixture. Stir in marshmallows until well blended. Form into eight logs. Roll in graham cracker crumbs. Wrap in foil and freeze. Slice to serve.

Candied Walnuts

1/2 cup brown sugar, packed
1/4 cup granulated sugar
1/4 cup sour cream

1/2 tsp. vanilla extract
1 1/2 cups walnut halves

Combine brown sugar, granulated sugar and sour cream in a saucepan. Cook to soft ball stage. Cool to lukewarm. Stir in vanilla. Stir in nuts until all are well coated. Dump out onto aluminum foil to cool.

Mom's Old Standbys

Mom's Old Standbys

Mom's Old Standbys

Easy Microwave Cooking

Using a microwave to prepare meals can cut cooking time considerably. You can defrost, warm and cook meals in minutes, not hours. Here are some rules specific to microwave cooking:

Use the Right Containers

• Do not use metal pans, dishes or utensils in the microwave.

• Do not use any container decorated with gold or metal trim.

• Do not use aluminum foil to cover dishes or cook in the microwave.

• Use heavy-duty paper plates or bowls, plastic wrap, waxed paper and paper towels in the microwave, especially when reheating or defrosting.

• For cooking larger meals, use only containers or cookware made from glass or microwave-safe material.

• If you microwave a lot, buy some microwave cookware. Look for the most versatile. An all-in-one microwave container can be used to cook food, serve meals and even store leftovers.

Be Aware of Safety

• When microwaving food with a tight-fitting lid, always open the lid facing away from you. Poke plastic covering with a fork before unwrapping so that you won't be burned by the steam.

• Because the food is hot, cooking dishes may be hot after microwaving. Use oven mitts when necessary.

Know Your Cooking Times

• The initial temperature of food will affect cooking time. Room temperature items require less time than frozen or cold foods.

• As you increase the amount of food to be cooked at one time, the cooking time must be increased as well.

• A cover speeds cooking, keeps food moist and reduces spattering.

• Food will continue to cook for a short time after it is removed from the microwave. Sometimes that's only from the time you take it from the oven until you sit down for the meal. But larger cuts of meat may need 15 to 30 minutes of standing time to finish cooking through.

• To avoid undercooking meat or poultry, check the internal temperature with a cooking thermometer right after removing from the microwave. If not hot enough, microwave a little longer.

....

Know Your Cooking Techniques

Microwave cooking requires stirring, turning and rearranging to obtain even cooking results. Stir contents, rotate the dish, or rearrange food at least once during cooking time.

When preparing cakes and other foods that cannot be stirred or rearranged, rotate the dish one quarter or one half turn during cooking.

When baking cakes, it's best to use a microwave cooking ring created especially for microwave baking.

Stirring. Microwaved food heats faster along the outside of the container than in the center. When cooking liquids, sauces, vegetables or casseroles, stir occasionally during cooking time to equalize temperature.

Arranging. Allow space between individual items when arranging food in the microwave. When cooking more than two items, place them in a circle. Leave the center open and free of food. Food should not be piled for cooking in the microwave.

The food should be uniform in size, whenever possible. When cooking food that is uneven in shape, such as chicken breasts, place the thicker part toward the outside of the dish and the thinner part toward the inside of the dish.

Browning. Most foods, especially meats, cook so quickly in the microwave that they do not have time to brown. To enhance the color of steaks, chops or hamburgers, put gravy, browning sauce, soy sauce, onion soup mix or dry gravy mix on the meat during cooking. Paprika will enhance the appearance of poultry.

Some stores carry microwave browning sleeves, pockets or wrap. You may also achieve browning by using a microwave browning grill or placing the microwaved food under the broiler of a conventional oven for a few minutes before serving.

Large cuts of meat, such as roasts or turkeys, usually do brown naturally while cooking in the microwave.

You can buy pre-packaged foods made especially for microwave cooking, such as chicken patties, fish sticks, pocket sandwiches, noodle meals, rice meals, popcorn, pot pies, pasta dishes, hot cereals, hot dogs, hot drinks, soups, premade dinners and individual-sized pizzas. Remember that, as with conventional meal preparation, the food you prepare on your own tastes better and is better for you.

Basic Bacon

Place two layers of paper towel onto a platter or large plate. Arrange single strips of bacon evenly on paper towel. Place another layer of paper towel on top of bacon. Microwave on high power for 45 seconds to one minute depending on thickness and crispness desired.

Steamy Baked Potato

Prick potato with fork several times to allow steam to escape. Place on paper towel. Microwave on high power for approximately five minutes per average size potato. Do not overcook.

Corn on the Cob

Husk the corn. Clean and rinse in cold water. Butter corn and loosely wrap in wax paper. Microwave on high power four to six minutes per cob of corn. Be careful when unwrapping – corn will be hot.

Cheesy Scrambled Eggs

3 tsp. butter or margarine	3 tsp. milk
3 eggs	1/4 cup cheese, grated

Place butter in microwave-safe dish. Microwave on high power until melted. Break eggs into dish then add milk. Scramble egg mixture with fork. Fold in grated cheese. Microwave eggs on high. Stir mixture every 30 seconds from the outside to the inside of the mixture. Cook until eggs are just past the runny stage. Let stand one to two minutes until eggs are set. Do not overcook – eggs can toughen quickly. *Do not cook eggs in the shell in a microwave. They will explode.*

Open-Face Cheese Sandwich

2 slices bread	Garlic powder or garlic salt
Butter or margarine	2 slices of cheese

Toast bread in toaster. Spread a thin layer of butter on toast. Sprinkle toast with garlic powder or garlic salt, if desired. Arrange slices of your favorite cheese on toast. Place on paper towel or paper plate. Microwave on high for ten to 15 seconds.

Microwave Baked Fruit

1 small apple
1 small pear
4 Tbsp. brown sugar

1 tsp. cinnamon
2 tsp. butter or margarine
4 Tbsp. water

Core the apple and peel the pear. Slit the skin around the middle of the apple to avoid bursting. Cut pear in half. Scoop out middle seeds. Arrange the fruit in a microwave-safe dish. Mix together sugar, cinnamon and butter. Fill each fruit middle with the mixture. Pour water into the dish around the fruit. Microwave on high power for two to four minutes per piece of fruit.

New Mexico Egg Bake

5 slices bacon, cooked and crumbled
3 Tbsp. canned green chilis, chopped
6 eggs
1 can cream-style corn

1 cup Monterey Jack cheese, grated
1 cup cheddar cheese, grated
1/2 tsp. salt
1/2 tsp. pepper

Cook bacon in microwave. Crumble and set aside. Reserve two tablespoons of bacon drippings. In large bowl, beat together drippings, eggs, chilis, cream corn, cheeses, salt and pepper. Pour into 3-quart microwave-safe dish. Microwave uncovered on medium power until eggs are set. Remove and top with crumbled bacon. Let stand a few minutes before serving.

Picky Eaters Cauliflower

1 medium head cauliflower
1/2 cup mayonnaise
2 tsp. mustard

1/4 tsp. salt
1/4 cup cheese, grated
Paprika

Cut off base of cauliflower, but leave whole head intact. Pierce bottom core with fork. Place in 2-quart microwave-safe dish. Microwave, covered, on high for six minutes per pound. Let stand for a few minutes. Mix mayonnaise, mustard and salt together. Spread over top of cauliflower. Sprinkle with cheese. Microwave for one minute or until cheese melts. Sprinkle with paprika.

Cream-Cheese Corn Chowder

1/4 cup onion, chopped
1/4 green pepper, chopped
8-oz. pkg. cream cheese, cubed
1 cup milk

1 cup chicken broth
1 can cream-style corn
1/2 tsp. salt
1/8 tsp. pepper

Place onion and green pepper in microwave-safe dish. Cover and microwave on high power for one to two minutes or until tender. Add cream cheese and milk. Microwave on medium power for three to six minutes, stirring once, until mixture is smooth. Stir in chicken broth, corn, salt and pepper. Microwave on medium power, stirring occasionally, for five to ten minutes or until chowder is hot.

Right and Ready Reuben

4 slices rye bread
Butter or margarine
1/2 cup Swiss cheese, shredded

1/4 lb. deli corned beef, thinly sliced
1/2 cup sauerkraut, drained and rinsed
1/4 cup Thousand Island dressing

Lightly toast bread in conventional toaster. Spread each slice lightly with butter or margarine. Place an equal amount of shredded cheese on each slice of toast. Place half each of corned beef on two slices of toast. Place half each of sauerkraut and dressing on remaining two slices. Pair the corned beef and sauerkraut slices of toast together to make each sandwich. Arrange on microwave-safe dish. Cover with paper towel. Microwave on high for one minute or until cheese melts.

Creamy Pita Rounds

1/2 cup creamy onion dip
2 Tbsp. milk
1 Tbsp. fresh parsley, chopped
1 clove garlic, minced

1 sweet red pepper, cut into strips
1/4 cup black olives, sliced
1 cup mozzarella cheese, grated
2 pita bread

In 1-quart microwave-safe dish, stir onion dip and milk. Add parsley and garlic. Cover and microwave on high power for three minutes, stirring once. Cut pita bread in half horizontally. Spread heaping spoonful of onion dip mixture over each pita round. Top with red peppers, olives and cheese. Arrange pita rounds on microwave-safe plate. Microwave, uncovered, on high power one to two minutes or until cheese melts. Place under broiler to brown, if desired.

Sloppy Joes

1 1/2 lbs. ground beef
2/3 cup onions, chopped
1/2 cup celery, diced
1/4 cup green pepper, diced

1/2 cup ketchup
1 Tbsp. Worcestershire sauce
1 tsp. salt
1/2 tsp. pepper

In 2-quart microwave-safe dish, crumble raw beef, onion, celery and green pepper. Cover and microwave on high for six minutes, stirring after three minutes. Drain grease. Add ketchup, Worcestershire, salt and pepper. Cover. Microwave on high for five to six minutes, stirring after three minutes. Serve on hamburger buns or French bread.

Beef Burger Stroganoff

1 lb. ground beef
1/2 cup onion, chopped
1 garlic clove, minced
1 can mushrooms, drained
1 can cream of mushroom soup

3 Tbsp. flour
1 tsp. salt
1/4 tsp. pepper
1 cup sour cream

In 2-quart microwave-safe dish, crumble raw beef, onion, garlic, mushrooms, soup, flour, salt and pepper. Cover and microwave on high 15 to 18 minutes. Mix thoroughly. Stir in sour cream.

Breaded Pecan Chicken

3 chicken breasts, boneless and skinless
1/2 cup sour cream
1 Tbsp. lemon juice
1 tsp. Worcestershire sauce
1/2 tsp. salt

1/2 tsp. paprika
1/4 tsp. garlic powder
1/4 tsp. celery salt
1/2 cup seasoned dried bread crumbs
1/4 cup pecans, chopped

Rinse and dry chicken breasts. Mix sour cream, lemon juice, Worcestershire, salt, paprika, garlic and celery salt in medium bowl. Add chicken breasts, coating each piece well. Cover and let stand in refrigerator overnight. When ready to cook, mix bread crumbs and pecans in large bowl. Roll chicken in crumbs, coating evenly. Arrange chicken breasts in a circle in a shallow microwave-safe dish, with the thickest portions toward the outside. Microwave on high power for six minutes per pound or until juices run clear.

Spicy Orange Roughy

1 lb. orange roughy fish fillets
1/4 cup mayonnaise
1/2 tsp. ground cumin
1/4 tsp. crushed red pepper

1/4 tsp. garlic powder
1/4 tsp. onion salt
1/2 cup crackers, crushed

Mix mayonnaise and spices. Coat fish with mixture. Roll in cracker crumbs. Arrange fish on microwave-safe dish with thickest portions toward outside. Microwave on high power for three to four minutes. Let stand a few seconds. Fish will flake easily when cooked well.

Mushroom-Chicken Rice

1 cup rice, uncooked
1 can mushrooms, drained
1 can cream of chicken soup
3/4 cup hot water

1/4 tsp. onion powder
1/4 tsp. garlic powder
1/4 tsp. salt

In 3-quart microwave-safe dish, mix all ingredients. Microwave, uncovered, on high power for five minutes until boiling. Reduce to medium power and microwave for 15 minutes. Fluff with fork. Let stand a few minutes before serving.

Risotto with Sweet Peas

3 Tbsp. butter or margarine
1 small onion, minced
1 clove garlic, minced
1 cup chicken broth

1 cup short-grain rice
1/2 cup frozen peas, thawed
1/4 cup parmesan cheese

In 3-quart microwave-safe dish, combine butter, onion and garlic. Microwave on high for two to three minutes. Set aside. Pour chicken broth into glass measuring cup. Microwave on high until hot. Stir rice into onions and butter. Add broth. Cover tightly and microwave on high for four to six minutes or until boiling. Microwave on medium for eight to ten minutes or until liquid is absorbed. Stir in peas and cheese. Cover. Let stand five minutes before serving.

Three-Cheese Potatoes

2 lbs. frozen hash-brown potatoes
1 can cream of mushroom soup
1/2 cup cheddar cheese, grated
1/2 cup Swiss cheese, grated
4-oz. pkg. cream cheese
2 cups sour cream

1 tsp. seasoned salt
1/4 tsp. pepper
1/4 tsp. Worcestershire sauce
1 cup corn flakes, crushed
Dash of pepper

Thaw potatoes and drain. In three-quart shallow microwave-safe dish, mix soup, cheeses, sour cream, salt, pepper and Worcestershire. Stir in potatoes. Sprinkle with corn flakes and paprika. Microwave, uncovered, on medium for 15 to 20 minutes or until bubbling.

10-Second Nachos

2 cups tortilla chips
2 Tbsp. canned green chilis
3 Tbsp. black olive, sliced

1/2 small onion, minced
1/4 cup Monterey Jack cheese, grated
1/4 cup cheddar cheese, grated

Place tortilla chips on a microwave dish or plate. Top with chilis, olives, onions and grated cheeses. Microwave ten to 15 seconds or until cheese melts completely over chips.

Quick German Chocolate Cake

1 pkg. chocolate cake mix
1 cup water
1/3 cup cooking oil

3 eggs
1 can coconut-pecan frosting

Combine cake mix, water, oil and eggs. Place frosting in bottom of microwave-safe bundt cake pan or 3-quart microwave-safe dish with cone in middle. Pour cake mixture on top of frosting. Let stand a minute or two before placing in microwave. Microwave uncovered on high power for ten to 15 minutes. Cool five to ten minutes. Invert cake onto serving dish. Serve warm or let cool completely then serve.

Brownies Now

2 squares unsweetened chocolate
1/2 cup butter or margarine
1 cup brown sugar
2 eggs, beaten

1 tsp. vanilla extract
2/3 cup flour
1/2 tsp. baking powder
1/2 cup nuts, chopped

In large microwave-safe dish, combine chocolate and butter. Microwave on medium power for two to three minutes then stir. Microwave at 30-second intervals, stirring each time, until melted. Stir in sugar and blend well. Beat in eggs. Stir in vanilla, flour, baking powder and nuts. Spread mixture evenly into 8 1/2-inch round or 8 x 8 microwave-safe cake dish. Place dish on top of microwave-safe cereal bowl in oven.

Microwave on medium power for eight minutes, then on high power for one to four minutes or until toothpick inserted into center of brownies comes out clean. Rotate one quarter turn at least twice during baking. Cool for ten to 20 minutes before serving. If you do not have chocolate squares, substitute 1/4 cup unsweetened cocoa powder.

Chocolate Fudge

1 lb. box powdered sugar
1/2 cup cocoa
1/2 tsp. salt
1/4 cup milk

1 tsp. vanilla extract
1/2 cup butter or margarine
1/2 cup nuts, chopped

Mix sugar, cocoa, salt, milk and vanilla until well-blended. Pour into a 2-quart microwave-safe dish. Top mixture with butter. Microwave on high for two minutes. Stir until smooth. Blend in nuts. Pour into a wax-lined 8 x 8 baking pan. Chill one hour.

Crunchy Peanut Brittle

1 cup granulated sugar
1/2 cup white corn syrup
1 cup roasted salted peanuts

1 tsp. butter
1 tsp. vanilla extract
1 tsp. baking soda

In two-quart microwave-safe dish, stir together sugar and corn syrup. Microwave on high for four minutes. Stir in peanuts. Microwave on high three to five minutes or until light brown. Add butter and vanilla to syrup, blending well. Microwave on high one to two minutes or until peanuts are lightly brown and syrup is very hot. Add baking soda and gently stir until light and foamy. Pour mixture onto a lightly greased cookie sheet. Let cool one hour. Break into small pieces.

Banana-Apricot Bread

1/3 cup olive oil

2/3 cup granulated sugar

1/2 tsp. orange peel, grated

2 eggs, beaten

1 cup bananas, mashed

1 1/2 cups flour

1/4 cup wheat germ

1/2 tsp. baking powder

3 fresh apricots, chopped

1/2 cup pecans, chopped

In large bowl, blend oil, sugar and orange peel until creamy. Beat in eggs and mashed bananas. In separate bowl, mix together flour, wheat germ and baking powder. Add dry ingredients to egg mixture, beating well until batter is smooth. Fold in apricots and pecans. Pour batter into microwave-safe ring cake pan. Microwave on high for six minutes, or until toothpick inserted into thickest part comes out clean. Turn out onto plate to cool before slicing.

When the Lights Go Out

Here are three recipes to help you through a short blackout: No oven, no toaster, no microwave. These treats require only a few things from the refrigerator and cupboard.

Diced Apple Salad

2 cups apples, diced

1/2 cup celery, diced

1/2 cup nuts, chopped

1/2 cup raisins

1/2 cup mayonnaise

2 tsp. sugar

Combine apples, celery, nuts and raisins in bowl. In a separate bowl, stir mayonnaise and sugar together. If needed, stir in one teaspoon milk to thin mixture. Coat salad well with dressing.

Tomato Tuna Boats

Small can tuna, drained

1/2 cup celery, chopped

2 Tbsp. onion, chopped

1/4 tsp. salt

Dash of black pepper

1/2 cup mayonnaise

3 tomatoes

3 lettuce leaves

Mix tuna, celery, onion, salt and pepper. Stir in mayonnaise. With stem end down, slice tomato into 6 wedges, cutting to, but not through, base of tomato. Spread wedges. Sprinkle with salt. Fill tomato with tuna. Serve on lettuce leaves.

Vienna Cabbage Toss

1 head cabbage, shredded

1/2 cup celery, chopped

3 Tbsp. onion, diced

1 can Vienna sausages, thinly sliced

1 cup mayonnaise

2 Tbsp. vinegar

1 tsp. salt

1/4 tsp. black pepper

In large bowl, mix cabbage, celery, onion and sausage together. In small bowl, combine mayonnaise, vinegar, salt and pepper. Beat well. Stir into salad until well coated.

Mom's Old Standbys

MOM'S OLD Standbys

Notes

5

Keeping up Appearances
Laundry & Clothing Repair

You overslept and you're in a big hurry to get dressed. You paw frantically through your drawers and dig through the clothes piled at one end of the closet. You're out of luck. Everything you own is either dirty, wrinkled, or in need of repair. The clock ticks on, and you stand by helplessly late.

You wend your way out of the theater and as you get into the glare of the lobby lights, you see it. A huge glob of mustard on the front of your new plaid shirt, absent without leave from the footlong hotdog you eagerly gobbled up in the first few minutes of the movie. It's your favorite shirt! Disaster? Not if you act quickly and know how to combat the stain.

What you wear and how you wear it is part of who you are. Your appearance, personal hygiene and the care you put into your clothes makes a statement about you – how you feel about yourself and what you represent. We're all judged on the basis of first impressions, and the condition of our clothing is a big part of that.

The Shrinking Laundry Pile

Keeping your clothes in good condition can be easy once you learn the basics of doing laundry, the secrets behind stain removal and the simple skill of mending. It all begins with choosing your clothes wisely.

Buy clothes that work for you. The best way to keep laundry manageable is to buy clothes that fit well and look good. Don't follow fashion fads. Instead, develop your own style. It's better to have a few clothes that look great on you than to have a huge wardrobe that takes a lot of upkeep. When most of it's dirty, you end up wearing something that looks awful. Throw out tight or baggy clothes.

Out with the old and in with the new. Every three months, go through clothes and make the change from winter clothing to spring clothing or from summer clothing to fall clothing. Store the out-of-season clothes in boxes for next year.

Throw away socks that are without mates or can't be mended. Avoid keeping clothes in the closet and drawers just for sentimental reasons. Either pack them away, donate them or throw them out.

Lay out your outfit for the next day before you go to bed. Then you won't forage on deadline for the perfect outfit, tossing rejects onto a dirty floor. When this happens, clean clothes end up in the dirty laundry pile, resulting in wasted time laundering.

Laundry Top 10

Do your laundry weekly or at least every two weeks. Don't let it pile up – it can become overwhelming.

1) Choose appropriate clothing.

2) Pretreat stains.

3) Put dirty clothes in hamper.

4) Sort whites, colors, delicates.

5) Mend holes, repair buttons.

6) Wash.

7) Dry.

8) Iron.

9) Hang and fold.

10) Put clothes away.

Sorting Is a Must

Do you want to keep whites white and colors bright? Take the time to sort your laundry before you dump it into the washing machine. Sorting is really quite simple.

Wash whites only with whites. To qualify for the white load, there cannot be any color at all on an article of clothing; not even a small red stripe around athletic socks.

Wash colored clothes with other colors of the same intensity. In other words, wash light-colored clothing with light-colored clothing and dark colors with dark colors.

Check labels and fabrics. If it says *dry clean only,* don't wash it. Wash delicate fabrics in their own load, even if it's small. Wash heavy fabrics, like jeans, in a load of their own. Also wash "fuzzies" like bathroom rugs and some sweaters in a separate load so that they won't deposit lint on all the other clothes. Be careful not to overload the washer.

Pay attention to how dirty your clothes are, too. If a few items are extremely dirty, wash them together in their own load. If you put heavily soiled clothes with clothes that are only lightly soiled, some of the soil may get distributed to the cleaner clothes and they may not come completely clean. If clothes are very soiled, try soaking them in soapy water and rinsing them before they are laundered.

As you sort, check the condition of your clothes. Look for loose buttons or torn seams, and repair them before washing. Keep a small sewing kit with your laundry supplies.

If you have pockets, check to make sure they're empty. You don't want an important phone number or address shredded into pieces in the bottom of the washer, or a pen leaking all over your white shirts, or a ruined ID card or driver's license. Remove pins or name badges. Brush off any loose dirt, lint or debris.

*M*om says: *Don't be a clothes horse. Have only one or two outfits that need dry cleaning. Have a small group of clothes for work or school, a few dress clothes for special occasions, some casual clothes for play and one or two grubby outfits for cleaning and dirty work.*

The Disappearing Spot

Heat sets stains. It's essential that you treat stains before you do the laundry. Once you have washed clothes in warm or hot water and dried them in the heat of a dryer, most stains are difficult, if not impossible, to remove. The faster you treat the spot, the greater your chances for successful removal.

For best results in removing a stain, treat it immediately. Fresh stains are easier to remove completely. The longer the stain is on the fabric, the more difficult it will be to get out. Even though you might not be doing your laundry until Saturday, take the time after dinner on Wednesday night to treat the stain made from the beef gravy you spilled. Once the stain has been treated, you can swish the item in the sink, hang it up to dry out and then wash it as usual on laundry day.

Before washing, check each item carefully for stains. You can expect extra soil on cuffs and necklines. Check the seat and knees of washable slacks or jeans and the front of everything. That's where spills are most likely to occur.

Purchase a stain remover or use your regular detergent. If you're using a powdered detergent, mix a little with water to make a paste and rub the paste into the stained area. If you're using a liquid or concentrate, rub a little into the stain. Use a fingernail brush to lightly scrub the stain, then launder as usual

For the most effective stain removal, use a good commercial product or a solution you make yourself in the kitchen.

Now Serving: Socks with Lemon

Do your white socks look like you walked a thousand miles in them? Then try this simple trick. Bring half a gallon of water to a boil in a large saucepan or kettle. Throw in a few slices of lemon and toss in your dingy, but freshly laundered, socks. Boil for half an hour, drain and launder again as usual. You'll be amazed at the difference!

Quick & Dirty Stain Removal

Alcohol. Stain may seem colorless but will brown without treatment. Rinse with water. Rub in liquid detergent or paste, then rinse. Sponge with vinegar. Rinse and launder as usual.

Ballpoint pen. Saturate stain with hairspray. Rub with clean cloth. Rinse and launder as usual. *OR* mix 1/2 cup rubbing alcohol with one cup water. Rub into stain until it disappears. Rinse and launder as usual.

Blood. Mix meat tenderizer and water. Rub into stain. Let set for 30 minutes. Rinse in two quarts cool water and one tablespoon of ammonia. Rinse and dry in sun. *OR* flush stain with cool water. Soak in cold water for 30 minutes. Rinse. Work detergent into stain. Wash using bleach safe for fabric. *OR* sponge stain with cool water. Work spoonful of 3% hydrogen peroxide into stain. When foaming stops, rinse in cool water. Launder as usual. *OR* make a paste of starch and water. Rub into stain. Let dry. Peel dried paste away. Rinse and launder.

Butter or margarine. For whites, rub stain with kitchen cleanser. Let stand for 15 to 30 minutes. Rinse with cool water. Launder as usual. *OR* mix borax, cleanser and water into paste. Test on concealed area of fabric. If fabric does not discolor, work paste into stain. Launder without first rinsing paste out of fabric.

Candle wax. Scrape wax off with dull knife. Place stained area between paper towels or pieces of brown paper sack. Press with warm iron until wax absorbs into towel or sack. Launder in hottest water safe for fabric.

Carbon paper. Make a paste of detergent and water, or use liquid detergent. Work into stain. Rinse with cool water. Launder as usual. If stain remains, before laundering, work a little household ammonia into stain and launder as usual.

Chewing gum. Put article of clothing into plastic bag in freezer. Scrape frozen gum off clothing with dull knife. *OR* sponge gum with turpentine before washing as usual. *OR* rub gum with beaten egg white

*M*om says:
The best way to deal with stains is to clean them up right when they happen. Don't let a stain soak or set in. Even if it means simply blotting it with a wet cloth and spraying with a spot remover until you have time to get it out completely.

243

until gum dissolves. Launder as usual. *OR* rub gum with ice cube. When hard, scrape with dull knife. Launder in hottest water safe for fabric. *OR* soak in white vinegar until gum dissolves.

Chocolate. Make a paste of borax and cold water. Rub into stain and let stand for 15 minutes. Rinse in cool water. Launder in hottest water safe for fabric.

Coffee or Tea. Rub stain with liquid detergent or paste. Rinse. Rub with vinegar, rinse and let dry. If stain remains, use 3% hydrogen peroxide. Launder as usual.

Cosmetics. To remove mascara, eye shadow, rouge, pancake powder or liquid foundation from clothing, rub a paste of powdered detergent and water into stain or use small amount of liquid detergent. Rinse with cool water. Launder as usual.

Crayon. Loosen crayon with shortening. Scrape off with dull knife. Rub detergent into stain. Wash in hottest water safe for fabric with detergent and two cups of baking soda. Repeat before putting clothing in dryer.

Deodorant. Sponge stain with ammonia, and launder as usual. If fabric is silk or wool, be sure to dilute ammonia with one part water. *OR* sponge stain with white vinegar. If stain remains, soak in rubbing alcohol for 30 minutes. Rinse thoroughly with cool water. Wash in hottest water safe for fabric.

Dye. If one article of clothing bleeds during washing and discolors other clothing, wash discolored clothing immediately with color-safe bleach. Treat hair dye or fabric dye stains immediately.

Egg. Scrape dried egg off fabric with dull knife. Soak in cold water for 30 minutes. Work detergent into stain. Launder in hottest water safe for fabric.

Fruit juice. Stretch stained area over large bowl. Pour boiling water through stain from height of two feet. Repeat until stain disappears. Launder as usual. *OR* rub lemon juice into stain. Let stand for 15 minutes. Rinse with cold water. Launder as usual. If stain is fresh, sponge area with cold water. Soak in cold water for 30 minutes. Launder with bleach safe for fabric.

Grass. Soak in cold water for 30 minutes. Rub detergent into stain. Wash in hottest water and bleach safe for fabric. *OR* for silk, wool, or colored fabrics, soak stained area with two cups water and one cup rubbing alcohol. Rinse. Launder as usual. *OR* dip strip of white fabric in kerosene. Rub stain with strip until saturated. Wash in warm sudsy water. Rinse thoroughly. Launder as usual.

Grease. Rub detergent into stain. Hand wash in warm sudsy water. Rinse thoroughly. Launder as usual. *OR* sprinkle talcum powder, cornstarch or cornmeal onto stain. Let stand 15 minutes. Brush. Work small amount of shampoo into stain. Wash in hottest water safe for fabric. *OR* for knits, rub stain with club soda. *OR* for suede, sponge with vinegar. Let dry. Brush to restore nap.

Fountain pen. Pour cold water through stain until gone or until no more color runs. Rub stain with paste of detergent and lemon juice. Let stand for ten minutes. Launder as usual.

Iodine. Moisten cotton ball with rubbing alcohol. Rub stain until gone. Rinse. Launder as usual. Dilute alcohol with two parts water for silk or wool fabrics. *OR* soak stain in cool water. Rub detergent in. Soak in warm sudsy water. Rinse and launder as usual.

Ketchup. Scrape off. Sponge with cool water. Soak stained area in cool water overnight. Work either powdered or liquid detergent into stain. Rinse with cool water. Launder as usual.

Lipstick. Rub stain with petroleum jelly. Wash in warm sudsy water. Rinse thoroughly. Launder as usual.

Mildew. Add 1/2 cup of disinfecting liquid to water in washing machine. *OR* mix one tablespoon chlorine bleach in two cups water. Test on concealed area of fabric. If fabric doesn't discolor, soak stain 15 minutes. Rinse and launder. Don't use this on wool or silk. *OR* mix one teaspoon of salt and the juice of one lemon. Rub into fabric. Without rinsing, let dry in sun. Launder using hottest water safe for fabric.

Milk products. Immediately flush with cold water. Soak stain in cold water 30 minutes. Rub detergent into stain. Wash. If stain hasn't disappeared, work 3% hydrogen peroxide into stain and wash again.

Mucus. Scrape away. Sponge with 1/4 cup salt dissolved in one quart water. Scrub slightly if necessary. Launder as usual.

Mud. Let mud dry completely. Scrape off or rub off dried mud with brush. Sponge stain with cool water. If stain remains, sponge with rubbing alcohol until gone. Launder as usual.

Mustard. Moisten stain with cool water, rub detergent into stain. Rinse with cool water. Soak overnight in warm sudsy water. Wash in hottest water safe for fabric.

Pencil. Try to erase stain with a clean pencil eraser. Rub detergent into stain. Rinse thoroughly. If stain remains, rub ammonia into stain. Rinse.

Perspiration. If the stain is still fresh, sponge immediately with warm water and detergent or ammonia. Soak for 30 minutes in warm water. Launder in hottest water safe for fabric. *OR* if stain has already dried, sponge with vinegar. Soak in warm water for 30 minutes. Launder in hottest water safe for fabric. *OR* rub stain with paste of warm water and meat tenderizer. Let stand for one hour. Rinse with cool water and launder as usual.

Rust. Spread stained area of fabric over bowl or pan of boiling water. Pour lemon juice through stain. Rinse thoroughly. Launder as usual. *OR* make paste of lemon juice and salt. Rub into stain. Let dry in sun. Rinse dried paste off fabric with warm water. Launder as usual.

Scorch. Put stained area on ironing board and cover with cloth that has been soaked in 3% hydrogen peroxide. Cover first cloth with clean dry cloth. Press with iron set at hottest temperature safe for fabric. Rinse thoroughly. Launder as usual.

Shoe polish. Rub stained area with rubbing alcohol. Use alcohol straight with white fabrics, and diluted with two parts of water on colored fabrics. Rinse thoroughly. Launder as usual.

Soft drinks. Sponge area immediately with rubbing alcohol diluted with one part water. Rinse thoroughly. Work liquid detergent or paste into stain. Rinse. Launder as usual. Note: At first it may not look like a soft drink has left a stain, but soft drinks leave a yellow stain when they dry.

Wine. On red wine stain, immediately pour white wine on soiled area. Then wash with cold water and ammonia. For white wine, wash with cold water and ammonia. Rinse and launder as usual.

Mildew in Bloom

If you live in a humid area, watch out when it gets warm. Molds that are always present in the air thrive in warm, moist surroundings and result in mildew on towels, sheets, white shirts, even books!

If you've never seen mildew, you might not recognize it. It's a dark, furry growth that smells dank and musty. It leaves behind a stain and when left too long, it can rot leather, paper and fabrics.

Avoid the appearance of mildew on clothing by checking to make sure that there isn't any mildew in the drawers or on the walls or shelves of the closet. If you do find mildew, wipe down the closet and inside of the drawers with vinegar. Leave the closet door open for a few day to air out. If possible, set your empty drawers outside in the sun for a day or two.

To Prevent Mildew:

Hang up wet towels after showering.

Leave shower curtain pulled closed so that it can dry.

Never put damp clothing in a laundry basket. Hang to dry first.

Don't leave damp or wet clothes or towels on floor.

Don't use starch in laundry. Mildew feeds on it.

Stay caught up on laundry. Don't leave clothing in hamper longer than a week.

If the air outside is cooler and drier than air inside, open some windows for ventilation while at home.

247

To get rid of mildew between bathroom tiles, mix a cup of liquid laundry bleach with a cup of water, apply the solution generously to the tiles. Rinse the solution off with clear water after half an hour. Make sure you don't breathe the fumes directly and don't get the solution on the shower curtain or your clothing.

Top 5 Laundry Goofs

Problem	To Avoid It
Bleach spots or holes	Place liquid bleach in the wash water *before* the clothes.
Whites turn gray or pink	Wash whites *only* with other whites. Not a speck of color.
Dingy laundry	Don't stuff it all into one load. Load washer *loosely*.
Shrinkage	Hang, don't dry, shrinkables. Never wash *dry clean only*. Wash cottons in warm. Wash wool in cold.
Bubbles all over!	*Never* use liquid dish soap or shampoo for detergent in the washing machine!

Homemade Stain Removers

Alcohol. Most commercial spot removers are simply a basic base of two parts water mixed with one part rubbing alcohol.

Cornmeal. Sprinkle on greasy stain to help absorb the grease. Combine with water for a paste or shake it right out of the box.

Cornstarch. Use while stain is fresh. Grease is absorbed as a powder or paste.

Hydrogen Peroxide. Use diluted for some of the most difficult stains such as blood, mildew and milk products.

Lemon Juice. Tackles fruit juice, mildew, ink and rust.

Petroleum Jelly. Gets off crusty part of many stains, such as tar or food. Use to loosen and soften residue then scrape or lift off.

Salt. Absorbs grease. Shake it right out of the shaker. The sooner salt gets on a stain, the more likely it will come right out.

Talcum Powder. Great grease absorber. Shake and rub it in.

White Vinegar. Removes acidic stains, like fruit juice.

Others: Ammonia, glycerine, borax, pepsin powder, diaper wash and sanitizer with sodium percarbonate. Look in pharmacy aisle of supermarket.

Time to Wash

A main cause of dingy wash is stuffing too many clothes into the washer. Most washing machines have a line that indicates maximum load capacity. Keep your load a little smaller than that. When the washer has filled and the cycle has started, lift the lid and check to make sure that the clothes are agitating freely. If you're washing knits, keep the load small to avoid wrinkling.

Detergent. There are hundreds of brands of detergents on the market and you can choose one in powdered, liquid, solid or concentrated form. The detergent you choose is a matter of personal preference, but read the label. Make sure you're getting a detergent that works in hard water if your have hard water. It is more difficult to get clothes clean in hard water than in soft water.

Regardless of the detergent you choose, follow label directions for amount. You'll need to consider

What's the Right Temperature?

The wrong water temperature can wreak considerable havoc on laundry day. Your clothes can shrink, colors can bleed and whites will turn gray. As a rule, use the following water temperatures for the fabric types listed.

HOT water wash, cold rinse: white shirts.

WARM water wash, cold rinse:
White underwear. Wash and wear colored fabrics. Elastic fabrics. Synthetic fabrics.

COLD water wash, cold rinse:
Delicate fabrics. Colored fabrics that bleed. Heavy sweaters.

size of load, type of fabric and amount of soil. Remember, some detergents are low-sudsing, designed to work without foamy suds. Don't pour more detergent into the washing machine just because you don't see bubbles.

To get better results, let the washer fill with water. Pour in designated amount of detergent and swish around by hand until it dissolves. Then add clothes. With the water shut off, let the clothes soak in the soapy water for 15 minutes. Then reactivate the washing cycle. Soaking will help loosen stubborn stains and will give the detergent time to start working on the clothing.

Bleach. In most cases, you won't need to use liquid bleach. Occasionally, bleach can be used to remove soil and stains and to brighten whites. Use a washer that has a separate port to add liquid to wash water or pour bleach in with detergent and let the wash water agitate before you add your clothes.

If you add bleach to the wash water after you've added your clothes, you risk dripping the bleach directly onto fabric which will cause holes. Washing certain clothes too often in liquid bleach also can cause holes and fraying.

Liquid bleach can be used safely on white cotton. For other fabrics, choose a color-safe powdered bleach. The powder dissolves slowly in water and doesn't damage the clothes.

Check all clothing labels before using any bleach. Some will warn you against using any kind of bleach at all. If you do use liquid bleach, use extreme care. Make sure none of it splashes on dry clothing and make sure the clothes are in the washer no longer than ten minutes after you add bleach to the wash water. *Don't soak clothes in bleach or bleach water as the fabric will fall apart.*

Fabric Softener. Fabric softener will help eliminate static cling from fabrics, resulting in softer, fresher laundry. Fabric softener can be found in liquid form that is added to rinse water, and a small sheet that goes in the dryer.

Both kinds have advantages. Liquid fabric softener dissolves in the rinse water, allowing for even distribution among clothing. It is best to use liquid softener if you plan to hang your clothes on a clothes line to dry, especially towels. Overuse of liquid fabric softener can compromise some fabrics. Fabric softener sheets are more convenient since they don't require measuring or monitoring of the wash cycle.

Rinsing. Rinsing is critical to clean laundry. You must remove all soapy residue from clothing for it to look clean and bright. Cold water rinsing is best. Besides saving energy, it cuts and removes soapy residue better than warm or hot water. If you add extra detergent for heavily soiled clothing, run them through an additional cold water rinse cycle to remove all traces of soap.

Drying. Before using a clothes dryer, clean all lint and dust from the lint filter (which usually looks like a screen). Select the right temperature if the dryer has a temperature control. You can dry most clothing on medium heat but use high heat for heavy fabrics, such as denims and towels.

It's best to slightly under dry. Check the load periodically to make sure the clothes don't get too dry or too hot. Many articles of clothing won't need to be ironed if you remove them from the dryer when they are slightly under dry and hang them on a hanger immediately. If you'll be ironing your clothes right away, remove them from the dryer while they're still slightly damp.

If you hang clothing on a clothesline, first shake the clothing so that some of the wrinkles fall out. Hang clothing as straight as possible and take it off the line while still slightly damp if you need to iron it.

Mom says:
Not every item has to be washed after you wear it one time, especially dry-clean only clothes, jackets, vests, suits, heavy sweaters and jeans. Just hang them up!

The Worst Ring of All

You have ring around the collar! If your shirt collars have grungy dark rings, try one of these easy methods:

1) Add enough vinegar to baking soda to make a thick paste. Rub it in with an old toothbrush. Launder as usual.

2) With an old toothbrush, rub shampoo into the collar and cuffs. Shampoo is specially designed to dissolve hair oils.

3) Mix 1/4 cup dish soap, 1/4 cup ammonia and 1/4 cup water. Pour a *little* on stain, rubbing well until fabric is saturated. Launder as usual. *(Don't use too much dish soap!)*

Putting Clothes Away

The best reason to put clothes away properly is so that they stay clean until you need them. Dumping a pile of clean laundry on the floor, bed or couch is a waste of your time and money.

Keep drawers organized so that you know what is clean and what is dirty and where to find what you need when you need it.

Neatly fold underwear, socks, shorts, T-shirts, sweat shirts, pants, pajamas, sweaters and jeans.

Hang blouses, dress shirts, slacks, suits, dresses, dry-clean only items, jackets and vests.

You may want to remove certain clothes from the dryer before they are totally dry. These include clothes that get too tight when dried completely, such as jeans and sweaters. You'll also want to pull out delicates, dresses and vests before completely dry. Hang them up immediately, smooth out any wrinkles and allow them to air dry.

Wool Takes a Bath

Wool blankets, and some wool clothing, can be washed in a normal washing machine if you follow certain steps. If not, your blanket may end up the size of a small bath towel. To avoid shrinkage and distortion:

1) Check for spots or heavy soil. Use vegetable brush and warm soapy water to remove obvious spots.

2) Fill washing machine with warm water, not hot. Use enough detergent for a full load. Agitate machine until soap dissolves.

3) Stop washer agitation. Submerge blanket in water and soak for 20 minutes. Swish blanket a few times by hand.

4) Turn dial to spin cycle and let washer spin until all water spins out of blanket.

5) Allow washer to fill with warm rinse water, then stop washer. Let blanket soak, submerged in the water for five minutes. Turn dial to spin so that water will drain from washer, but don't let washer spin yet. Repeat rinsing process, letting the blanket soak in clear water another five minutes. Swish blanket by hand a few times.

6) Turn dial to spin, let the washer drain and let blanket spin to get rid of all excess water.

7) Put five or six large bath towels in dryer and run it on high heat for five minutes. Remove towels and wrap the blanket gently around them, then return the towels and blanket to the dryer.

8) Dry on high heat for 15 minutes. Check often and remove blanket from dryer while still slightly damp. *Drying blanket completely will cause it to shrink.*

9) With another person on the other end of blanket, pull and stretch it vigorously to reshape. Brush it with a nylon or metal bristle bush to raise the nap and make the blanket look like new.

10) Drape blanket over a rack or rod, outdoors if possible, until dry. *Do not hang it on clothesline with clothes pins.*

Keeping Clothes in Good Repair

Check your clothes to see if any item needs mending. Common problem areas are hems, buttons, armhole seams and crotch seams. The old adage "A stitch in time saves nine" is true. Take time to fix a problem now, or you might face a bigger problem later.

When you sew by hand, always double the thread. Put one end of the thread through the needle, pull it even with the other end and tie a firm knot, holding both ends of the thread together.

Keep the length of thread relatively short. Long thread tangles and knots. Use a sharp needle. Blunt needles are hard to work with and can snag.

Never pull threads hanging from a hem or seam. Cut them off and do the necessary mending.

Sewing on Buttons

Check buttons regularly. It's better to repair a loose button than to try to find a button that matches after losing the original. It's also easier to sew the button aligned with the buttonhole before the button has fallen off completely.

To sew on a button, thread the needle and tie a knot in the end. Begin with the needle on the underside of the fabric. Push the needle up through the fabric and through one of the holes in the button, holding the button down firmly with the edge of your thumb. Pull the thread all the way through until the knotted end is taut against the underside of the fabric. Push the needle down through the other hole, pulling the thread all the way through again. Repeat until finished.

While buttons should be sewn firmly to the fabric, they should not be so tight that they can't be buttoned and unbuttoned easily. Check periodically as you sew to make sure that you aren't pulling the thread too tight. A helpful hint to allow for this spacing is to slip a straight pin between the fabric and the button and proceed to sew the button on, then remove the pin when finished.

To finish, make sure you knot the thread well on the underside of the fabric. If you have a button on a coat or suit jacket that is constantly coming loose, try sewing it with fine fishing line.

Repairing a Seam

To make the repair durable, use doubled thread.

Turn garment inside out. Match thread used to sew garment originally as closely as possible. Never use anything but white thread on white clothing. Use black or navy on dark clothing, gray on gray clothing and white on light-colored clothing.

With item turned inside out, locate tear. Matching edges of seam together, use straight pins to hold seam securely closed.

Use running stitch to repair seam. Keep stitches small and overlap them slightly. On knitted fabric, sew stitches in a slight zig-zag pattern to allow for stretch.

If seam is stressed, such as an armhole or crotch seam, sew a double line of stitching for reinforcement.

Knot thread securely. Press seam flat open on inside, spritzing with a little vinegar to set the seam. Turn garment right-side-out and press seam on outside for a finished look.

Repairing a Hem

Use the old crease as a guide. Pin hem in place.

With thread doubled, take small stitches around the hem. As each stitch is completed, take up only a few threads of the fabric on the right side of the garment.

Knot the thread securely when finished.

Press the hem on inside, dampening it or using the steam setting on the iron. Turn garment right side out and press the hem on the outside again, dampening or using steam.

Button, Button Who's Got the Button?

There's nothing worse than losing a button off a shirt, skirt or slacks. Unless it's tearing the inseam out of your pants in public, that is!

If you want to keep your shirt on *(and* be very popular with your friends) always have a small sewing kit in your purse, backpack or briefcase.

No one is so panicked and in need as a friend missing a button from a strategic place. Provide them with a quick solution, and you'll be a hero. The sewing kit will save *you* from a number of potentially embarrassing moments, too.

You can purchase a small, prepackaged mending kit or assemble your own. This is easy and inexpensive.

You will need to find something to store a few basic supplies in. It doesn't have to be fancy – even an empty bandage tin will do the job.

Checklist

Sewing Kit

❑ **Thread.** White, black and gray are usually enough. Use the white thread for light clothing and the black for navy and dark clothing.

❑ **Needles.** Needles come in a small pack of assorted sizes from any fabric store or supermarket.

❑ **Straight pins.** You'll only need a few. Stick them into a chunk of Styrofoam, a pin cushion or a short strip of masking tape.

❑ **Safety pins.** These are for emergencies. Resist the urge to permanently hold yourself together with a maze of skillfully placed safety pins. Eventually, this will cramp your style.

❑ **Buttons.** Visit a fabric store or supermarket and choose buttons that closely match your suits and shirts.

❑ **Small Scissors.** Don't use your teeth very often to nip thread. After a few years of that, you'll wear down the enamel on your front top and bottom teeth.

*M*om says:
In a pinch, you can use masking tape or a stapler to temporarily fix a torn seam or hem. But it's very temporary. Get to the nearest needle and thread as soon as possible.

Pressing Matters

Want the crispest shirt in town? It's not really that difficult. By following a few simple steps, you can master the art of ironing.

To get started, you need an iron and an ironing board. The ironing board should have a snug-fitting cover to make the job easier and to prevent bunching and wrinkling while ironing. The iron can either be a dry or a steam iron. Without a steam iron, slightly dampen clothes before ironing them. Don't dampen or steam silks as they will get water spots. Regardless of what you're ironing, follow these guidelines:

Take clothes that need ironing out of dryer while still damp. Lay them neatly on ironing board. If ironing clothes later, use a spray bottle to dampen each item of clothing while ironing.

Start out cool. To prevent accidental scorching, begin with a low temperature and iron items that need a lower temperature first. Iron clothes that need a hot temperature last.

Use a light hand. Don't exert a lot of pressure while ironing. Use a basic back-and-forth motion. Don't stretch or pull the fabric.

Iron double-thick fabric on the inside first. Where the fabric is doubled, such as cuffs, collars, hems, pocket flaps and some yokes, iron the outside last.

To get crisp seams, dampen first. Spritz seams with a mixture of one part water to one part white vinegar, then press them open from the inside before pressing on the outside.

Start with the smallest parts of a piece of clothing. For example, on a shirt, iron the cuffs and collars first, then move on to the sleeves, then the front and finally the back.

Iron wools, silks, rayons and dark fabrics on wrong side. When doing a minor touch-up on the right side of the fabric, put a light weight clean cloth between the iron and the fabric.

To get a sharp crease, dampen it a little more than usual. Then press. If necessary, dampen again and press again. To iron lace, put it on a clean bath towel and use a lightweight clean cloth between the iron and the lace. *TIP: Never iron over buttons, snaps, zippers or hooks.*

No One Wants a Shiny Seat

Many of us have experienced a shine on the seat off our pants or skirts after repeated wearing of a particular garment. This shine is the result of fibers being repeatedly pressed and packed. To get rid of the shine, those fibers need to be released.

Dip a clean soft cloth in white vinegar, slightly wring it out, then vigorously rub the shiny area. Do not press the fabric afterwards unless it is absolutely necessary, but if you do, be sure to use a clean cloth between the iron and the fabric.

If there still seems to be too much shine, try rubbing a very fine grade of sandpaper gently over the shiny area. Before using the sandpaper, test a hidden area to see if the sandpaper might do too much damage.

A Fresh Blast of Steam

To prevent hard water and mineral deposits from building up in a steam iron, fill it only with distilled water. Buy it in the store as such or you can scrape the frost from your refrigerator freezer compartment, melt the desired amount and use that. If you don't have access to distilled water and your iron is hopelessly clogged, here's how to blast it free:

• Dump out any water that is still in the iron.

• Fill the iron with white vinegar, set the control on steam and let the iron heat for at least five minutes.

• Unplug the iron and let it cool completely. It's important that the iron is not hot. Empty the vinegar out of the iron and refill it with distilled water.

• Plug the iron back in, set the control on steam and iron a rag or scrap of fabric that can be thrown away. Loosened residue will escape with the steam and deposit itself on the cloth. Keep ironing until no more residue escapes.

• Empty the water out of the iron, refill the iron with clean water and resume ironing.

Notes

Easing the Pain
Basic First Aid

It's happened. You've burned yourself on the stove. Gotten a nosebleed. Scalded yourself in the shower. Fallen off your bike. Blistered with a sunburn. Then you try to remember: What did Mom do when I got myself into these scrapes?

Most minor accidents can be handled with simple first aid, but learn to use common sense. You've heard it before, "An ounce of prevention is worth a pound of cure." Use safety equipment essential to any physical activity you undertake.

Don't do anything remotely dangerous if you are intoxicated at all.

If you plan to be in a hazardous area, take clean water, a first aid kit, a flare gun and a cell phone, if possible. Be more cautious than you feel you need to be. Think before you leap.

First aid, of course, is only a temporary measure for more serious accidents like head injuries, fractures, severe burns or deep lacerations. Do what you can to help yourself or someone else, then seek medical attention immediately.

Rule 1: Do no harm. If you or someone is injured and down, do not move them, or let anyone else move you, unless doing so will remove them from harm's way and prevent further injury.

Rule 2: Know what you are doing. Take a CPR (cardiopulmonary resuscitation) class. Most CPR classes are free and taught by the Red Cross in your area. With that knowledge, you could save a life.

Rule 3: Always seek medical attention if you have a burn that has blistered, if you suspect you have a broken bone or if you have signs of infection, like redness, pain, swelling and fever.

To Soothe Minor Hurts

Bleeding

1) Grab the cleanest material you can find – a washcloth or sterile gauze.

2) Cover wound with cloth and apply firm pressure to wound with your hand, holding the edges of wound together.

3) Keep firm pressure on wound until bleeding stops.

4) Sponge wound gently with antiseptic, such as or hydrogen peroxide. Spread thin layer of antiseptic or antibiotic ointment over wound. Cover with bandage.

If bleeding can't be controlled within a few minutes, seek medical attention. Stitches may be needed.

Blisters

1) Sterilize end of needle or pin in flame of a match.

2) Carefully puncture edge of blister next to skin.

3) Gently squeeze fluid out. Leave skin intact as it guards against infection.

4) Treat blister with antibiotic ointment or rubbing alcohol. Cover with gauze. Tape loosely.

To prevent blisters, use layers of sterile gauze at the first sign of discomfort. Purchase some mole skin – a flesh-colored felt material with sticky backing that adheres to skin. Cut to size and put on areas most likely to blister, like the heel and sides of toes.

Boils

1) Soak boil for 30 minutes at a time in hottest water you can stand. If boil is on hand or foot, immerse it in hot water. If boil is somewhere that cannot be immersed, soak it with washcloth dipped in hot water. Rewet cloth often to keep temperature up.

2) Do not puncture the boil. It will eventually come to a head

and burst on its own. Apply gentle pressure and keep bathing boil to drain infection.

3) Apply an antibiotic ointment and cover with a bandage.

Breathing Difficulties

To help a person who has stopped breathing.

1) Position victim on his or her back. Take precautions if you think the person has a back or neck injury.

2) Place a hand under the victim's neck to tilt head so the chin is pointing up. Lift up gently while you press down on the victim's forehead. Check to make sure that the victim's tongue is not blocking the throat. If it is, move it so that it no longer obstructs airway.

3) Using the hand that is on the victim's forehead, pinch nostrils shut to prevent leakage of air. Open your mouth wide, take a deep breath and seal your mouth over the victim's mouth. Blow four quick breaths into the victim. Pause between each breath only long enough to lift your head and inhale.

4) If the victim does not begin to breathe after the four quick breaths, continue to breathe into the person's mouth, one breath every five seconds, or twelve times per minute. Continue until help arrives.

If victim is an infant, breathe gentle puffs of air at the rate of one every three seconds, or 20 times per minute. On babies, *cover the mouth and nose with your mouth and breathe gently but thoroughly.*

If the victim has no heartbeat or pulse, continue administering CPR until help arrives.

If done improperly, CPR can result in life-threatening injury. You should first receive training from a licensed practitioner.

Bruises

1) Immediately place cold compress on bruise. A cold, wet washcloth will work.

2) Apply compresses 15 minutes at a time several times a day.

Burns

1) Immerse burn in cold water until you no longer feel pain. *Don't* put butter on burn as this will hold heat in and do more harm.

2) Apply burn ointment, thick layer of honey or thin paste of baking soda and water.

3) Cover loosely with bandage to allow exposure to air.

Chemical Burns

1) Irrigate area with running cold water to flush chemical.

2) Apply burn ointment, thick layer of honey or thin paste of baking soda and water.

3) Cover area with a loose protective bandage.

If chemical burn involves the eye, flush with water immediately. Cover eye with a sterile pad and seek medical help immediately.

Choking

An item stuck in the throat that cuts off breathing is a life-threatening emergency. If *you* are choking, signal for help. If you see someone choking and not getting air, help them. Learn the Heimlich Maneuver. *The worst thing do is slap the victim on the back.* A forceful blow to the back can push food further into windpipe. Don't attempt to reach the stuck object with your fingers as that too will likely push it further into the windpipe.

The Heimlich Maneuver, which can save the life of a choking victim, can be used on victims who are conscious or unconscious and those who are standing, sitting or lying down. You can even perform the maneuver on yourself.

For a victim who is standing:
1) Stand behind the victim and wrap your arms around the victim's waist, grasping your hands in front of them. The hand resting against the victim's abdomen should be in a fist. Make sure the fist is positioned between the tip of the breastbone the navel.

2) With your hands tightly grasped, press your fist into the victim's abdomen, using a quick, upward thrust. The lodged item should come flying out. If it doesn't repeat this procedure until it is dislodged.

For a victim who is sitting:
Repeat procedure as with victim who is standing. Stand behind the chair and grasp victim around waist. Repeat the other steps.

For a victim who is lying down:
1) Roll the victim on their back. and kneel at their side or straddle the hips. Choose the position most comfortable that allows greatest strength as you thrust. Do not place all your weight on the victim.

2) Place one hand on top of the other. The heel of your bottom hand should be between the tip of the breastbone and navel. Move your shoulders above the victim's abdomen.

3) Press your hands forcefully into the victim's abdomen with a rapid, upward thrust. Repeat the thrusting motion until you can see the object. You may have to fish it out. Act quickly so the victim doesn't breathe it in again.

For a victim who is a child:
1) Place the child on his or her back across your thigh.

2) Position two or three of your fingers between the tip of the breastbone and navel.

3) With a quick thrust, push fingers into child's abdomen. Continue the movement until the object is dislodged. Don't use as much force as you would use on an adult.

To perform the maneuver on yourself:
1) Quickly locate a firm, rigid, preferably non-movable object about the height of your abdomen – the edge of a counter, the edge of a table or back of a chair will do.

2) Rest your abdomen across the object so that it is positioned between the tip of your breastbone and your navel.

3) Press your weight quickly and forcefully downward so that the object thrusts upward into your abdomen.

4) Repeat thrusting until the food or object is dislodged. Work quickly to avoid passing out

Cuts

1) Wash thoroughly with warm soapy water.

2) If bleeding is severe, apply pressure as described in the *Bleeding* section. If minor, apply moderate pressure until it stops.

3) Apply alcohol to cleanse wound thoroughly and remove any debris, such as gravel.

4) Cover with an adhesive strip. If the cut is large, use sterile gauze and tape.

5) To relieve pain or throbbing, hold ice pack over bandaged cut for 15 to 20 minutes.

6) Change bandage daily and check the cut for infection. Apply antibiotic ointment each time you change the bandage.

Fainting

1) If you feel faint, lie down immediately. If you cannot lie down, sit and put your head between your knees. Stay in this position for at least ten minutes.

2) If someone faints, help the victim lie down in a comfortable position, preferably with the head lower than the body.

Foreign Object in Ear

1) Lay on your side with the affected ear up.

2) Put several drops of warm mineral oil or olive oil into ear until it feels full. Wait five minutes.

3) Sit up and tilt your head to the side, with the affected ear pointed downward. If the object was small, it should float out in the oil.

Note: Don't use this method if the object is one that would swell like a bean, wood, or any other absorbent object. If a large object is lodged in the ear, or if your first aid treatment is unsuccessful, seek medical help. Do not try to dislodge objects with a hair pin or cotton swab as this may force it deeper into the ear.

Foreign Object in Eye

1) If you can see the object, lift it gently from your eye with the tip of a clean cotton swab.

2) If you can't see the object, gently pull your upper eyelid out and down over your lower lid. Leave it there for a few moments. The tears should wash the particle from your eye.

3) If you still aren't successful, gently pull upper lid upward, inverting it. If you see object, remove it with a cotton swab or corner of a handkerchief.

4) If you still haven't found the object, check the lower lid by gently pulling it outward.

5) Irrigate your eye gently with clear, cool water.

*M*om *says:*
Do not use a hair pin to remove ear wax or anything else that might get stuck or go too far in your ear. Use cotton tips to carefully clean ears after bath or shower.

Mom says:
When out in the sun,
wear sun screen and
drink plenty of water
to avoid heat
exhaustion.
Be prepared for
outings at the park,
sporting events, lake
and mountains,
especially if you will
be involved in
physical activity in
the heat.

If you are unable to remove an object or if you have particles of metal in your eye, seek medical help immediately. Also seek help if your eye burns for a long time after removing object or if the surface of your eye is scratched or cut. Sometimes a scratch or cut feels like an object is still there.

Fractures

Fractures must receive medical attention. To avoid further injury, do not move the fractured area. If you suspect injury to the neck or spine, DO NOT move the person at all and do not allow anyone to move you. If the fracture is compound (the bone sticking out of the skin) take measures to stop bleeding while waiting for help to arrive.

Frostbite

Frostbite initially looks like a reddened first-degree burn. A tingling sensation follows, ice crystals may form in the skin, the skin will become a yellowish-gray color and feel numb. Frostbite usually affects the nose, cheeks, ears, fingers and toes.

1) Rewarm frozen skin by submerging it in warm, not hot, water. *Do not rub the skin to warm it with friction.*

2) You may also use body heat to gently but rapidly rewarm affected parts. For instance, wrap your hands around their toes, wrap your palms around their ears, or put their fingers under your armpits.

3) When a reddish color returns to the frostbitten skin, take it out of the warm water and gently pat it dry. Take care not to break any blisters that may have formed and *do not rub the skin.*

4) Cover the skin with a loose bandage and seek medical help immediately. If the feet or legs are affected, don't attempt to walk. The best cure for frostbite is prevention.

Hypothermia

Victims of frostbite often suffer from hypothermia, where the internal body temperature drops below 98.6 degrees. The victim may experience intense shivering, muscle stiffness or trembling, discolored skin or puffy face, lethargy, coordination problems, unconsciousness and, in severe cases, heart attack. Seek medical help immediately. Handle victim gently, move to warm place and wrap in blankets.

Heat Exhaustion

If you've been in the sun without a hat or exerting yourself in the heat, watch for the signs of heat exhaustion. They may include: pallor, sweating, faintness, nausea, muscle twitching, cramping pain, confusion, weakness and vomiting.

1) Move to a cool area out of the heat and sun.

2) Lay down with your feet elevated higher than your head.

3) Drink plenty of water or clear fluids.

4) Apply cool wet cloths to head, face and body.

Nosebleed

For minor nosebleeds caused by injury, allergy, or change in altitude, follow these guidelines:

1) Sit and tilt your head back.

2) Apply pressure to your nose by firmly grasping the area just below the bridge of the nose between the thumb and forefinger. Apply pressure for five to ten minutes.

3) If bleeding does not stop within ten minutes, pack nostril with sterile gauze and apply firm pressure at tip of nose.

4) Apply cold compress or ice pack to base of skull at the neck.

5) Once bleeding stops, remain quiet and avoid laughing or blowing your nose.

If you suspect that your nose is broken, do not try to treat it yourself. Seek medical help.

And if you cannot control bleeding within 15 to 20 minutes, seek medical help. The nosebleed may be due to high blood pressure or a fracture.

Puncture Wounds

1) Wash the wound well with soap and hot water.

2) If bleeding, control it by applying direct pressure.

3) When bleeding stops, cover the wound with sterile gauze.

4) Seek medical help in cases of deep puncture wounds. A tetanus shot may be needed if you have not been immunized against tetanus within the previous five years.

Seizure

The signs of seizure are falling, rigid muscles, uncontrolled movements, jerking and loss of bladder control. Usually this is followed by a sleepy state or confused period.

1) Don't put anything in the mouth.

2) Do not restrain or try to stop seizures but do protect the victim from hard or sharp objects.

3) After seizure, lay victim down and turn head to the side.

4) Make sure victim is breathing. If not, begin administering mouth-to-mouth resuscitation.

Shock

Shock, which generally occurs to some degree after any injury, can cause death when severe. A person in shock may look dazed and confused, may either be pale or flushed, and breathing may be irregular and weak. The person may vomit and may lose consciousness. Immediate medical attention is needed. Until medical help arrives, follow these guidelines:

1) Have the person lie down on his or her back. Keep the head level with the body or slightly elevated above the body. *Do not tilt the person so that the head is lower than the body.*

2) Loosen tight clothing at the chest and neck.

3) If the victim's skin is pale and cool, cover them with a blanket or two for warmth, but be careful not to overheat them. If

Mom says:
Take special care of
your skin when you
are young. Severe
sunburns early in life
or continuous
exposure to the sun
without sunscreen
will increase your
risk for skin cancer
and melanoma later
in life.

the skin is hot and red, apply bath towels soaked in cool water until the skin returns to normal temperature and color. Then cover the victim with a blanket to keep warm.

4) Never give a person in severe shock anything to eat or drink.

Splinters

1) Wash the area around the splinter with warm soapy water. Rinse well. Swab with alcohol.

2) If the end of the splinter sticks out of the skin, use tweezers to gently pull it out. Do this slowly and gently to avoid breaking the splinter off beneath the surface of the skin.

3) If the end of the splinter is visible but beneath the skin, use a sterilized needle gently to loosen skin and expose splinter end. Then grasp the end firmly with tweezers and remove. Needle can be sterilized by holding sharp end in flame of a match for ten seconds. The tip will get dark.

4) Squeeze the wound until it starts to bleed to wash out any bacteria.

5) Apply an antibiotic ointment or swab the wound with alcohol and cover it with a bandage.

Seek medical help if the splinter is too deep to be removed at home, if you are unable to remove all of it or if an infection develops. If the splinter is deep and you have not had a tetanus shot in five years, you may need medical attention.

Sprains

1) Immediately immerse sprain in ice water for 20 minutes to control swelling. Use ice water or cold compresses every four hours until swelling stops.

2) Elevate the sprained limb to at least waist level until swelling has stopped.

3) Once swelling stops, soak the sprain in very warm water for 20 minutes first, then in icy water for 20 minutes. Do this three times a day.

4) Once swelling stops, gently exercise the sprained area by carefully moving it from side to side. This is important to maintain flexibility. Be careful not to overdo it. Continue these exercises several times daily until the pain begins to diminish.

5) Limit use of sprained area. If it is an ankle, use crutches until the motion of walking slowly heel-to-toe no longer hurts. If it is a wrist, avoid using your hand to eat, write or do other tasks until a waving motion no longer causes pain. For extra support, wrap an elastic bandage around sprained area.

Sunburn

1) Apply cool compresses to the burned area to reduce pain and swelling, or take a cool shower. If the sunburn involves an area you can't reach, soak in tub of cool water.

2) Take aspirin or a non-aspirin pain reliever to reduce pain, and drink plenty of water.

3) Gently apply a thin paste of baking soda and water to alleviate pain. Calamine lotion (also used for insect bites) can also be applied to relieve pain and reduce swelling.

4) If blisters form, never break them intentionally. If they do break, liberally apply antibiotic ointment and cover them with a sterile dressing.

5) For chapped skin, lips, hands or feet, apply petroleum jelly. Always apply sunblock early when you plan to be outdoors for a long period of time

Most sunburn is minor, but seek medical help if the sunburn is severe, covers more than one-fourth your body or involves extensive blistering.

Checklist

First Aid Essentials

Keep a full first-aid kit in your bathroom. You might want to put a mini-kit in your car or strap one to your bicycle.

These are must haves:

- ☐ Antibiotic ointment
- ☐ Adhesive bandages
- ☐ Bottle of rubbing alcohol
- ☐ Clean absorbent cloth
- ☐ Cotton balls and swabs
- ☐ Digital thermometer
- ☐ Elastic bandages for sprains
- ☐ Instant heat pack or hot-water bottle
- ☐ Instant ice pack
- ☐ Matches or lighter
- ☐ Pain reliever
- ☐ Roll of adhesive tape
- ☐ Roll of gauze
- ☐ Safety pins or needle
- ☐ Small scissors
- ☐ Sunblock
- ☐ Tweezers

Eventually get these:

- ☐ Antacid/antigas medicine
- ☐ Antibacterial gel
- ☐ Bottle of calamine lotion for sunburn, hives or insect bites
- ☐ Diarrhea remedy
- ☐ Disposable wipes
- ☐ Hydrogen peroxide
- ☐ Tube of burn ointment
- ☐ Tube of petroleum jelly

Notes

7

Just a Cold or Pneumonia?
When to See a Doctor

You've felt it before. The scratchy throat. The throbbing head. The burning brow. The queasy stomach. It's natural to worry a little when you don't feel well – but how can you tell when your worry is unfounded and when you should indeed seek medical help?

If you are suffering from a stabbing pain, an itching eye or a spotty rash, find your symptoms (and any of a dozen others) in this chapter to determine when you should visit the doctor, clinic or hospital and when you can safely tough it out at home.

Regardless of any symptoms you may have, you should seek medical attention in two general situations: First, if your symptoms worsen with the passage of time and despite your attempts to treat them. Second, when you feel intuitively that something is just not right, that you've never felt this bad before or that you may be very ill. It's always better to make an unnecessary visit to the doctor than to risk a serious illness going undetected and untreated.

Common Illnesses

Canker Sores. Red welt-like sores occurring inside the mouth which follow illness or irritation to the mouth. Some people get canker sores from eating too many nuts, spicy foods, salty foods or foods high in acid, including tomatoes and citrus fruits.

Treatment: Add one half teaspoon of salt or baking soda to a cup of warm water and rinse your mouth with the solution several times a day. Take a pain reliever if soreness of cankers becomes intolerable. Don't eat or drink anything irritating to the mouth.

See a doctor if: Gums begin to bleed, canker sores bleed, a fever higher than 101 degrees develops or multiple sores form.

Cold Sores. Usually occurring outside of the mouth on or near the lips, cold sores look like blisters. They are caused by the herpes simplex virus (HSV1), which is not the same virus that causes genital herpes (HSV2), although HSV1 can be spread to the genital area. The sores are highly contagious and easily spread from one person to another. As sores heal, they crust over and dry up. Don't pick at the sores or remove the scabs as this will impede healing.

Treatment: Dab sores with alcohol or witch hazel to help dry them. Apply some anesthetic ointment to relieve pain. Apply an antibiotic cream if sores appear to be infected.

See a doctor if: Sore gets larger, sores begin to spread, more sores form near original, sore lasts longer than a week or if self-treatment doesn't help.

At-Home RX

If you learn to manage stress, you'll decrease your risk for cankers and cold sores. A sensitive mouth registers stress early on. Overwork, emotional upset, worry or illness can trigger mouth sores. Take time for yourself every day to breathe deeply, get some sun, do something fun or relax in the tub. Let go of the stress of the day.

Common Cold. Colds are caused by viruses; sadly, there is no cure. Certain treatments can provide relief from symptoms while a cold runs its course.

Treatment: A vaporizer or humidifier will keep respiratory tract moist, easing sore throat and breathing. Gargle with hot salt water for throat. Take pain reliever for fever and aches. Use cough syrup or drops at night if coughing keeps you awake.

See a doctor if: Fever climbs higher than 101 degrees, cough lasts more than a day, nasal discharge is greenish, thick or has a foul odor, sore throat lasts more than two days, you have severe earache or cold lasts more than ten days.

Constipation. Some occasional constipation is normal, resulting from stress, not enough liquids or not enough fiber, eating too fast, and ignoring urge to use the bathroom. You should have a bowel movement daily. If you cannot get regular, see a doctor.

Treatment: Drink eight full glasses of water per day. Eat unprocessed bran, vegetables, whole grains and fruits with skins and seeds. Use a mild laxative or a mineral oil enema if condition becomes uncomfortable and does not respond to dietary changes.

See a doctor if: You have sharp stomach pains, you have sudden weight loss, you notice blood in stool, you suffer repeatedly each week or you have dizzy spells.

Please note:
This chapter is intended as an informational guide only.

The author and Aspen West assumes no responsibility or liability for any administration of these basic suggestions.

Chicken Soup Really Works!

Scientists have confirmed what moms and grandmothers have known for centuries – chicken soup is good for colds. Homemade chicken soup contains ingredients beneficial to the immune system. Anti-inflammatory properties in the soup soothe sore throats and ease the symptoms of colds and flu.

Researchers tested a recipe of chicken, onions, sweet potatoes, parsnips, turnips, carrots, celery and parsley. Many ingredients helped decrease the body's release of mucus which causes the cough and stuffy nose brought on by respiratory infections. The steam from the soup calms inflamed airways. Of course, the tender loving care factor of someone preparing homemade soup for you may also speed healing.

271

Cough. A cough is usually a symptom of upper respiratory tract infection. Many coughs result from irritated bronchial tubes brought on by a cold.

Treatment: Use a vaporizer at night. Take a cough suppressant before bed. Keep head elevated to reduce irritation from mucus drainage.

See a doctor if: Fever climbs higher than 101 degrees, you cough throughout the day, cough persists for a week, you have difficulty breathing, you begin wheezing, you cough up thick, foamy phlegm or you have chest pains.

Diarrhea. Diarrhea can be a symptom of many illnesses. Be concerned about loose, watery stools passed more than six times a day. Dehydration is a major danger.

Treatment: Use anti-diarrhea medications. Drink liquids but avoid milk. Eat bland foods until stools are firm.

See a doctor if: You have blood or mucus in stools, you are vomiting, you have a very high fever, you do not urinate for eight hours or if diarrhea continues.

Earache. Swimmer's ear, or *external otitis*, is an infection of the ear canal. It should be treated with prescription antibiotic ear drops. The more common *otitis media* affects the middle ear. A stabbing earache may be preceded by a cold. Pain may subside after a few hours, but infection usually continues. Since infection is on the other side of the eardrum, ear drops are not effective. Get a prescription for antibiotics.

Treatment: Take a non-aspirin pain reliever and fever reducer. Apply heat to ear with a hot water bottle or with a warm washcloth. Take a decongestant for inflammation. For swimmer's ear, avoid water in ears for two weeks. Use ear plugs or cotton balls coated with petroleum jelly while swimming and bathing. For otitis media, avoid changes in pressure and altitude, such as airplane trips or mountain climbing.

See a doctor if: Severe pain persists longer than an hour, nagging pain lasts longer than two hours, fever climbs higher that 101 degrees, there is discharge from ears or your teeth hurt or feel loose.

Fever. Usually, fever is the body's response to infection, but there can be other causes including some medications, antibiotics, chronic disease, vigorous exercise or heatstroke. The main danger from fever is dehydration. Convulsions may result with fevers above 105 degrees Use a thermometer to diagnose a fever correctly.
Treatment: Use a pain reliever designed to reduce fever. Take proper dosage until fever is gone for 24 hours. Take a bath in lukewarm, not cold, water. Get plenty of rest. Eat light foods to keep strength up. Drink plenty of fluids. You should generally let a fever run its course for 24 hours to eliminate any harmful agents in the body. Consult a doctor immediately for a child with high fever.
See a doctor if: Fever suddenly reaches 105 degrees or higher, fever lasts more than a day, you also experience vomiting, nausea or severe headache, condition continues to worsen after you have been treating it for 24 hours or more, you feel extremely ill, you are confused, you feel disoriented or you cannot stay awake.

Headache. There are different types of headaches. *Tension* headaches result from stress which causes neck and shoulders to tighten. *Migraine* headaches are caused by too much blood circulating to the brain; pain results from increased pressure. Migraines usually involve one side of the head, may affect vision and can cause nausea. *Infection/allergy* headaches may be caused by hay fever and may be accompanied by runny nose, sneezing and itchy, irritated eyes. *Sinus* headaches result from infection and are accompanied by tenderness in face, especially around the eyes, toothache and foul smelling nasal discharge. *Eyestrain* does not actually cause a headache, but can cause pain in that general area.
Treatment: Take a pain reliever every four hours. If you have a cold or hay fever, also take a decongestant. Get some sleep. If tension related, lie down with heating pad on shoulders and neck or gently massage area.
See a doctor if: Headache follows blow to head, severe headache interferes with normal activities, you become clumsy or dizzy, your vision is blurred, you suffer chronic headaches or the pain is sudden and fierce.

Influenza (Flu). Usually, a flu must run its course. Prescription medications may help symptoms which include fever, fatigue, aches, nausea, sore throat and cough.
Treatment: Get bed rest for at least four hours or more as soon as symptoms appear. Drink fluids to fight dehydration and keep lungs clear. Take pain reliever and cough medicine, if needed.
See a doctor if: Fever reaches 104 degrees, symptoms last a week or more, you have trouble sleeping or if a low grade fever of 100 degrees lingers.

Ingrown Toenail. When the corner of a toenail penetrates the soft skin around it, the area will throb, swell, turn red and, if not treated, become infected.
Treatment: Soak feet in very warm water for 20 minutes. Use alcohol to clean area. Apply antibiotic ointment or medicine. Wear clean socks and loose shoes.
See a doctor if: You have severe pain or pus, self-treatment does not work and it gets worse, you have diabetes or poor circulation in your feet

Jock Itch. Caused by a fungus that thrives in warm, dark, moist places. It causes itching in groin, thigh or anal area, and a raised, red rash with blisters.
Treatment: To prevent and treat jock itch, keep skin, clothes, athletic supporters, underwear, sheets and towels clean and dry. Don't reuse soiled gym clothes. Use antifungal cream. Bathe daily. Wash area well, then dry completely. Wear loose cotton undergarments. Never share a towel with anyone.
See a doctor if: Jock itch is recurrent and does not improve with self-treatment.

Pink Eye (conjunctivitis). A highly contagious infection of the inner eyelid membranes. The white part of eye and insides of eyelids turn dark pink or red.
Treatment: Wipe away discharge with moist cotton ball. Lie down with a cool cloth over eyes to relieve discomfort. Avoid spreading infection – don't share wash cloth or towel.
See a doctor if: Symptoms last longer than a day. You will need prescription antibiotic drops or ointment.

Rash. Because a rash can signal a variety of problems, some quite severe, you should get medical attention for any rash lasting longer than a day.

See a doctor if: Rash lasts longer than 24 hours, you suspect you may have a contagious disease, a rash from contact dermatitis affects large area of skin or a rash from an insect bite causes breathing difficulties.

Common Causes of Rash:

Hives, a reaction caused by allergy to food or medication, are small, itchy reddened bumps or large, welt-like raised areas.

Treatment: Discontinue any new medication or food that may have caused the hives. Bathe in lukewarm water and baking soda. Use an antihistamine to stop itching or apply calamine lotion, witch hazel or alcohol.

Heat rash results from overdressing or overexposure to high temperatures. Skin, usually rough and reddened, is covered with pinhead sized pimples. Can itch severely.

Treatment: Dust affected areas with cornstarch to stay dry. Use hydrocortisone cream. Avoid wearing wool, and dress in light, loose cotton clothing.

Eczema is a rough rash that itches and may bleed. Common in knee and elbow creases, it can occur many places on the skin.

Treatment: Consult doctor for antihistamine for itching. Wash areas infrequently to prevent drying. Apply cortisone cream if area is not infected or antibiotic cream if infected.

Contact dermatitis results when skin becomes irritated by certain fabrics or detergents left in clothes. The red rash is rough, itchy and may weep or blister.

Treatment: Wash area with mild soap. Apply lukewarm compresses and calamine lotion. Apply cortisone creams and use an antihistamine.

Impetigo, a very contagious infection, looks like whiteheads or oozing blisters that itch severely and eventually scab. Over-the-counter antibiotic creams are effective in some cases. In severe cases, you might need a prescription from your physician.

*M*om says:
To soothe a minor rash or hives, fill the tub with cool to lukewarm water and a cup of baking soda. Soak until itch and redness subsides.

275

At-Home RX

Echinacea, a native North American wildflower first used by the Plains Indians, is still a popular healing herb. Properties in the herb boost the immune system by normalizing the number of white blood cells and helping them destroy bacteria and viruses in the body. Taken at the first sign of the flu, a cold, or sore throat, echinacea can help slow infection, flush toxins and speed recovery. Find it in lozenges and tea.

Treatment: Wash the area gently with mild soap and water. Do not pick scabs, scrub or scratch area as this may spread infection. Use nonprescription or prescription antibiotic cream. Treat promptly as scarring may occur. Avoid contact with other people.

Sore Throat: Often a result of a respiratory infection, a sore throat is occasionally caused by a bacterial infection or strep. Sore throat may also result from excessive talking, breathing heavily polluted air or breathing through your mouth during sleep.

Treatment: Pain reliever every four hours. Suck on lozenges, hard candy or mints. Gargle hourly with hot salt water.

See a doctor if: Sore throat interferes with breathing, glands in neck swell, fever is 101 degrees or higher, you have a rash, you begin drooling or the inside throat is bright red.

Stomach Ache. Commonly a stomachache results from overeating, eating rich foods or from a build-up of painful gas. Other stomachaches may be caused by food-borne illness or a viral infection. A common stomachache hurts beneath the navel with cramping throughout the abdomen. A stomachache from appendicitis is sharp and stabbing or dull and intense in the lower abdomen on either side (not just the left side).

Treatment: Eat a clear diet of broths, juices and herbal teas. Follow with bland diet of soft foods. Avoid spicy or fried foods and milk products. If you have diarrhea, eat only a clear diet until you pass firm stools. Never take a laxative for a stomachache. Take an over-the-counter antacid or anti-gas medicine if gas pains are severe. Apply gentle heat to abdomen with hot water bottle.

See a doctor if: Stabbing pain or intense dull ache in lower abdomen lasts longer than two hours, ache is less intense but lasts longer than 24 hours, fever climbs higher than 101 degrees, diarrhea has blood or mucus, vomit has blood, mucus, green bile or black grit resembling coffee grounds.

Sty. A pimple-like swelling of the upper or lower eyelid, a sty is usually red and tender.

Treatment: Soak sty with a hot washcloth for 30 minutes every three hours until it comes to a head, bursts and drains. Wipe drainage gently. Never squeeze or lance a sty. Apply antibiotic ointment.

See a doctor if: Sty interferes with vision, sty does not come to head, pain or fever develops, there is more than one sty on the same eye or one on both eyelids.

Testicular Pain. Most often, pain in the testicles results from a blunt trauma. Other reasons may include twisted spermatic cord, inflammation of sperm tube, varicose veins in scrotum, hernia or kidney stones.

Treatment: For sudden, excruciating testicular pain that is not caused by injury, seek medical care immediately.

See a doctor if: Pain develops gradually and doesn't subside, one testicle is elevated and you have swelling, nausea or fever or if you notice a lump.

Urinary Pain. Painful urination can result from a kidney, bladder or urinary tract infection, a narrowing of urinary tract, or an irritation of the genitals. A fever indicates infection and should be checked by a physician. Burning during urination usually means a bladder or urinary tract infection. Straining during urination, less common and more serious, can result from narrowing of the urinary tract.

Treatment: If genital irritation is present, wash area with mild soap and warm water. Rinse, dry, then apply zinc oxide (diaper rash) ointment. If swollen, use an icepack. If you cannot urinate because of pain, soak in warm tub and urinate directly into the bathtub then take a shower afterward. If you suspect a urinary infection, have your physician test the urine to rule out infection.

See a doctor if: Irritation doesn't clear up after treatment, fever climbs higher than 100 degrees, burning during urination lasts longer than 24 hours, you urinate more than every two hours over a 24-hour period, you have dull throbbing pain in lower back or trouble urinating.

Vaginal Discharge. It's normal to have some vaginal discharge that is clear and odorless. The troublesome kind is different. Ranging from frothy and foul-smelling to the consistency of cottage cheese, the irritation may cause pain and severe itching. Most often vaginal discharge is related to an imbalance in beneficial bacteria levels in the vagina, resulting in a yeast infection.

Treatment: Wash area with mild soap and warm water. Rinse and dry thoroughly. Avoid nylon undergarments that trap heat and perspiration – wear cotton that can absorb moisture and let skin breathe. To relieve pain and itching, sit in a lukewarm tub twice a day. Do not douche – it will aggravate a yeast infection. If you know you have a yeast infection, you can use nonprescription medication to relieve itch and clear infection.

See a doctor if: You have pain during urination. If home treatment is not effective within 48 hours, see a doctor because some sexually transmitted diseases can also cause discharge.

Vomiting. Don't try to stop vomiting. The process usually rids the body of harmful substances or signals another illness that needs attention. Be aware that vomiting will likely bring dehydration. Promptly treat symptoms of dehydration. Although you may not feel like ingesting any fluids, do so. Drink juices, water or liquid made to help balance electrolytes. Vomiting accompanies many illnesses and rarely occurs alone. Sudden or violent vomiting in absence of another illness can signal a food-borne illness, and you should seek immediate medical attention.

Treatment: No solid food for eight hours after vomiting stops. If vomiting is severe, stick with clear liquids for 24 hours or more. Take fever-reducing pain reliever, if needed.

See a doctor if: You have vomiting spells for more than 24 hours, you vomit mucus or blood, you vomit green or bile-stained material more than once, you vomit dark material resembling coffee grounds, vomiting is sudden and intense without symptoms of illness or disease or fever remains higher than 101 degrees for more than a day.

Serious & Chronic Diseases

Often, symptoms of illness are simply signals that something isn't running smoothly in the body, and that you may have an infection or mild malady that needs attention. If your symptoms persist, however, or if you notice definite patterns over a prolonged period of time, read through this chapter to see if you might have a more serious condition, then see your doctor immediately to discuss your concerns and schedule any necessary medical tests.

Remember: Just because you may have many or all of the symptoms listed under a certain illness or disease, that does not mean you have that illness. Use this list as a guide to help you decide whether you should consult a doctor. Only a licensed physician can accurately diagnose and treat any disease.

Anemia. Condition results from a lack of red blood cells or hemoglobin in the blood. Red blood cells are the body's oxygen transportation system. When the system is compromised, the body tissues don't receive enough oxygen and serious illness can result. Anemia can arise from too little iron in the diet or prolonged internal bleeding such as with a peptic ulcer.

Symptoms: Breathlessness, fatigue or drowsiness, dizziness, ringing in ears, muscle weakness, pounding or racing heart, increased thirst, confusion or loss of acuity, swollen, flabby, sore tongue, pale coloring, especially on the linings of eyelids and mouth and the beds of fingernails

Treatment: See your doctor to determine whether the anemia is due to a loss of blood or dietary problems. If anemia is due to loss of blood, the source of bleeding must be detected and corrected by your physician. If the source of anemia is dietary, you will need to eat an iron-rich diet including dark green vegetables, eggs, molasses, liver, whole grains and possibly a supplement. Follow your doctor's recommendations.

Mom says:
Pay attention to what your body is telling you, especially when you have pain or symptoms of infection. If in doubt, check it out with your doctor.

279

Appendicitis. The appendix, a worm-like extension from the colon, usually lies in lower right abdomen but is occasionally found on other side or toward the center. Medical researchers know of no real purpose for the appendix. Once it's removed surgically, you continue to function as usual. When the appendix becomes infected, it gets swollen, tender and can become gangrenous or rupture. If the appendix ruptures, it can lead to peritonitis, a sometimes fatal disease. Appendicitis is usually accompanied by an elevated white blood cell count, which a doctor can determine with a lab test.

Symptoms: Pain in the abdomen, usually on lower right side, or rigidity in lower right side of the abdomen, a fever of 100 degrees or higher, loss of appetite, indigestion, nausea or vomiting.

Treatment: The only treatment for appendicitis is surgical removal of the appendix. Delay can result in rupture. If you suspect appendicitis, don't take a laxative or give yourself an enema as this might cause rupture if infected. Don't apply heat to your abdomen.

Asthma. An illness where the victim struggles to breathe, asthma can be caused by an infection, allergy or stress. For most people with asthma, the attacks are broken up by long periods in which there is no problem. Problem-free periods become shorter and asthma attacks become more frequent and more intense. Unfortunately, some people with asthma also develop allergies or sensitivities to the drugs used in treatment, including aspirin.

Symptoms: Tightness and constriction in the chest, severe difficulty breathing, noisy and wheezy breathing, pale, bluish face, violent cough that produces thick mucus.

Treatment: Asthma treatment requires a physician's supervision. Many cases can be easily controlled with prescription medication. People with asthma should not smoke and must take extra measures to avoid colds and respiratory infections.

Athlete's Foot. A common malady among men, athlete's foot is caused by a fungus that thrives in warm, damp places, such as between the toes and in tight, closed shoes that do not allow feet to breathe. You can pick up the fungus by walking barefoot in locker rooms, gymnasiums or around swimming pools.

Symptoms: Severe itching, redness of the skin, skin cracks between toes, white patches of skin, blistering or bleeding.

Treatment: Once every two hours, wash your feet with soap and warm water, rinse well and make sure your feet are dry. Sprinkle feet liberally with an antifungal powder or cream.

Bronchitis. Either bacteria or a virus can cause bronchitis, an illness that inflames bronchial tubes and results in breathing difficulties. Without proper treatment the infection can develop into pleurisy (painful inflammation of lining around lungs) or even bronchial pneumonia.

Symptoms: Severe pain in the back, pain under the breastbone, pain when taking deep breaths, violent cough which is at first nonproductive but then produces thick phlegm, fever more than 101 degrees.

Treatment: If bacteria causes the bronchitis, your doctor will prescribe an antibiotic. Stay in bed, drink plenty of fluids and keep the air warm and moist with a humidifier.

Bacteria vs. Virus

Bacteria are germs that multiply by splitting into two cells. Those cells keep dividing and release poisons, causing the body to react to them. Bacterial infections are usually treated with antibiotic drugs. Some bacterial infections can be prevented with vaccines, which create immunity.

Viruses are simpler in structure. They multiply by invading cells and taking them over to make copies of themselves. Viruses make you sick by interfering with how those cells work. Our immune system can fight most viruses. The symptoms of some viruses can be treated with drugs, but antibiotics don't work for viral infections.

281

*M*om says:
The best way to defeat or avoid cancer is to prevent it. Eat cancer-fighting foods. Exercise. Stay at a healthy weight. Don't smoke or chew tobacco. Get checked for breast, prostate, colon and cervical cancer. Have your doctor check any suspect skin lesions.

Bursitis. Sometimes called tennis elbow, bursitis can occur in any joint but is most common in shoulder, elbow and knee. Bursitis occurs with constant irritation to the bursa, or the membranous sac between joints. This irritation can come from calcium deposits, constant bruising or improper grip of a racquet. Your doctor may want to x-ray the joint to make sure there is no bone damage.

Symptoms: Severe pain upon movement of a joint, dull aching while the joint is not being used, sensation of extreme tension in the joint.

Treatment: Pain can be partially relieved by cold packs and keeping the joint immobile. If calcium deposits cause the irritation, they may need to be surgically removed or controlled by medication.

Cancer. A complex disease that can manifest itself many ways, cancer has numerous and varied possible symptoms. As a guideline, the American Cancer Society has *Seven Warning Signs Of Cancer*. The presence of any of these symptoms for a period longer than two weeks should be reason to see a doctor.

Symptoms (Seven Warning Signs): Change in bowel or bladder habits, sore that does not heal, unusual bleeding or discharge, thickening or lump in breast or elsewhere, indigestion or difficulty in swallowing, obvious change in wart or mole, prolonged cough or hoarseness.

Treatment and Prevention: Treatment may include surgery, radiation or chemotherapy.

Take these steps to reduce your risk: Eat fiber-rich foods. Avoid exposure to sun. Don't smoke cigarettes. Maintain proper weight. Women should do monthly breast self-exams. Older women should have yearly mammograms. Get frequent medical checkups. Older men should have yearly colon and prostate screenings.

Cystitis. This bacterial disease, also known as *bladder infection*, causes inflammation of the bladder and pain during urination. It is most common among women of childbearing age, but can also affect men, particularly those with an enlarged prostate.

Symptoms: Frequent need to urinate, burning or pain during urination, scanty urine, body aches, general fatigue.

Treatment: Contact your doctor for antibiotics. If you feel a bladder infection coming on, drink up to four glasses of cranberry juice a day to acidify urine and kill the bacteria. Also drink a lot of water to flush out bacteria.

Diabetes. Diabetes occurs when the body does not produce enough insulin, a hormone essential to digest fat, protein and carbohydrates. As a result, the body cannot utilize sugar and blood sugar levels become dangerously elevated.

Symptoms: Unexplained weight loss, excessive hunger and thirst, excessive or frequent urination, cramps in the legs, dryness of mouth and throat, frequent skin infections, boils, numbness or tingling in limbs.

More than Melancholy

We all have ups and downs, but if you feel down frequently or feelings of sadness interfere with usual activities, you may be clinically depressed.

Depression is a disease resulting from an imbalance of brain chemicals. Symptoms range from mild, temporary feelings of sadness to severe, chronic feelings of despair.

Symptoms include recurrent feelings of sadness, loss of interest in activities once enjoyed, loss of appetite or excessive eating, fatigue, sleeping problems, loss of concentration, uncontrollable weeping, frequent feelings of worthlessness and sometimes suicidal thoughts. If you have thoughts of suicide, call a crisis hotline and seek help from your doctor.

The majority of depressed people can be treated. Most feel better within weeks. Treatment may include mental health counseling, talk therapy and medication.

You can also: Exercise. Avoid use of alcohol, marijuana or any other drug to cope with your problems. Learn to relax to reduce tension and stress. Join a support group for people with depression. Do things that brought you joy as a child, like blowing bubbles, playing in the park, finger painting, flying a kite, running through sprinklers or planting some flowers.

Participate in an artistic activity like drawing, painting, singing, writing, dancing or playing an instrument. You don't have to be good at it! The activity alone will help you work through your feelings.

Treatment: In some cases diabetes can be controlled by diet and exercise. In many cases, the diabetic must take medication or insulin injections. If not controlled, the disease may lead to blindness, kidney disease, coma or even death.

Gastroenteritis. A catch-all phrase for inflammation of the stomach and intestinal lining, gastroenteritis can result from food allergy, virus, intestinal flu, food poisoning or too much food and alcohol. Vomiting and diarrhea can lead to dehydration.
Symptoms: Cold, sweaty skin, fatigue, weakness, nausea or vomiting, intestinal cramps, diarrhea, pain in abdomen.
Treatment: Avoid food and drinks while vomiting and diarrhea continue. Once it has stopped, eat only a clear liquid diet. If vomiting persists, you should contact a doctor who can prescribe medication or give intravenous liquids to correct dehydration.

Hay Fever. An allergic reaction to wind-borne pollens can occur in the spring, summer or autumn. Hay fever occurs seasonally, unlike allergies to cat dander or household dustmites.
Symptoms: Headache isolated in front, violent sneezing, thin nasal discharge, itchy eyes, nose, throat, fatigue.
Treatment: Take antihistamines. Your doctor can also isolate the cause of hay fever by a skin patch test. then a desensitization program can develop immunity.

Hemorrhoids. Simply put, hemorrhoids are varicose veins in the anus or rectum. They can result from stress, chronic constipation, sedentary lifestyle and heredity. External hemorrhoids protrude from the anus and look like wrinkly brown folds of skin. Internal hemorrhoids can't be seen without a physician's tools.
Symptoms: Itching, pain, irritation or burning during or after a bowel movement, blood streaks on stools, bleeding or passage of clots.

Treatment: Only severe hemorrhoids need surgery. Your doctor can help you treat mild cases. Avoid straining during bowel movements. Drink plenty of fluids and eat fiber-rich foods. See a doctor if you have bleeding to rule out other more serious conditions.

Hepatitis. A viral infection affecting the liver, hepatitis can result from poor sanitation, infected food or can be spread from person to person through bodily contact. The intensity of the disease varies. Some victims are debilitated while others are unaware of it.
Symptoms: Nausea and/or vomiting, cramping and diarrhea, loss of appetite, pain and tenderness on right side below the ribcage, high fever, dark urine and light stools.
Treatment: There is currently no effective cure for hepatitis. Since hepatitis is contagious during the first few weeks, take extreme caution not to spread it to others. Wash your hands well in soap and hot water after using the bathroom.

Hernia. The most common types of hernia occur exclusively in men when part of the intestine pushes through an internal opening into the groin or scrotum. Inguinal hernias usually result from physical overexertion or improper lifting. If your doctor is unable to push tissue back into place, surgery may be necessary.
Symptoms: Unusual pressure in groin, discomfort when lifting, painful lump or bulge in groin or scrotum, scrotum pain, swelling.
Treatment and Prevention: Eat high fiber foods. Don't strain during bowel movements. If any activity places strain on lower back, use a support belt. Learn proper lifting techniques. Keep physically fit.

Hypoglycemia. Also known as low blood sugar, hypoglycemia results when the body produces too much insulin and cannot handle sugars normally. The illness is most common in young , overweight women, but may also result from illnesses like liver disease.

At-Home RX

To ease the pain of hemorrhoids, take a 15 minute sitz bath in warm water twice a day, then apply a cool cloth soaked in diluted witch hazel.

To lessen itch and aid in healing, you can use any nonprescription ointment specifically for the affliction or try Bag Balm, which is an antibiotic ointment developed originally to treat the infected udders of cows. Well known for its skin-healing properties, Bag Balm can be found on store shelves with hand and body lotions.

Symptoms: Dizziness and shakiness, inability to concentrate, mild to severe headache, excessive sweating, fatigue and weakness.

Treatment: After a diagnosis of hypoglycemia from a glucose tolerance test, your doctor will advise you about diet and exercise that can help control the disease. Eating well and often throughout the day will help.

Kidney Infection. Caused by a variety of factors, even something as simple as a boil, this bacterial infection usually responds well to antibiotics. Neglect or failure to treat kidney infection, however, can lead to long-term damage of the kidneys.

Symptoms: Scanty and cloudy urine, flu symptoms and fever, painful urination, urine containing pus, foul-smelling urine, severe lower back pain.

Treatment: See your doctor. Treatment usually involves antibiotics and bed rest with plenty of fluids. People with diabetes should get treatment immediately to avoid kidney disease.

Kidney Stones. Made of calcium or uric acids, kidney stones form in the kidneys and can get lodged anywhere along the urinary tract – in the kidneys themselves, the ureter, bladder or urethra. As stones pass through the urinary tract they cause excruciating pain.

Symptoms: Pain radiating across back, blood in urine, fever and chills, pain in the groin and genitals.

Treatment: Stones must either pass through the urinary tract or be removed surgically. Your doctor can administer pain medication to help pass smaller stones.

Mononucleosis. Known as the kissing disease, mononucleosis is spread through saliva and mainly affects adolescents. Caused by a virus, mono can vary in severity. It causes the spleen to enlarge. Victims should not engage in physical activities that could rupture the spleen.

Symptoms: Low-grade fever, loss of appetite, nausea and/or vomiting, fatigue and headache, enlarged lymph nodes, severe sore throat, general body rash, yellowish skin and eyes.

Treatment: Bed rest during active stage of illness when most symptoms are present. Take medication to reduce fever. If nausea is severe, your doctor may prescribe medication to help. Avoid strenuous physical activity. While you cannot be reinfected, you can suffer a relapse if you become run down.

Perforated Eardrum. A cotton swab or bobby pin can rupture an eardrum. It can also be perforated by severe suction to the ear, a blow to the side of the head or severe infection in middle ear. Perforated eardrum can lead to permanent hearing loss.

Symptoms: Sudden, severe ear pain, hollow sensation, nausea and/or vomiting, dizziness, drainage from ear.

Treatment: Don't put any drops in ear. Place sterile cotton loosely in ear and call a doctor. Immediate care will help ensure hearing can be protected even in the case of a large rupture.

Peptic Ulcer. A bacterium causes more than 70 percent of all peptic ulcers (irritations in stomach and small intestine). Antibiotics can quickly eradicate the bacteria and liberate millions of people who have suffered through years of abdominal pain and bland diets.

Symptoms: Gnawing or burning in upper abdomen usually worse on an empty stomach, upper abdominal pain made worse by drinking alcohol or eating spicy, heavy or fibrous foods, sometimes bloating, nausea, vomiting, excessive belching indigestion, heartburn, weight loss, black or tarry stools.

Treatment: Ask doctor if antibiotics will cure your ulcer. Use antacids to neutralize stomach acids. Avoid high-fat, overly fibrous or very spicy foods. Eat six small meals a day instead of three large ones. Avoid alcohol, milk and cigarettes. Learn relaxation techniques to reduce stress and calm stomach acids.

Mom says:
Find a way to relax and reduce stress. Many illnesses are caused or made worse by stress. Check into meditation, tai-chi, yoga, biofeedback, self-hypnosis to get your mind and body working together. Don't under estimate the value of a brisk daily walk or an aromatic warm bath.

Pneumonia. An inflammation of air cells in lungs, pneumonia is commonly caused by bacteria, but can also result from a virus or chemicals. Pneumonia caused by bacteria or virus is contagious and can be spread through coughing or sneezing. You can be exposed to pneumonia without developing it, but are at risk if you are run down. The mortality rate from pneumonia used to be high, but medical advances have improved recovery rates.

Symptoms: Violent shaking and chills, extremely high fever, eruptions of cold sores, flushed, hot, moist skin, profuse sweating, rapid pulse, difficulty breathing, wheezing, fatigue and weakness, painful burning cough, bloody sputum.

Treatment: If you suspect pneumonia, see your physician immediately. If the pneumonia is caused by bacteria, prescription antibiotic therapy will help. Bed rest is essential until fever has eased completely. In severe cases, the doctor may need to administer oxygen. Avoid contact with small children and the elderly as they are quite susceptible to the illness.

Shingles. Anyone who has had chicken pox can get shingles. Unlike chicken pox, the discomfort you experience may not go away when blisters disappear. Almost half of the people who experience shingles develop chronic neuralgia, which is a lingering soft-tissue pain.

Symptoms: Pain or tingling on skin, rash, small blisters filled with clear fluid that cloud and crust over after a few days, flu-like symptoms.

Treatment: Get a prescription from a doctor. Apply an antibiotic ointment to blisters. Keep blisters covered to avoid spreading the disease. Apply cool, wet compresses to relieve pain.

Sinusitis. When sinuses become filled with fluid due to infection, sinusitis is the result. Sinuses no longer drain and the dark, warm spaces encourage bacterial growth. Sinusitis is common among those with frequent head colds, allergies or a deviated septum.

Symptoms: Severe, constant headache, soreness around the eyes, toothache in the upper row, fever, chills, sore throat, dizziness, nausea or vomiting, thick nasal discharge.
Treatment: Sinusitis must be treated with prescribed antibiotics. Your doctor may also need to drain the sinuses. You can treat pain with a pain reliever and heat packs. Sinusitis usually persists for about four weeks. Don't use nasal sprays.

Strep Throat. Caused by the invasion of streptococcal bacteria in the throat, a strep throat can lead to possible complications of abscess or rheumatic fever if left untreated. With antibiotic treatment, most strep throat is responsive without complication.
Symptoms: Severe sore throat, painful swallowing, chills and fever, swollen lymph glands.
Treatment: Take prescribed antibiotics. Take over-the-counter pain reliever and suck on ice chips to relieve pain. Get plenty of fluids from broths and warm drinks.

Tooth Abscess. Usually caused by bacteria but sometimes a fungus, tooth abscess is a pocket of infection inside at the tooth root. Untreated, an abscess can spread infection to the blood stream.
Symptoms: Relentless, gnawing toothache, severe pain while chewing, swollen gums around the aching tooth, swollen jaw.
Treatment: Your dentist will prescribe antibiotics for the infection and treat an early abscess with a root canal. In this case, the tooth is opened, the nerve cut out and the abscess allowed to drain before the tooth is packed and sealed. If the abscess is too large or has done too much damage, the dentist will, as a last resort, pull the tooth.

Toxic Shock. This rare but potentially fatal disease is caused by bacteria that are often present in the nose, skin or vagina. However, a deep wound, surgery or the use of highly absorbent tampons can cause the bacteria to release life-threatening poisons.

Mom says:
When a virus or illness is going around, take precautions. Increase your intake of vitamin C. Wash your hands with antibacterial soap after you use the toilet and before you handle food. Don't drink out of other people's cups or eat off their plates. Use a disinfectant and spray it on telephones and doorknobs in the office and at home.

*M*om says:
Everyone suffers some type of personal malady, like acne or bad breath, at times in their lives. Usually these things are easily treated and will pass. Just remain patient and persistent until things clear up.

Symptoms: Sudden high fever, severe vomiting, diarrhea, sunburn-like rash on palms and soles of feet, muscle aches, dizziness or fainting, sore throat.

Treatment and Prevention: Use sanitary napkins instead of tampons during menstruation or use the lowest absorbency tampon. Change tampons frequently during the day. Do not wear tampons overnight. Wash hands with soap and water before and after changing tampons.

Trench Mouth. Mildly contagious, trench mouth is caused by bacteria, poor nutrition and poor dental hygiene. Untreated, trench mouth can loosen all teeth and may cause damage to jaw bones.

Symptoms: Dirty, gray membrane inside of mouth, red, spongy gums, bleeding, sore gums.

Treatment: Your dentist likely will prescribe antibiotics. Rinse mouth every two hours with hydrogen peroxide diluted with two parts of water. Eat soft bland foods.

Up Close and Personal

Acne. Most experts agree that acne is linked to heredity and hormone levels, not too dietary preferences. Hormones stimulate oil production in glands around hair follicles, the ducts surrounding follicles become clogged and a whitehead or blackhead results. An inflamed skin clog becomes a red pimple.

Treatment: Keep all acne-prone areas clean, using warm soapy water. Rinse well. Pat areas dry, don't rub or scrub. Try soaps or astringents designed to dry out the skin. Use acne medications that contain benzoyl peroxide.

Seek Medical Help If: You have extremely painful, cyst-like lesions that leave scars. See doctor if a cyst or pimple becomes infected.

Bad Breath. Obvious causes of bad breath – bad dental hygiene, smoking, and poor diet – are treatable at home. But other problems such as liver disease, lung disease, respiratory infections, digestive disorders and kidney failure can cause bad breath.

Treatment: Brush and floss teeth two or three times daily. Brush and rinse your tongue. Have teeth professionally cleaned and examined every six months. Rinse mouth often with antiseptic mouthwash. Avoid eating garlic, onions, hot peppers and cheeses.
Seek Medical Help If: Breath smells like urine or feces, or has an unusually fishy or fruity odor. Bad breath does not just go away.

Dandruff. A dry, itchy scalp can signal dandruff, but the most noticeable symptom is white or gray flakes on hair or clothing.
Treatment: Shampoo daily with a nonprescription dandruff shampoo. If you notice no improvement after three weeks, see your doctor about a prescription. Shampoos with selenium sulfide or zinc pyrithione work quickly and slow down flaking. Preparations with salicylic acid and sulfur will loosen flakes so that they can be washed away more easily.
Seek Medical Help If: Heavy dandruff does not improve after treatment, you have scaly patches of skin on sides of nose, in eyebrows or on chest or if dandruff flakes are accompanied by spots where scalp is inflamed.

Warts. A skin growth caused by a mildly contagious virus, almost any wart will go away on its own. But that can take two years! The raised pinkish growths, hard or rough on the surface, sometimes have dark dots or specks in center. Most warts are small, granular and painless except for larger, painful foot warts.
Treatment: Apply nonprescription wart medicine containing salicylic acid then cover with an adhesive bandage. Avoid irritating skin around wart. For foot warts, use wart ointment or powder. Keep your feet dry. Never cut or burn a wart off by yourself.
Seek Medical Help If: A wart drains fluid or becomes irritated, painful or inflamed, you have a wart on the neck or face or have a growth that may not be a wart.

Sexually Transmitted Diseases

The risk taken by having unprotected sex is high and the consequences can be devastating. When you engage in unprotected sex (including oral sex) or have multiple sexual partners, you are at high risk for serious sexually transmitted diseases (STDs) such as *pubic lice, genital warts, syphilis, gonorrhea and chlamydia.* Worst of all, you are also at risk for the incurable diseases of *genital herpes* and *acquired immune deficiency syndrome or AIDS.*

AIDS. A disease caused by the human immunodeficiency virus or (HIV) destroys the white blood cells and immune system. AIDS is fatal. The disease leaves its victims unable to fight opportunistic infections and cancers which lead to death. At this time, there is no cure for AIDS. Antiretroviral drugs, however, can slow its progression.

The AIDS virus can be transmitted through the vulva, vagina, penis, rectum or mouth during sexual contact. HIV is also spread through infected blood and contaminated needles.

The HIV infection can be present without symptoms for up to a decade – thus, HIV can be passed on and acquired without your knowledge, or the knowledge of your partner. The only sure way to know if you are free of HIV is to be tested.

Some people with HIV experience flu-like symptoms within a few months of exposure that usually disappear quickly. Then the person enters an asymptomatic phase that can last up to ten years. During this time, there are no symptoms of illness, but the virus is multiplying rapidly, killing off or disabling white blood cells.

Early Symptoms: Recurrent fever, night sweats, fatigue, body aches, diarrhea, decreased appetite, white spots in mouth, sore throat, nausea and vomiting, swollen lymph glands in neck, underarms or groin.

Advanced Symptoms: Lymph nodes remain swollen

for more than three months, weight loss, severe fatigue and weakness, frequent fevers, frequent yeast infections in mouth or genitals, frequent herpes infections, short-term memory loss.

HIV protection and Prevention: Abstain from intercourse, or use condoms and a diaphram each time, especially if neither of you has been tested for HIV.

If your partner refuses to use a condom, don't have sex. If a person does not want to use a condom with you, it is likely that person has not used them with others, increasing your risk for HIV.

If you or your partner have had other sexual partners, both of you should have an HIV test.

Don't inject illegal drugs. If you do, don't share needles. Any drug use increases risk because under the influence you are less likely to make wise sexual decisions.

> ### Respect Yourself, Protect Yourself
>
> Abstain from having sex. If you are a teenager or young adult, avoid having sexual relations (including oral sex) as long as possible. The younger you are the first time you have sex, the more at risk you are for STDs.
>
> Use a condom every time, especially if you or your partner have had other sexual partners.
>
> The only time you can safely not use a condom is if you and your partner have only had sex with each other, ever, or after both test negative for all STDs and remain monogamous.
>
> Birth control pills do not protect from STDs.
>
> Ask questions of your sexual partner and be honest in return. If you are too embarrassed to talk about sex, then you don't know each other well enough to have sex.
>
> Get tested for all STDs if you have multiple partners or before sex with a new partner. Insist your partner be tested.
>
> Limit your number of sexual partners as the risk for STDs increases.
>
> If you suspect you have an STD, end all sexual contact until you have been diagnosed and treated.

If you have another STD, do not have sex with an HIV-infected partner as you will be more at risk.

If you think you have been exposed to HIV or have symptoms, see your doctor. If your HIV test is positive, talk with your doctor about starting drug therapy.

Genital Herpes. Caused by the herpes simplex virus (HSV), genital herpes is most often spread through sexual intercourse, but can also be spread by kissing. The virus comes in two types: HSV1 which causes cold sores and can also infect the genital area through oral sex, and HSV2, the chief reason for genital sores, which can also cause infections in the mouth. No cure exists, but medication is available to manage outbreaks of sores. Use a condom to protect your partner.

Symptoms: Pain in legs, buttocks, genitals, vaginal discharge, pressure in abdomen, fever, headache, muscle aches, sores at site of infection, lesions that progress to blisters or open sores which crust over and eventually heal, painful or difficult urination, swollen glands in groin area.

Treatment: If you have symptoms of genital herpes, see your doctor. If the diagnosis is confirmed, your doctor may prescribe an antiviral medication that shortens the first outbreak. Sprinkle cornstarch in underwear to keep sores dry. Avoid touching sores, and wash hands with soap and water after contact. Avoid sexual contact until all sores have healed completely.

Chlamydia. A bacterial disease, chlamydia is transmitted through unprotected sexual intercourse or an exchange of bodily fluids through the mucous membranes in the genital areas, mouth and anus. It is the leading STD in the United States mainly due to the fact that half of all women and a quarter of all men with the disease have no obvious symptoms. If left untreated, chlamydia can lead to pelvic inflammatory disease, infertility, an inflamed rectum and conjunctivitis.

Symptoms: Abnormal genital discharge, pain with urination. Often there are no symptoms.

Treatment: Your doctor can prescribe an antibiotic to eliminate the infection. You should get tested regularly for chlamydia if you are 25 or younger and have had sexual intercourse with more than one partner. Women should avoid douching as it removes beneficial bacteria.

Gonorrhea. Also known as *the clap*, gonorrhea is caused by bacteria that multiply rapidly in the cervix, urethra, mouth and rectum. Many people with this disease have no obvious symptoms. If left untreated, the disease can spread to the uterus and fallopian tubes, causing pelvic inflammatory disease, sterility or tubal pregnancy. In men, the disease can spread to the prostate gland, and the urethra can narrow, making urination difficult. If left untreated, gonorrhea can also infect joints, heart valves and the brain.

Symptoms: Fever, vomiting, painful urination, vaginal discharge, abdominal pain, bleeding between periods, anal itching or discharge.

Treatment: Although symptoms are mild, visit your doctor if you suspect you have gonorrhea. Since the disease often occurs with chlamydia, your doctor may prescribe a combination of antibiotics to treat both diseases. Your sexual partner should also be tested for the diseases.

Syphilis. A serious, highly contagious, multiple-stage sexually transmitted disease, syphilis is caused by bacteria spread from sores of an infected person to mucous membranes of another through sexual contact. It can also pass through broken skin on other areas of the body. Early symptoms are mild, yet this is when the disease is most contagious. Left untreated, syphilis can cause heart problems, mental disorders, blindness and death.

Symptoms: Chancre sores on penis, vulva, tongue or lips, skin rash, mild fever, fatigue, headache, sore throat, patchy hair loss, swollen lymph glands.

Treatment: Although early symptoms are mild, your doctor can make a diagnosis through a blood test. Syphilis can be treated with prescription antibiotics. Avoid sexual relations until you complete treatment and all sores have healed. Using a condom can help prevent the spread of syphilis. If you have multiple partners, get checked regularly for this disease.

Genital Warts. Also called venereal warts, the malady is caused by a virus spread through sexual contact. If untreated, the warts may grow to resemble tiny cauliflower or develop into large masses that can block the vagina, urethra or anus. The warts may also be too small to see or may grow in places such as the cervix where they can't be seen. The virus may cause a pap smear to register abnormal.

Symptoms: Warts appear as small, flat, soft, flesh-colored bumps, or as tiny, cauliflower-like bumps. In women, they may appear on vulva, perineal area, vagina and cervix. In men, they may appear on penis, near anus or between penis and scrotum. They may also appear on mouth, lips and throat.

Treatment: If you have genital warts, your doctor can remove them using freezing, laser or chemicals. However, the virus does remain in your body. If left untreated, the infection can lead to cervical cancer in women and cancer of the penis in men. A person can be infected for months or years before warts appear.

Pubic Lice. Known as *crabs,* pubic lice are blood-sucking insects that resemble tiny pale crabs. They are found in pubic hair, around anus, and occasionally in underarm hair, eyebrows or eyelashes. Pubic lice are highly contagious and spread by intimate contact.

Symptoms: Intense itching in pubic area, minute, flat crab-like insects, mild fever, fatigue, irratibility.

Treatment: A nonprescription treatment to kill lice may clear up crabs. If not, see a doctor. Wash clothes, bedding and towels. Crabs can survive 24 hours without a host.

Drug Use, Abuse & Addiction

Drug abuse is defined as the harmful use of mind-altering or physically addictive substances, including illegal and prescription drugs as well as legal drugs, like alcohol.

Some people take drugs due to curiosity or peer pressure. Others use drugs to escape reality, alleviate depression or rebel against parents and society.

Alcohol, nicotine, cocaine, marijuana, hallucinogens like psilocybin mushrooms or LSD, ecstacy, and chemicals in glue and solvents are habit-forming. Regular use of them can cause psychological dependence. Some of these drugs can also be physically addictive.

The user of a habit-forming drug is compelled to continue using in order to maintain the state of well-being it produces. When deprived of the drug, the habitual user often becomes restless, irritable and anxious.

Heroin, barbiturates, speed, methamphetamine and crack are physically addictive. They alter body chemistry so that the drug becomes necessary to function. An addict develops painful, physical withdrawal if the drug is suddenly stopped. The addict will also develop tolerance to the drug so that larger doses are necessary to produce the desired effects.

Experimentation with drugs does not always lead to abuse or addiction, but psychological dependence can come on rapidly. Drug experimentation poses real dangers. Even trying some drugs once can lead to death or mental disability, as with sniffing or huffing solvents or glue – one huge sniff can be fatal and regular huffing leads to brain damage. The first try of crack or heroin can bring a fatal overdose.

Symptoms of drug abuse and addiction include alterations in behavior, such as apathy or unusual aggressiveness, lack of interest in activities you once enjoyed, like school and work, borrowing or stealing money to pay for drugs, indifference to personal appearance, hanging out with known drug users and suppliers, being exposed to harder drugs and recruited to try them, mental disturbances, and depression, aggression or physical withdrawal when drug use is stopped.

Treatment: Seek medical attention and psychological counseling if you find that drug use interferes with healthy behavior patterns. You may need to check yourself into a rehabilitation facility if you are physically addicted.

Notes

8

Getting From Here to There
Maintenance & Safe Traveling

Transportation can come in all sizes and shapes, from a shiny new car to a well-worn bicycle. Whatever the mode, it's critical that your transportation be reliable. If you've ever been stranded at the edge of the highway as traffic screeches past unrelentingly, you know the wisdom of proper vehicle maintenance and being prepared for an emergency.

In this chapter, you will find tips to keep your bicycle and your automobile in good running condition. You will also learn some basic tips about safety on the road and in your home.

Not everyone has a bicycle or car to get around. The old reliable is a pair of feet and some good walking shoes, but traveling in unfamiliar territory, walking anywhere at night, even using public transportation, a skateboard, scooter or roller blades all have their inherent risks. Knowing a few safety rules and basic self-defense techniques will better ensure that you get where you want to go on time and in one piece.

Mom says:
Always wear a
bicycle helmet.
When you plan to
go on long bike trips,
tell someone where
you are going and
when you expect to
return. For nighttime
bicycle trips, wear
light colors or clothes
with iridescent strips.
Buy a headlight if
you plan to go on
frequent night rides.

Keeping up a Bicycle

If you're in the market for transportation, consider buying the less expensive bicycle as opposed to a car. In addition to getting you around more economically, a bicycle also gives you daily exercise and means there's one less automobile on the road to pollute the air.

Selecting a size. As a rule, you should be able to straddle the horizontal bar with one inch of clearance. If your legs are 30 to 34 inches long, you need a frame between 21 and 22 inches tall.

Adjusting the seat. The heel of your foot should barely reach the low pedal, while the ball of your foot should rest on the high pedal with your knee slightly bent.

Brakes. Test brakes by squeezing them to be sure they are in good condition. They should come no closer than halfway to the handlebar. Check the brake cables for fraying and make sure the brake pedals are not worn.

Cables. Check for fraying and wear.

Chains. Check for damage, stress and rust. Lubricate with lightweight oil every three months.

Handlebars. Handlebars should be tight. Replace worn tape or grips. Adjust handle bars for comfort.

Nuts and Bolts. Quickly check all nuts, bolts and other hardware items before you begin riding to make sure they are tight. Keep an eye out for damaged or worn parts.

Reflectors. Check that reflectors are in place. It's best to have front, back and wheel reflectors.

Sprockets. Check that sprockets are tight on the cranks. Replace the sprockets if teeth are bent or broken.

Tires. Each time you ride, check both tires. They should be fully inflated as per specifications. Check to make sure they are not splitting, tearing or pulling away from rims. Check for bulging, puncture holes and nails.

Wheels. The front wheel should be centered between the fork. Check that the fork is not bent or broken. Make sure the axle nut is tight. The rear wheel should be centered within the chain stays. Keep the spoke tight. Both the rear and front wheels should rotate smoothly without any noticeable wobbling.

Note: Study the owner's manual for your bicycle and keep it handy for repairs and regular maintenance.

Automobile Maintenance

In general, you should know how to check the air in your tires, how to change a tire, how to maintain your battery and battery cables, and how to check all fluids including oil, antifreeze/coolant, brake, power steering and windshield wiper fluids. To keep your car in good condition, perform the following maintenance:

Air Conditioning/Heater. Check or have a mechanic check the operation of controls, belts and hoses for leaks, tears or brittleness every six months.

Air Filter. Check at every oil change and replace if dirty.

Battery. If your car battery uses water, make sure the reservoirs are full. Keep the cables free of encrusted battery acid. If cables are worn or frayed, have them replaced.

Defroster. If weather conditions indicate, check to make sure defroster works. Also check your windshield wiper fluid levels. If you do not have automatic windshield cleaning, carry glass cleaner and paper towels in the car.

Engine Oil. Change the oil every 2,000 to 3,000 miles. You should check your oil level every other time you fill up for gas to make sure you are not leaking oil. If your car runs out of oil, the engine will freeze up and you'll have an expensive problem.

Checklist

Bicycle Repair Kit

❏ **Allen Key.** or six mm "T" wrench for light bikes.

❏ **Crescent Wrench.** Get a 6-inch adjustable-end wrench. Get one with a forged body, milled and hardened jaws and a precise adjusting action. To test it, open the adjustable jaw and see if you can wiggle it. A good wrench won't wiggle.

❏ **Screwdriver.** Or a pocket knife with a screwdriver. Get one with a forged steel shank and thin blade end. The tip should be 1/4 inch wide and the shank four or five inches long.

❏ **Tire Irons.** Each tire iron should have a smooth, thin, rounded prying end and a hook at the other end to fit onto the spokes.

❏ **Tire Patch Kit.** Tire glue, small and large patches, and sandpaper to scrape a rough spot on a damaged tube. Carry a spare tube.

❏ **Tire Pump.** Get one that fits on frame bracket or between top tube and bottom bracket of frame.

Fuel Filter. Replace every 15,000 miles.

Horn. Sound the horn to make sure it works.

Hood and Door Hinges. Lubricate every six months.

Oil Filter. Change the filter every time you change the oil.

Power Steering Fluid. Check every time you change the oil. Replace when level is low.

Seatbelts. Check for fraying or fuzzing. Check to make sure the buckles totally engage and disengage as designed. Check to make sure retractor locks.

Spark Plugs. Replace every 15,000 miles if you use leaded gasoline or every 30,000 miles if you used unleaded gasoline.

Tires. Rotate every 10,000 miles.

Auto Quick Check

Check the following items every month and certainly before taking a long trip:

Battery Jumper Cables. You'll need these if your battery dies. They may also come in handy should someone need your help with their battery.

Brake Lights. Make sure that the brake lights are working and clean.

Headlights. Check that headlights on both sides work. Snow and mud can cut down on headlight efficiency. Also check the high beams. See to it that the lights are aimed properly – not too high or too low.

Jack. Make sure you have a jack and flares in case of a flat tire.

Signal Lights. Check signal lights on both sides, front and rear.

Spare Tire. The spare should be in good condition and fully inflated. If possible, buy a spare the same size as the original tires.

Steering. The steering wheel should function smoothly. If your car has automatic power steering or makes a groaning sound when you turn the steering wheel, it is a sign that you are low on power steering fluid.

Tires. Check that tires are all fully inflated. Be sure that there are no bulges, splits or nails and that tires are not pulling away from the rim.

Windshield wipers. If worn, wipers should be replaced. Check that they are working. Keep windshield wiper fluid filled.

Personal, Travel & Home Safety

Top 10 Rules for Personal Safety

1) Learn and practice basic self-defense techniques.

2) If attacker is a man, kick or knee him in the groin.

3) Scream and continue screaming while you run.

4) In a face-to-face attack, ram the heel of your hand as hard as you can into the base of the attacker's nose.

5) If grabbed from behind, kick your leg backward into attacker's shin or throw your head back into attacker's nose.

6) Observe what's going on and who is around you.

7) Carry pepper spray around your neck or in an accessible pocket.

8) Avoid situations that might compromise your safety.

9) Agree with a friend to keep an eye on each other.

10) Keep an eye on your drink and never accept a drink from someone you do not know.

Top 10 Rules for Travel Safety

On Foot or Bicycle:

1) Know where you are going.

2) Learn and practice self-defense techniques.

3) Tuck some money into the bottom of one sock.

4) Always have your photo identification with you.

5) Walk (or ride) quickly and confidently. Attackers are less likely to prey on the strong.

Checklist

Emergency Road Kit

Every vehicle should have an emergency road kit, especially when traveling in severe heat or cold. Kit should include:

❑ **Blanket**

❑ **Gloves**

❑ **Water.** Keep a gallon for the radiator.

❑ **Flashlight**

❑ **Tire Pressure Gauge**

❑ **Antifreeze/Coolant**

❑ **Motor Oil**. Keep two quarts of the correct kind.

❑ **Gas Container**

❑ **Kitty Litter.** Put a bag in your trunk during winter. The weight will stabilize your car on snowy roads. If you get stuck, the litter provides good traction dumped around wheels.

❑ **"Call Police" Sign.** Put it in the window facing traffic. It's safer than flagging down a stranger for help. Only use it in an emergency.

❑ **Emergency Cell Phone.** Keep the battery charged.

❑ **Roadside Service.** Invest in roadside assistance service so that you have someone to call for help.

*M*om says:
Be good. Keep your feet dry, your eyes open and your heart in the right place. Oh, and call home or write once in a while just to let me know how you're doing. OK?

6) Carry a cell phone, change or a calling card.

7) Always wear the appropriate safety gear for recreational activities.

8) Carry pepper spray around neck or in easily accessible pocket.

9) Be aware of surroundings, who's around you and what's going on around you.

10) Travel only with people you know and trust – walk with the wise, and you are wise.

In Automobile:

1) Do not speed. Allow plenty of time to get where you're going.

2) Always wear your seatbelt.

3) Carry a cell phone in case you get stranded.

4) Have enough gas in the car to make the trip.

5 Slow down in unfamiliar areas and bad weather.

6) Check outside surroundings before leaving a building to go to your car. If possible, have someone walk to your car with you at night.

7) Lock car doors when you leave your vehicle and after you get into your vehicle.

8) Do not eat, apply makeup or talk on cell phone while driving.

9) Do not drive drunk or high on drugs. Do not ride with a driver who is drunk or high.

10) Carry car keys with pointed ends exposed through fingers of fist to use as a weapon.

Top 10 Rules for Home Safety

1) Keep a phone next to your bed.

2) Never tell anyone you are home alone.

3) Install a deadbolt and chain lock on all doors.

4) Make sure the porch lights work, or install motion detector lights outside.

5) Have peep holes installed in your front and back doors. Never answer the door unless you are sure who is there.

6) Keep pepper spray near the front door of your home and by your bed, but out of the reach of children.

7) Lock the doors to your house when you leave and when you are at home alone.

8) Have emergency police numbers on automatic dial on your phone and use them if you feel unsafe.

9) Know what you can use as a weapon in your house and don't hesitate to use it.

10) Keep your windows locked, especially at night. Install window locks or stop locks that allow the window to open only a short way.

Where's Dad Now That I Need Him?

Not all necessary tips on how to survive away from home come from Mom. Dad, too, has some tricks up his sleeve.

That's why we've also published *Where's Dad Now That I Need Him?* While times have changed, expectations of what a man should know and what a father should teach his sons and daughters have pretty much remained the same. *Where's Dad?* offers father-specific advice such as how to rent your first apartment, buy your first car, fix a flat tire, carve a turkey, prepare a resume, deal with contracts, invest your money, paint a room, and do almost anything else including tie a tie, hold a baby, fold an American flag and set a table.

Together, *Where's Mom?* and *Where's Dad?* provide all you need to know to live happily and successfully on your own. These books will teach you not only how to survive—but also how to thrive—away from home.

Mom's Best Advice

Mom's Best Advice

Index

A

abbreviations, in recipes... 48
abscessed tooth 289
acne................... 290
adrenaline 2
AIDS 292
air conditioning
   automobile........... 301
   increasing efficiency 63
Alaska 6
alcohol, stain.......... 243
amino acids........... 2, 4
anemia................ 279
animal proteins......... 2
ant killer 70
appendicitis........... 280
apple(s)
   Apple banana pudding . 202
   Apple-nutmeg muffins.. 180
   Breakfast apple pie 79
   Bubbly apple topping ... 78
   Cabbage-apple slaw 118
   Diced apple salad 234
   Easy apple pie 200
   Golden apple rings..... 81
   how to select/store 30
   Sweet cherry-apple
   punch 189
applesauce
   Applesauce brownies .. 211
   Applesauce cake...... 197
   Applesauce cookies ... 208
   Applesauce roll pancakes 74
   Cherry applesauce
   salad 121
apricot(s)
   Apricot-nut muffins ... 180
   Banana-apricot bread .. 234
   how to select/store 30
artichoke(s)
   how to select/store 32
asparagus
   how to select/store 32
   Sweet and tender
   asparagus........... 165
   Tender asparagus 165

chicken 131
asthma................ 280
athlete's foot........... 281
automobile
   emergency road kit ... 303
   maintenance of 301
   safety.............. 304
avocado(s)
   how to select/store 30

B

bad breath............. 290
bake, definition of....... 53
baking chocolate
   how to measure 49
baking soda
   drop biscuits......... 183
   how to measure 48
   uses of.............. 69
banana(s)
   Apple banana pudding . 202
   Banana-apricot bread .. 234
   Banana-orange sauce ... 78
   Bran banana bread 178
   how to select/store..... 30
   Strawberry-banana pie . 200
   Sweet banana shake ... 190
barley
   Barley mushroom stew 155
   Italian barley casserole . 155
bars
   Chocolate chip bars ... 210
   Easy cheesy breakfast
   bars................ 82
   English toffee bars..... 210
   Spicy nut bars 211
basic four food groups.... 17
basil.................. 58
baste, definition of 53
beans
   Barbecue beans and
   franks.............. 100
   Barbecued hot dog
   beans.............. 148
   Beef with chili beans... 140
   Easy baked beans 165

French almond green
   beans............... 166
   Green bean casserole.. 165
   Island baked beans 165
   Mexican rice and beans 171
   snap, how to select..... 34
   substitutions for chili ... 52
   Three bean salad 116
beat, definition of 53
beef
   Beef rolls and gravy ... 136
   Beef burger stroganoff . 230
   Beef with chili beans... 140
   Beefy mushroom
   casserole............ 141
   Best beef nachos...... 137
   Chinese beef casserole. 140
   Corned beef and eggs .. 89
   Corned beef casserole . 144
   Corned beef potpourri 143
   Corned beef and slaw .. 96
   Ground beef and
   noodles 134
   how to roast.........37, 41
   how to select/store 35
   Oriental beef stir-fry .. 141
   Philly beef and swiss.... 98
   Quickest-ever beef stew 106
   Simply beef stew 133
   Tender pot roast...... 142
   Vegetable beef
   casserole............ 142
   Western eggs and beef. 100
beer, substitution for 51
beets
   Harvard.............. 166
   how to select/store 32
   tips on cooking........ 56
berries
   Creamy berry floats ... 191
   how to select/store 30
   in muffins............ 180
beverages
   Bubbly grapefruit ice .. 189
   Cherry soda 192
   Creamy berry floats..... 191

Easy strawberry soda . . 192
Fresh lemonade 189
Hot cider punch 193
Jiffy hot chocolate 191
Limeade zing 189
Mexican hot chocolate . 193
No-cook eggnog 192
Orange slush 190
Orange jubilee 190
Pineapple floats 191
Spiced grape juice 193
Steaming autumn treat . 191
Sweet banana shake . . . 190
Sweet cherry-apple
  punch 189
Tangy citrus punch 190
Traditional eggnog 192
Triple fruit punch 190
Winter wassail 191
bicycle
  maintenance of 300
  repair kit 301
  safety tips 303
biotin 10
biscuits
  Baking soda drop biscuits 183
  reheating 55
  Rich buttermilk biscuits 183
blanch, definition of 53
bleach
  to purify water 65
  used in laundry 250
bleeding, first aid for 260
blend, definition of 53
blisters, first aid for 260
blood stains, removing . . . 243
boil, definition of 53
boils, first aid for 260
botulism 41
braise, definition of 53
brakes
  bicycle 300
bread
  Baking soda drop
    biscuits 183
  Basic muffin mix 180

Basic rolls 176
baking hints 55
Banana-apricot bread . . 234
Bran banana bread . . . 178
Buttermilk oatmeal
  muffins 181
Caramel pecan rolls . . . 182
Cinnamon puffs 176
cooking terms 53
Early American brown
  bread 179
Easy bread sticks 184
Easy cheese puffs 176
Healthy carrot muffins . 183
how to store 34
Muffin mix variations . . 180
90-minute white bread . 177
Pizza dough 179
Pizza wheat crust 179
Quick and easy donuts . 182
Rich buttermilk biscuits 183
Simple cinnamon rolls . 182
Simple corn bread 178
Simple pretzels 184
60-minute wheat bread 177
Soft zucchini bread 178
Spiced pumpkin bread . 181
30-minute hamburger
  buns 177
Universal dough 175
Zesty lemon bread 181
bread crumbs
  measuring 49
  substitution for 52
breakfast
  Apple granola crunch . . . 80
  Applesauce roll pancakes . 74
  Bacon and cheese waffles . 77
  Banana-orange sauce 78
  Best-ever waffles 76
  Breakfast apple pie 79
  Breakfast sandwiches 79
  Brown sugar syrup 78
  Bubbly apple topping 78
  Caramelized French toast . 81
  Cinnamon breakfast cake . 80

Cinnamon spice toast 81
Creamy cinnamon syrup . . 78
Easy cheesy breakfast bars 82
Easy granola 80
Easy maple syrup 78
Easy pancakes 74
Easy waffles 76
Four-fruit cocktail 81
Fruited grits 80
German pancakes 75
Gingerbread waffles 77
Golden apple rings 81
Honey maple syrup 79
importance of 39
Moist oatmeal pancakes . 75
Nutty granola 79
Nutty whole-wheat waffles 77
Potato pancakes 75
Quick breakfast cookies . . 82
Swedish pancakes 76
Whole-wheat pancakes . 76
breathing difficulty
  first aid for 261
broccoli
  Broccoli and ham
    noodles 146
  Broccoli ricotta lasagna 156
  Cheesy broccoli bake . . 166
  how to select/store 32
broil, definition of 53
bronchitis 281
brown rice 171
brown sugar
  how to measure 48
  how to store 34
brownies
  Applesauce brownies . . 211
  Brownies now 233
  Chewy chocolate
    brownies 212
  Easy brownies 211
  Peanut butter brownies 212
bruises, first aid for 261
brussels sprouts
  how to select/store 32
burns, treatment for 261

bursitis 282
butter
  Easy butter frosting . . . 198
  how to select/store 34
  measurement of 49
  stains. 243
  substitutions for 50
buttermilk
  Buttermilk oatmeal
    muffins 181
  Rich buttermilk biscuits 183
  substitution for. 50
Butterscotch freeze 218
button, how to sew on . . 253

C
cabbage
  Cabbage-apple slaw . . . 118
  German red cabbage . . 167
  how to select/store 33
  New England cabbage
    bake. 144
  removing odor of 62
  Vienna cabbage toss. . . 234
cables
  bicycle. 300
  jumper 302
cake
  Applesauce cake. 197
  Carrot cake 197
  Chocolate-mayonnaise
    surprise. 197
  Cinnamon breakfast cake 80
  cooking tips 55
  Dump-it cake 198
  Easy lemon cake. 198
  microwave tips 226
  Quick German chocolate
    cake. 232
cake flour, substitution 51
calcium 11
calories
  in fast foods 25
  in weight loss or gain . . . 19
cancer, warning signs 282
candies & sweet treats. . . 217
  Butterscotch freeze . . . 218

Candied walnuts. 220
Caramel corn 217
Chewy corn flake
  clusters 220
Eggnogsicles 218
Five-minute fudge. 219
Fudgesicles 218
Holiday candy logs 220
Marshmallow squares. . 217
Mixed-up candy 217
Peanut brittle 219
Puffed rice balls 218
Raspberry popcorn balls 217
Rocky road fudge. 219
candle wax
  stains, how to remove . 243
canker sores. 270
cantaloupe
  how to select/store 30
canned produce
  how to select/store 35
caramel
  Caramel corn 217
  Caramel pecan rolls . . . 182
  Caramelized French
    toast 81
  Creamy caramel frosting 199
  No-bake caramel drops 212
carbohydrates. 1, 3
  complex 4
  simple 4
cardiopulmonary
  resuscitation 260
carpet cleaner. 71
carrot(s)
  Carrot cake 197
  Carrot cookies. 208
  Creamy carrot salad. . . 117
  Healthy carrot muffins . 183
  how to select/store 33
  10-minute carrot soup . 105
casaba melon
  how to select/store 31
casseroles
  Beefy mushroom
    casserole. 141
  Cheeseburger casserole 140

Cheesy broccoli bake. . 166
Chinese beef casserole. 140
Corned beef casserole. 144
Crunchy tuna casserole 146
Easy chicken bake. 129
Green bean casserole. . 165
Hamburger rice
  casserole 141
Hot dog potato bake . . 149
Italian barley casserole. 155
Oven macaroni and
  cheese. 157
Penny-wise salmon bake 145
Stuffed zucchini
  casserole. 159
Vegetable beef casserole 142
cauliflower
  how to select/store 33
  Picky eaters cauliflower 228
  tips on cooking. 56
celery
  how to select/store 33
  measuring chopped 49
cereal, soggy 57
check lists
  Bicycle repair kit. 301
  Cooking essentials 50
  Emergency road kit . . . 303
  First aid essentials 267
  Herbs and spices 60
  Kitchen essentials. 48
  Laundry essentials 250
  Sewing kit 255
cheese
  Bacon and cheese
    waffles. 77
  Baked cheese puffs 95
  Baked cheese fries 168
  Barbecued cheese buns . 99
  Cheesy broccoli bake. . 166
  Cheese-garlic muffins . . 180
  Cheese make-aheads . . . 98
  Cheesy pigs in blankets. 148
  Cheesy scrambled eggs 227
  Cheesy tuna burgers . . . 96
  Chops and cheesy
    potatoes 150
  cooking tips 55

Cream-cheese corn
chowder 229
Creamy cheese soup . . 107
Deviled ham and cheese . 96
Double cheese linguini . 156
Easy cheesy breakfast bars 82
Easy cheesy omelet. 88
Easy cheese puffs 176
Ham, egg and cheese pie 147
Hamburger cheese
patties 136
hints in using. 55
how to select/store 34
measuring grated 49
Open-face cheese
sandwich. 227
Oven macaroni and
cheese. 157
Three-cheese potatoes. 232
chemical burns 261
cherry
Cherry-applesauce salad 121
Cherry soda 192
Sweet cherry-apple
punch 189
chicken
Best barbecued chicken 129
Bleu chicken with
mushrooms. 127
Breaded pecan chicken. 230
broth. 107
Chicken and dumplings 107
Chicken filled dumplings 129
Chicken soup 271
Creamy chicken divan . . 130
Easy chicken bake. 129
Easy chicken pie 131
Easy chicken salad 119
Golden chicken bake . . 130
Herbed lemon 130
Mushroom-chicken rice. 231
Roasted citrus chicken. . 127
Tangy skillet chicken. . . 131
Tender asparagus
chicken 131
tips for cooking 56
Toasted chicken salad. . 100

chili
Beef with chili beans . . 140
chili powder 59
Easy meaty chili 106
Fast chili mac 139
Southwestern white chili 157
substitutions for 52
Tastiest vegetarian chili 159
chill, definition of 53
chlamydia 294
chocolate
baking chocolate,
measuring 49
Chewy chocolate
brownies. 212
Chocolate fudge. 233
Chocolate-mayonnaise
surprise. 197
Classic chocolate chip
cookies 207
how to melt 55
Jiffy hot chocolate 191
Mexican hot chocolate. 193
Quick German chocolate
cake. 232
Simple chocolate
frosting. 199
stains, removing 244
unsweetened chocolate,
substitute for 51
chocolate chip
Chocolate chip bars. . . 210
Classic chocolate chip
cookies 207
choking, treatment for . . . 262
cholesterol
consumption of dietary . . 5
chop, definition of. 53
chow mein noodles
substitution for. 52
chowder
Corn and bacon
chowder 108
Cream-cheese corn
chowder 229
Easy clam chowder. . . . 108
10-minute corn chowder 105

Potato and ham chowder 109
cinnamon
uses for 59
Cinnamon breakfast cake 80
Cinnamon puffs. 176
Cinnamon rolls 175
Cinnamon spice toast. . . 81
Creamy cinnamon syrup 78
Simple cinnamon rolls . 182
clam chowder (Easy) 108
cleaners, recipes for . . . 70, 71
clothing repair 253
cobbler
Any fruit cobbler 198
coconut(s)
how to select/store 31
Incredible coconut pie . 201
Nutty coconut frosting 199
cold, common. 271
cold sores. 270
cold water fish 6
condom 293
conjunctivitis. 274
constipation 271
cookies & bars
Applesauce cookies . . . 208
Applesauce brownies . . 211
Carrot cookies 208
Chewy chocolate
brownies. 212
Chewy oatmeal cookies 207
Chocolate chip bars . . . 210
Classic chocolate chip
cookies 207
Easy brownies 211
English toffee bars 210
Lemon drifts 210
Moist sugar cookies . . . 208
No-bake caramel drops 212
Orange cookies 209
Peanut butter cookies . 207
Peanut butter
brownies. 212
Pumpkin cookies 209
Quick breakfast cookies. 82
Soft zucchini cookies . . 209
Spicy nut bars 211

cooking terms. 52
cool, definition of 53
copper 13
coriander, uses for 59
corn
    10-minute corn chowder 105
    Corn and bacon chowder 108
    Cream-cheese corn
    chowder 229
    Crunchy corn dogs. . . . 149
    Easy corn and franks . . 149
    how to select/store 33
    on the cob 227
    Simple corn bread 178
corned beef
    Corned beef and eggs . . 89
    Corned beef and slaw . . 96
    Corned beef casserole. 144
    Corned beef potpourri 143
cornmeal
    as stain remover. 248
cornstarch
    as stain remover . . . 68, 248
cottage cheese
    how to store. 35
cough 272
cracker crumbs
    how to measure. 49
crackers
    how to store. 35
    soggy. 57
cream
    definition of. 53
    how to store. 35
    whipped 57
cream of celery soup
    substitution for. 51
creamy wheat. 4
crenshaw melon
    how to select/store 31
Crete 6
crust
    Easiest-ever pie crust. . 201
    Graham cracker crust . 201
    Never-fail pie crust. . . . 202
    Pizza wheat. 179
cucumbers

how to select/store 33
cut in, definition of 53
cuts 263
cystitis. 282

D

daily calories. 4
daily fiber I
    how to increase 15
daily mineral needs. 11
daily nutritional needs 3
daily percentage 3
daily vitamin needs. 11
dairy products
    cottage cheese 35, 101
    cream 35, 101
    for lunch 101
    how to select/store 34
    pudding. 101
    substitutions for 50
    yogurt. 101
dandruff 291
defroster, automobile. . . . 301
Denis Spanek 125, 126
depression 283
dermatitis, contact 275
detergent, how to choose 249
diabetes 283
diarrhea 272
dip
    Authentic guacamole . . 122
    Easy fruit dip. 121
    Hummus 160
    The real thing salsa. . . . 122
    Vegetable garden dip . . 119
dough
    Pizza 179
    Universal. 175
donuts
    Quick and easy donuts. 182
dredge, definition of 53
dried fruits 4
drug abuse 296
dry mustard
    substitution for. 51
dumplings
    Chicken and dumplings 107

Chicken filled dumplings 129
dusting cloths 71

E

ear, foreign object in. 263
earache. 272
eardrum, perforated. 287
eczema 275
egg(s)
    baked. 88
    Cheesy scrambled eggs 227
    Classic quiche lorraine. . 89
    cooking tips 55
    Corned beef and eggs . . 89
    Creamed ham and eggs . 89
    Easy cheesy omelet 88
    Easy fried eggs 87
    Easy oven omelet 90
    Exactly egg salad. 97
    hard-boiled 87
    how to buy 34, 39
    how to store. 34, 55
    New Mexico egg bake . 228
    poached 88
    Quick quiche 90
    scrambled 87
    soft-boiled. 87
    South-of-the-border
    scramble 90
    The camel's eye 88
    substitution for. 50
    Western eggs and beef. 100
egg white
    how to measure 49
    substitution for. 50
egg yolk
    how to measure 49
    how to store. 55
eggnog
    No-cook eggnog. 192
    Traditional eggnog 192
eggplant
    Eggplant spinach roll ups 158
    Eggplant zucchini bake . 158
    how to select/store 33
empty calories 18
enchiladas

Extra-tasty enchiladas. . 138
energy 4, 19
  costs, how to cut 62
English
  English toffee bars 210
enzymes 2
essential fatty acids. 5
external otitis 272
eye, foreign object in 263

F
fabric softener, how to use 250
fainting, first aid for 263
farmers' market 28
fast foods, calories in 25
fats
  bad 4, 5
  good 4, 5
  monounsaturated 5
  polyunsaturated 5
  saturated. 3, 5
fatty acids
  essential 5, 6
fever 273
fiber. 1, 3, 14
  bran muffin 101
  essential to diet 14
  how to increase intake. . 15
  insoluble 14
  prevent constipation . . 14
  soluble. 14
  35 grams daily. 14
  wheat crackers 101
  whole-grain bread 101
first aid essentials 267
fish
  Citrus halibut steaks . . 145
  Easy fried fish 144
  how to buy and store . . 35
  oils 5
  Spicy orange roughy. . . 231
  tips on preparing 38
five a day 17
five food groups 17
floats
  Creamy berry floats . . . 191
  Pineapple floats. 191

flour, as a thickener 55
  how to measure 48
  how to store. 35
  substitutions for 51
flu 274
fold in, definition of 53
folic acid 10
food-borne illnesses 40
food groups, basic four. . . . 17
food guide pyramid. . . . 17, 18
food poisoning 40, 41
food warehouses 28
foods
  choosing best quality 30
  staples 50
Four-fruit cocktail. 81
fractures 264
freezer
  defrosting. 61
  increasing efficiency. 64
  temperature. 40
French
  Caramelized French toast 81
  Classic French onion soup 110
  French almond green
    beans 166
  French-American
    connection 101
  French dressing 120
  French hamwiches 97
  French vegetable stew . 161
fricassee, definition of. 53
frostbite, first aid for 264
frosting
  Creamy caramel frosting 199
  Easy butter frosting . . . 198
  Nutty coconut frosting 199
  Simple chocolate frosting 199
frozen
  butterscotch freeze . . . 218
  eggnogsicles 218
  fudgesicles. 218
  juice. 101
  peas. 52
  produce. 35
fruit(s)
  Any fruit cobbler 198

apples 30
apricots 30
avocados 30
bananas 30
berries. 30
cantaloupe. 30
casaba melon 31
coconuts 31
crenshaw melon 31
dried 4, 12, 16
Easy fruit dip. 121
Easy fruit salad 115
Four-fruit cocktail. 81
Fruit whip delight. 115
Fruity emerald salad. . . 121
grapefruit 31
grapes 31
honeydew melon 31
in diet 22, 23
lemons 31
limes 31
Marshmallow fruit salad 117
Microwave baked 228
nectarines 31
oranges 31
peaches 31
pears 32
pineapples 32
plums. 32
pomegranates 32
Sour cream fruit salad . 117
tomatoes. 32
Triple fruit punch 190
watermelon. 32
fruit group. 17, 18
fruit juice, stains from . . . 244
Fruited grits 80
fry, definition of 53
fudge
  Chocolate fudge 233
  Five-minute fudge 219
  Fudgesicles 218
  Rocky road fudge 219
fuel filter, automobile 302
furniture polish
  recipe for 70

G

garlic
    breath 35
    Cheese garlic muffins . . 180
    cloves, how to store. . . . 35
    cloves, uses for 60
    how to store. 35
    use for. 60
gastroenteritis 284
gelatin salads
    Cherry-applesauce 121
    Easy raspberry cooler . 121
    Fruit whip delight. 115
    Fruity emerald salad. . . 121
genital herpes. 293
genital warts. 295
Gingerbread waffles 77
glaze
    definition of. 54
    Lemon glaze 199
gonorrhea. 294
good health. 1
graham cracker crust. . . . 201
    substitution for. 51
grains. 2
granola
    Apple granola crunch. . . 80
    Easy Granola. 80
    Nutty Granola 79
grapefruit
    how to select/store 31
grapes
    how to select/store 31
grate, definition of 54
gravy
    Basic gravy 134
    how to thicken. 106
    Instant gravy 134
green pepper 33
    how to select/store 33
    measuring, diced 49
grill, definition of. 54
grits, fruited 80
grocery stores 28
growth 4
guacamole, authentic 122

H

halibut
    Citrus halibut steaks . . 145
ham
    Broccoli and ham
    noodles. 146
    Creamed ham and eggs . 89
    Deviled ham and cheese 96
    Favorite ham salad 118
    French hamwiches 97
    Ham and scalloped
    potatoes 147
    Ham egg and cheese pie 147
    how to roast. 37
    Potato and ham chowder 109
    Quick Hawaiian delight 148
    substitution for. 52
hamburger(s)
    Best-ever hamburgers . . 95
    Best hamburger stew. . 133
    browning. 226
    Easy hamburger pie . . . 132
    Easy sloppy joes 144
    Hamburger cheese
    patties 136
    Hamburger rice
    casserole. 141
    Hamburger soup 105
    Hamburger stroganoff . 134
    making them juicy. 56
    measuring 49
    30-minute hamburger
    buns 177
handlebars, bicycle 300
Harvard beets 166
hay fever. 284
headache. 273
healthy joints 4
heat exhaustion 264
heat rash. 275
Heimlich maneuver 262
hem, how to repair 254
hemorrhoids. 284
hepatitis, infectious. 285
hernia 285
HIV 293
hives 275

Holiday candy logs 220
home safety 305
hominy, substitution for . . . 52
honey
    as substitute for
    molasses 51
    how to store. 35
    substitutions for 51
honey butter
    substitutions for 50
honeydew melon
    how to select/store 31
hormones. 2
horn, automobile 302
hot chocolate
    Jiffy hot chocolate 191
    Mexican hot chocolate. 193
hot dog(s)
    Barbecued hot dog
    beans. 148
    Barbecue beans and
    franks 100
    Cheesy pigs in blankets. 148
    Crunchy corn dogs. . . . 149
    Easy corn and franks . . 149
    Fast franks and potatoes 149
    Hot dog potato bake . . 149
    how to select/store 35
how much is one serving. . 18
hydrogen peroxide
    as stain remover. 248
hypoglycemia 285
hypothermia 264

I

ice cream, how to store. . . 35
impetigo 275
infectious hepatitis 285
influenza 274
ingrown toenail 274
instant onion
    as a substitution 52
insulin 2
iodine
    definition of. 13
    stains. 245
    to purify water 65

iron
    definition of. 13
ironing. 256
Italian dressing 120

J

jack, automobile 302
jam
    how to store. 35
    muffins 180
jelly
    how to store. 35
jock itch 274

K

kidney
    infection 286
    stones 286
knead, definition of. 54

L

labels
    how to read 44
    importance of reading . . 28
lamb, how to roast. 37
laundry
    basics for. 240
    bleaching. 250
    drying 251
    essentials. 250
    goofs 248
    removing stains. 242
    rinsing 251
    sorting. 241
    top 10 240
    washing. 249
    water temperature. . . . 249
lemon(s)
    as stain remover. 248
    Easy lemon cake. 198
    for whitening socks . . . 242
    Fresh lemonade 189
    Lemon glaze 199
    grated, measuring 49
    Herbed lemon chicken. 130
    how to select/store 31
    juice, measuring 49

Lemon cream pie 201
Lemon drifts 210
lemon pepper 60
Lemon-sugar muffins . . 180
    peel, measuring 49
    Zesty lemon bread. . . . 181
lemonade, fresh 189
lettuce
    how to select/store 33
    to absorb grease. 56
    washing 56
limes
    how to select/store 31
lipoproteins. 6
    HDL high-density 6
    LDL low-density 6
lunch. 101
lunchbox foods. 101

M

macaroni
    Best-yet macaroni salad 116
    Oven macaroni and
    cheese. 157
macrominerals 11
magnesium 11
main dishes, beef
    Beef rolls and gravy. . . . 136
    Beef with chili beans . . 140
    Beefy mushroom casserole 141
    Best beef nachos 137
    Best hamburger stew. . 133
    Cheeseburger casserole 140
    Chinese beef casserole. 140
    Easiest-ever pizza 138
    Easiest meat loaf. 133
    Easy foil roast. 142
    Easy hamburger pie . . . 132
    Easy savory meatballs. . 135
    Easy sloppy joes 144
    Easy tamale pie 137
    Extra-tasty enchiladas. . 138
    Fast chili mac 139
    Ground beef and
    noodles. 134
    Hamburger cheese
    patties. 136

Hamburger rice
    casserole 141
Hamburger stroganoff . 134
Meat patties in sauce . . 136
Meatballs with potatoes 135
Oriental beef stir-fry . . 141
Pepper steak. 143
Pizza burger 138
Porcupine meatballs . . . 135
Quick quesadillas 137
Savory swiss steak 143
Simply beef stew. 133
Stove top meatloaf. . . . 133
Spaghetti and meatballs 139
Swift and spicy spaghetti 139
Tender pot roast 142
Upside down meat pie. 132
Vegetable beef casserole 142
main dishes, chicken
    A chicken standing up . 125
    Best barbecued chicken 129
    Bleu chicken with
    mushrooms. 127
    Chicken filled
    dumplings. 129
    Creamy chicken divan . 130
    Easy chicken bake. 129
    Easy chicken pie 131
    Golden chicken bake . . 130
    Herbed lemon chicken. 130
    Roasted citrus chicken. 127
    Tangy skillet chicken. . . 131
    Tender asparagus
    chicken. 131
main dishes, corned beef
    Corned beef casserole. 144
    Corned beef potpourri 143
    New England cabbage
    bake 144
main dishes, fish
    Citrus halibut steaks . . 145
    Crunchy tuna casserole 146
    Easy fried fish 144
    Penny-wise salmon bake 145
    Scalloped tuna and
    potatoes. 146
    Simple salmon patties. . 145

main dishes, ham
Broccoli and ham noodles 146
Ham, egg and cheese
pie 147
Ham and scalloped
potatoes 147
Quick Hawaiian delight 148
main dishes, hot dogs
Barbecued hot dog
beans 148
Cheesy pigs in blankets 148
Crunchy corn dogs 149
Easy corn and franks . . 149
Fast franks and potatoes 149
Hot dog potato bake . . 149
main dishes, pork
Chops and cheesy
potatoes 150
Easy pineapple pork . . . 150
Mandarin almond pork . 151
Pepper pork and rice . . 150
Pork tenders with
carrots 151
Stove top Kielbasa and
rice 150
Stuffed pork chops 151
Mandarin oranges
substitutions for 52
maple syrup (Easy) 78
margarine
how to store 34
stains 243
marinate, definition of 54
marshmallow(s)
how to store 35
Marshmallow fruit salad 117
Marshmallow squares . . 217
substitutions for 51
tips on how to use 55
mashed potato flakes
as thickener 56
mayonnaise
Chocolate-mayonnaise
surprise 197
recipe for 121
meat

cooking tips 37, 55
how to select/store 35
signs of spoilage in 42
meat food group 17, 22
meatballs
Easy savory meatballs . . 135
Meatballs with potatoes 135
Porcupine meatballs . . . 135
Spaghetti and meatballs 139
meatless protein 101
meatloaf
cooking tips 56
Stove top meatloaf 133
melon
casaba 31
crenshaw 31
honeydew 31
watermelon 32
metabolism 4
metric conversions 56
Mexican
Mexican hot chocolate . 193
Mexican rice and beans 171
Speedy Mexican pizza . . 157
microwave cooking 225
arranging 226
Banana-apricot bread . . 234
Basic bacon 227
Beef burger stroganoff . 230
Breaded pecan chicken . 230
Brownies now 233
Cream-cheese corn
chowder 229
Cheesy scrambled eggs 227
Chocolate fudge 233
containers 225
cooking techniques 226
cooking times 225
Corn on the cob 227
Cream-cheese corn
chowder 229
Creamy pita rounds . . . 229
Crunchy peanut brittle . 233
Microwave baked fruit . 228
Mushroom-chicken rice 231
New Mexico egg bake . 228

Open-face cheese
sandwich 227
Picky eaters cauliflower 228
Quick German chocolate
cake 232
Right and ready reuben 229
Risotto with sweet peas 231
safety 225
Sloppy joes 230
Spicy orange roughy . . . 231
Steamy baked potato . . . 227
stirring 226
10-second nachos 232
Three-cheese potatoes . 232
migraine headache 273
mildew
how to get rid of . 245, 247
prevention 247
milk
food group 17, 22
how to measure 48
instant, select/store 34
skim, substitution for . . . 50
sour, substitution for . . . 50
substitutions for 50
stains from 246
tips on buying 29
whole, substitution for . . 50
mince, definition of 54
minerals 1
minerals, macro 11
calcium 11
chloride 11
magnesium 11
phosphorus 12
potassium 12
sodium 11
minerals, trace 13
chromium 13
copper 13
iodine 13
iron 13
manganese 13
molybdenum 13
selenium 13
zinc 14

mix, definition of. 54
molasses, substitution for. . 51
mononucleosis 286
muffins
    Apple-nutmeg muffins . 180
    Apricot-nut muffins . . . 180
    Basic muffin mix 180
    Berry muffins 180
    Buttermilk oatmeal
    muffins 181
    Cheese garlic muffins . . 180
    Healthy carrot muffins . 183
    Jam muffins 180
    Lemon-sugar muffins . . 180
    Orange muffins. 180
    Pineapple muffins 180
multivitamin supplement . . 9
mushrooms
    how to select/store 33
    substitutions for 52
mustard
    as a substitution for dry. 51
    stains, removal of 246
    uses for 60

N

nectarines
    how to select/store 31
niacin. 10
no lumps. 106
noodles
    Broccoli and ham
    noodles. 146
    Ground beef and noodles 134
    measuring 49
non-stick pans 106
nosebleed, first aid for . . . 265
nutmeg, uses for 60
nutrition
    information on labels . . . 44
    in lunchbox meals. 101
nuts
    measuring chopped 49

O

oatmeal
    Buttermilk oatmeal

muffins 181
    Chewy oatmeal cookies 207
    Moist oatmeal pancakes . 75
odors, how to remove 62
oil 106
    automobile engine 301
    filter, automobile. 302
    olive. 6
okra
    how to select/store 33
Omega-3 fatty acids 5
Omega-6 fatty acids 5
omelet
    Easy cheesy omelet 88
    Easy oven omelet 90
onion rings (Golden) 167
onions
    how to select/store 33
    measuring chopped 49
    substitution for. 51
orange(s)
    Banana-orange sauce . . . 78
    how to select/store 31
    juice, measuring 49
    liqueur. 51
    Orange cookies 209
    Orange jubilee 190
    Orange muffins. 180
    Orange slush. 190
    Spicy orange roughy . . . 231
otitis media. 272

P

packaged foods. 4
pan broil, definition of 53
pan juices 126
pan-fry, definition of 53
pancakes
    Applesauce roll. 74
    batter, left over 57
    Easy pancakes 74
    German pancakes. 75
    Moist oatmeal pancakes . 75
    Potato pancakes 75
    Swedish pancakes 76
    Whole-wheat pancakes . 76
pantothenic acid 11

parboil, definition of 54
parsley
    substitution for 52
    use for. 60
parsnips
    how to select/store 33
pasta 4
peach(es)
    Fresh peach pie. 63
    how to select/store 31
peaks
    soft 54
    stiff 54
peanut
    Peanut brittle 219
    Crunchy peanut brittle. 233
peanut butter
    how to store. 35
    Peanut butter brownies 212
    Peanut butter cookies . 207
    Raisins and peanut butter 97
pears
    how to select/store 32
peas
    Creamed potatoes and
    peas. 168
    how to select/store 33
    Minted carrots and snow
    peas. 167
    Rissotto with sweet peas 231
pecans
    Breaded pecan chicken. 230
    Caramel pecan rolls . . . 182
    as a substitute. 52
petroleum jelly
    as stain remover. 248
phosphorus. 12
pie
    Breakfast apple pie 79
    Easiest-ever pie crust. . 201
    Easy apple pie 200
    Easy chicken pie 131
    Easy hamburger pie . . . 132
    Easy tamale pie 137
    Fresh peach pie 200
    Graham cracker crust . 201
    Ham, egg and cheese pie 147

Incredible coconut pie . 201
Lemon cream pie 201
Never-fail pie crust. . . . 202
No-bake pumpkin pie. . 200
Strawberry-banana pie . 200
Upside Down Meat Pie 132
pigs in blankets (Cheesy) . 148
pineapple(s)
Easy pineapple pork . . . 150
how to select/store 32
Pineapple floats. 191
Pineapple muffins 180
pink eye 274
pizza
Easiest-ever pizza 138
Pizza burger 138
Pizza dough. 179
Pizza on a roll. 99
Quick pizza. 99
Wheat pizza crust 179
plums
how to select/store 32
pneumonia 288
poach, definition of. 54
pomegranates
how to select/store 32
popcorn
balls, cooking tips 55
Caramel corn 217
how to store. 35
Raspberry popcorn balls 217
pork
Chops and cheesy
potatoes 150
Easy pineapple pork . . . 150
how to roast. 37, 41
how to select/store 36
Mandarin almond pork. 151
Pepper pork and rice . . 150
Pork tenders with
carrots 151
Stuffed pork chops. . . . 151
substitution for. 52
potassium 12
potato(es)
Chops and cheesy
potatoes 150

Creamed potatoes and
peas. 168
Easiest-ever scalloped
potatoes 169
Fast franks and potatoes 149
Grandma's potato salad 119
Ham and scalloped
potatoes 147
Hot dog potato bake. . . 149
Hot Dutch potato salad 119
how to select/store 34
Meatballs with potatoes 135
Potato and ham chowder 109
Potato pancakes 75
Ranchero potatoes. . . . 168
Scalloped tuna and
potatoes 146
Seasoned sliced potatoes 169
Skillet scalloped
potatoes 169
Speedy potato soup . . . 109
Steamy baked 227
sweet, select/store 34
Three-cheese 232
potato chips, soggy. 57
pot-roast, definition of 54
poultry
cooking tips. 41, 56
how to select/store 36
powdered sugar
how to measure 48, 49
power steering fluid. 302
preparing meat. 125
prescription drugs 296
pretzels, (Simple) 184
produce
canned, storing 35
frozen, storing. 35
tips on buying 28, 29
protein 3
animal sources of 3
complete. 2, 3
dairy 2
food group 23
for lunch 101
incomplete 2
meat 2

plant sources of 3
power packed. 2
pubic lice 296
pudding
Apple banana pudding . 202
One-pan rice pudding . 202
Puffed rice balls 218
pumpkin
No-bake pumpkin pie. . 200
Pumpkin cookies 209
Spiced pumpkin bread . 181
punch
Hot cider punch. 193
Sweet cherry-apple
punch 189
Tangy citrus punch 190
Triple fruit punch 190
puncture wounds
first aid for 265
purée, definition of. 54

Q
quiche
Classic quiche Lorraine . 89
Quick quiche 90

R
RDA (recommended daily
allowance). 8
raisin(s)
baking tip 55
Raisins and peanut butter 97
rash. 275
raspberry
Easy raspberry cooler . 121
Raspberry popcorn balls 217
refrigerator
increasing efficiency of . . 64
rhubarb
how to select/store 34
riboflavin. 9
rice
brown 171
Chinese fried rice. 170
Hamburger rice
casserole. 141
Hearty tomato-rice soup 109

how to measure 49
long-grain 171
medium-grain 171
Mexican rice and beans 171
Mushroom-chicken rice 231
One-Pan rice pudding . 202
Pepper pork and rice . . 150
Perfect rice 170
short-grain 171
Stove top Kielbasa and
rice 150
substitution for 52
types of 171
uses of 171
roast
cooking tips 56
definition of 54
Easy foil roast 142
how to cook 36
pot-roast 54
Tender pot roast 142
rolls
basic 175, 176
Beef rolls and gravy . . . 136
Caramel pecan rolls . . . 182
Simple cinnamon rolls . 182
Roquefort dressing 120

S

salad dressings
French dressing 120
Green salad dressing . . 120
Homemade mayonnaise 121
Italian dressing 120
Real Roquefort dressing. 120
Thousand Island dressing 120
salads
Best-yet macaroni salad 116
Cabbage-apple salad . . . 118
Cherry-applesauce salad 121
Classic Waldorf salad . . 115
Cool summer salad . . . 115
Creamy carrot salad . . . 117
Easy chicken salad 119
Easy fruit salad 115
Easy raspberry cooler . 121
Easy seven-layer salad . . 117

Easy taco salad 122
Favorite ham salad 118
Fruit whip delight 115
Fruity emerald salad . . . 121
Grandma's potato salad 119
Hot dutch potato salad 119
Marshmallow fruit salad 117
Quick cole slaw 118
Sour cream fruit salad . 117
Spinach parmesan salad 116
Stuffed tomatoes 116
Tempting turkey salad . 118
Three-bean 116
Vienna cabbage toss . . . 234
salmon
Heated creamy salmon . . 97
Penny-wise salmon bake 145
Simple salmon patties . . 145
salt
as a stain remover 248
dangers of excess 12
how to measure 48
sandwiches
Baked cheese puffs 95
Barbeque beans 'n franks 100
Barbecued cheese buns . 99
Best-ever hamburger . . . 95
Breakfast sandwiches . . . 79
Cheese make-aheads . . . 98
Cheesy tuna burger 96
Corned beef and slaw . . 96
Creamed tuna on toast . 96
Deviled ham and cheese 96
Easy tuna salad sandwich . 95
Exactly egg salad 97
French-American
connection 101
French hamwiches 97
Heated creamy salmon . . 97
Hoagie sandwich 101
Hot tuna boats 98
how to store 101
Philly beef and Swiss 98
Picnic sandwiches 98
Pizza on a roll 99
Pizza quick 99
Raisins and peanut butter. 97

Toasted chicken salad
sandwich 100
Western eggs and beef
sandwich 100
sauces, to thicken 106
sauté, definition of 54
scald, definition of 54
scones 175
seafood
food poisoning from 43
how to prepare 43
seams
how to press 256
how to repair 254
sear, definition of 54
seatbelts 302
secrets 125
seeds 3
septic tank recharger 71
shake
Sweet banana shake . . . 190
seizure, first aid for 265
sexually transmitted
diseases 292
shellfish 5
shingles 288
shock, first aid for 265
shopping for food 28
shortening
how to measure 48, 49
how to select/store 34
shred, definition of 54
simple sugars 4
side dishes
Baked cheese fries 168
Cabbage with bacon . . . 166
Cheesy broccoli bake . . 166
Chinese fried rice 170
Creamed potatoes and
peas 168
Easiest-ever scalloped
potatoes 169
Easy baked beans 165
French almond green
beans 166
German red cabbage . . 167
Golden onion rings . . . 167

Green bean casserole. . 165
Harvard beets. 166
Island baked beans 165
Mexican rice and beans. 171
Minted carrots and peas 167
Perfect rice. 170
Ranchero potatoes. . . . 168
Seasoned sliced
potatoes 169
Skillet scalloped potatoes 169
Sweet and tender
asparagus 165
Swiss baked vegetables . 170
Zucchini bacon fry. 167
Zesty zucchini bake. . . . 169
simmer, definition of. 54
sinusitis 288
sloppy joes 144, 230
slush, (Orange) 190
soda
baking 69
Cherry soda 192
Easy strawberry soda. . 192
soft drinks
stains from 247
sugar content of 16
soft peaks, definition of . . . 54
sore throat. 276
soup(s)
absorbing grease in. 56
Chicken and dumplings 107
Classic French onion . . 110
cooking tips 55
Corn and bacon
chowder 108
Cream of turkey soup . 108
Creamy cheese soup . . 107
Easy clam chowder. . . . 108
Easy meaty chili 106
Easy soup-in-a-hurry . . 105
Hamburger soup 105
Hearty tomato-rice . . 109
how to store 35
no lumps in. 106
Potato and ham
chowder 109
Quickest-ever beef

stew 106
Simple minestrone 110
Speedy potato soup . . . 109
Spicy tomato soup 110
storing. 35
10-minute carrot soup. 105
10-minute corn
chowder. 105
sour cream
substitution for 50
sour milk
substitution for 50
soy. 36
bean. 3
spaghetti
Spaghetti and meatballs 139
Swift and spicy spaghetti 139
Spanek vertical roaster . . 125
spare tire 302
spark plugs 302
spices
allspice. 59
basil. 58
bay leaves 58
cardamon 59
celery salt 60
chili powder 59
cinnamon 59
cloves 59
coriander 59
crushed red pepper 59
cumin 59
curry powder 60
dill 58
garlic salt. 60
ginger 60
how to buy 59
how to measure 48
how to store. 35
how to use 59
lemon pepper 60
mace 60
marjoram 58
mustard. 60
nutmeg 60
onion salt 60
oregano. 58

paprika 60
parsley. 60
peppermint 58
rosemary. 59
saffron 59
sage 59
salt. 12
savory 59
tarragon 59
turmeric 60
uses for 59
spinach
Eggplant spinach rollups. 158
Spinach parmesan salad 116
splinters, first aid for 266
sprains, first aid for. 266
sprockets, bicycle 300
squash
how to select/store 34
stains, removing
alcohol 243
ballpoint pen. 243
blood. 243
butter 243
candle wax 243
carbon paper 243
chewing gum. 243
chocolate 244
coffee 244
cosmetics 244
crayon 244
deodorant. 244
dye 244
egg. 244
fruit juice 244
grass 245
grease 245
iodine 245
ketchup 245
lipstick. 245
mildew 245
milk products 246
mucus 246
mud. 246
mustard. 246
pencil. 246
perspiration 246

rust 246
tea 244
scorch 246
shoe polish 246
soft drinks 247
wine 247
steak
    Pepper steak 143
    Savory Swiss steak 143
steam, definition of 54
steam iron, how to clean . 257
steep, definition of 54
stew
    absorbing grease in 56
    absorbing salt in 56
    Barley mushroom stew 155
    Best hamburger stew . . 133
    cooking tips 56
    definition of 54
    French vegetable stew . 161
    how to thicken 56
    Quickest-ever beef stew 106
    Simply beef stew 133
stiff peaks, definition of . . . 54
stir, definition of 55
stock pot 126
stomach ache 276
strawberry(ies)
    Easy strawberry soda . . 192
    measuring 49
    Strawberry-banana pie . 200
strep throat 289
stroganoff
    Beef burger stroganoff . 234
    Hamburger stroganoff . 134
sty 277
substitutions 50
sugar
    brown 34, 48
    danger of excess 15, 16
    granulated 48
    how to measure 48
    how to store 35
    Moist sugar cookies . . . 208
    powdered 48
sunburn, first aid for 266
Sweet and tender
    asparagus 165

Swiss baked vegetables . . 170
sweet potatoes
    how to select/store 34
swimmer's ear 272
Swiss steak (Savory) 143
syphilis 295
syrup
    Brown sugar syrup 78
    Creamy cinnamon syrup 78
    Easy maple syrup 78
    Honey maple syrup 79

T
talcum powder
    as stain remover 249
tamale pie (Easy) 137
testicular pain 277
Thousand Island dressing . 120
throat
    sore 276
    strep 289
tires
    automobile 302
    bicycle 300
    spare 302
The Original Spanek
    Roaster 125, 126
toffee bars (English) 210
tomato juice
    substitution for 51
tomato soup
    cold (Gazpacho) 160
    Spicy tomato soup 110
tomatoes
    how to select/store 32
    substitution for 52
tooth, abscessed 289
toss, definition of 55
toxic shock 289
trace minerals 13
trench mouth 290
tuna
    Cheesy tuna burgers . . . 96
    Creamed tuna on toast . 96
    Crunchy tuna casserole 146
    Easy tuna salad sandwich . 95
    Hot tuna boats 98

Scalloped tuna and
    potatoes 146
    Tomato tuna boats 234
turkey
    Cream of turkey soup . 108
    Tempting turkey salad . 118
thermos 101
thickeners
    cornstarch 106
    flour 106
thyroxin 2
2,000-calorie diet 4, 11
tofu 2

U
ulcer, peptic 287
urinary pain 277
USDA food guide pyramid . 17

V
vaginal discharge 278
veal, how to roast 37
vegetable(s)
    artichokes 32
    asparagus 32
    beets 32
    broccoli 32
    brussels sprouts 32
    cabbage 33
    carrots 33
    cauliflower 33
    celery 33
    corn 33
    cucumbers 33
    eggplant 33
    food group 17
    French vegetable stew
    (Ratatouille) 161
    green peppers 33
    lettuce 33
    mushrooms 33
    okra 33
    onions 33
    parsnips 33
    peas 33
    potatoes 34
    rhubarb 34

serving sizes 18
snap beans 52
squash 34
substitutions 52
sweet potatoes 34
Swiss baked vegetables. 170
tips on cooking 56
Vegetable beef casserole 142
Vegetable garden dip . . 119
vegetarian main dishes . . . 155
   Barley mushroom stew 155
   Broccoli ricotta lasagna 156
   Double cheese linguine 156
   Eggplant spinach rollups 158
   Eggplant zucchini bake . 158
   Gazpacho 160
   Hummus 160
   Italian barley casserole . 155
   Little Italy tomatoes . . . 159
   Mushroom penne pasta 156
   Oven macaroni and
   cheese 157
   Ratatouille 161
   Southwestern white chili 157
   Speedy Mexican pizzas . 157
   Stuffed zucchini
   casserole 159
   Tabbouleh 161
   Tastiest vegetarian chili 159
   Zucchini mushroom
   frittata 160
vertical poultry roaster . . 125
Vienna cabbage toss 234
vitamin(s)
   A 8
   B-1 9
   B-2 9
   B-3 10
   B-6 10
   B-12 10
   C 10
   D 8
   E 8
   K 9
   biotin 10
   fat-soluble 8
   folic acid 10

pantothenic acid 11
   water-soluble 9
vomiting 278

W
waffles
   Bacon and cheese waffles 77
   Best-ever waffles 76
   Easy waffles 76
   Gingerbread waffles 77
   Nutty whole-wheat
   waffles 77
wall cleaner 71
walnuts, candied 220
   as substitute for pecans . 52
warts 291
washing machine
   how to load 241
wassail (Winter) 191
water
   contaminated 41
   daily nutritional need . . . 3, 7
   how to measure 48
   how to purify 65
   the importance of 7
water heater
   increasing efficiency of . . 64
watermelon
   how to select/store 32
weight management 18
well-balanced meals 101
whip, definition of 55
whipped cream
   how to sweeten 57
   increasing volume . . . 55, 57
   substitutions for 50
white vinegar
   as stain remover 249
window cleaner
   recipe for 70
whole wheat
   Nutty whole-wheat
   waffles 77
   Pizza wheat crust 179
   60-minute wheat bread 177
   Whole-wheat pancakes . 76
wine, substitutions for 51

wool
   how to launder 252
wounds, puncture 265

Y
yeast, substitutions for 51
yeast infection 278
yogurt
   benefits of 38
   how to use 38

Z
zinc 14
zucchini
   Eggplant zucchini bake . 158
   Soft zucchini bread 178
   Soft zucchini cookies . . 209
   Stuffed zucchini
   casserole 159
   Zucchini bacon fry 167
   Zucchini mushroom
   frittata 160
   Zesty zucchini bake . . . 169

A Cookbook with a Difference

When you leave home for the first time and venture on your own into the world, take clean underwear and this book. *Where's Mom Now That I Need Her? Surviving Away From Home* is your guide to domestic living. Here you'll find the secrets and know-how that Mom practiced daily to fill your belly, keep a clean home, save your clothes from permanent damage and make sure you were healthy, safe and happy.

Now it's your turn to do all those necessary life tasks for yourself. And just in case you weren't taking notes, we've compiled the most essential tips.

You'll find information on nutrition and health, shopping and cooking, an extensive laundry and stain removal guide, a succinct first-aid section, symptoms of common illnesses and home remedies, a guide to let you know when to see a doctor, a quick car and bicycle maintenance guide and important safety tips.

And you thought this was just a cookbook. Yes, you will find recipes for delicious meals packed between the covers, and the recipes for steamy soups, crusty loaves of bread, seasoned casseroles, crispy salads and chewy cookies all have one thing in common: *They are easy to make even for a beginner.* Most require less than an hour to prepare. All you will need is a kitchen and an appetite to make what you find here.

Because you'll be missing Mom, we've also added blank pages at the end of each recipe section where you, or Mom, can pen in her Old Standbys, those time-honored recipes that have been passed down from generation to generation.

Keep this book handy to use as a daily reference guide. You'll be surprised how easy it is to make it on your own – with a little help from Mom.

For more information on retail, premium sales or quantity discounts, *please contact* **ASPEN WEST** *at 801-867-4502 or aspenwestpub@gmail.com.*

About the Author

Kent P. Frandsen was born and raised in Utah. When he was very young, his parents purchased a mountain ranch to raise cattle. Faced with feeding a growing family plus ranch hands, Kent's mother learned to fix quick, easy and healthy meals. Sharing the household with four siblings, Kent was given chores at an early age and taught home management skills as part of his upbringing.

Upon leaving home for the first time, Kent realized the need for a survival manual filled with all the things he had been taught growing up. Collaborating with his Mom, Betty Rae Frandsen, they compiled the first edition of *Where's Mom Now That I Need Her?*, which has sold more than a million copies.

Kent continues to "survive on his own" in Utah where he earned a degree in business management from Brigham Young University, and is the president of *Aspen West Publishing and Distribution*.

With the printing of the new, updated version of *Where's Mom?*, here's solid proof that if Kent can do it, you can survive on your own too!